THE WORLD OF THE BURGLAR

THE WORLD OF THE BURGLAR

Five Criminal Lives

Edited by **PEDRO R. DAVID**

UNIVERSITY OF NEW MEXICO PRESS
Albuquerque

© 1974 by Pedro R. David. All rights reserved. Manufactured in the United States of America. Library of Congress Catalog Card No. 73-82774. ISBN No. (clothbound) 0-8263-0304-8. ISBN No. (paperbound) 0-8263-0332-3.
First Edition

TO MARIA ELISA, AGUSTIN PEDRO,
MARIA SOFIA, AND MARIA TERESA

Preface

This book represents the findings and interpretation of a research project I designed and carried out while Research Director of the Criminal Justice Program of the University of New Mexico.

The five ex-convicts who tell their stories in this book have lived typical criminal lives. All five are burglars or robbers, most of them have either sold drugs or been addicted to them, and all are between twenty and thirty-five years old. They were interviewed as part of a research project intended to explore the criminal justice system of the city of Albuquerque and Bernalillo County, an area with a high rate of serious crime, from the point of view of the offender.

The decision to study property offenders was a result of a recommendation adopted in November 1971 by a planning conference of key criminal justice agency representatives of the city of Albuquerque and the state of New Mexico. The resolution adopted at the meeting stated that the "principal objective of the 1972 Albuquerque Bernalillo County Criminal Justice improvement plan shall be the development of a system-wide program for the reduction of property crime. This program shall include related high-priority improvements in the areas of prevention, enforcement, prosecution, the courts and corrections. Special attention shall be given to immediate and underlying causative factors." The priority emphasized by the resolution seemed to me appropriate and urgent, since Albuquerque has one of the highest burglary rates in the nation.

The research was designed to produce the following:

Detailed interviews describing the careers of five criminal offenders who appear to be typical of various ethnic groups in the Albuquerque area. This description will include:

(1) Socioeconomic conditions, family relationships, community environment, cultural values and educational experience having influence on the personality of the offender and his concrete conduct.

(2) Experience with law enforcement agencies, courts, corrections, probation and parole officers, as well as problems in adapting to community life after release.

(3) An overview of the patterns apparent in the careers of these individuals as they relate to current theories of criminology and sociology and policies and practices within the criminal justice system.

(4) Recommendations for criminal justice system improvement.

The offenders to be researched represented then paradigmatic examples of certain types of persons who commit property crimes, namely burglaries. The methodology employed consisted of extensive in-depth interviews, according to an interview guide previously constructed. Subjects were allowed, however, to comment freely on any topic they wished.

The interview guide covered, in sequence, topics encompassing the family structure, the school years, peer groups, early involvement with deviant or criminal acts, first exposures to the police, experiences related to detention or incarceration (juvenile homes, jails, correctional institutions, and so on), and the judicial process.

Important also was the overall description of their lives of crime, techniques, motivations, and problems of disposing of stolen property, as well as profiles of their day-to-day existences. It was considered important to learn how they viewed law enforcement, the judiciary, and correctional institutions, and their reactions to probation and parole. Life in prison was to be researched extensively.

The selection of the cases involved a careful study of those to be interviewed, securing at least, among the five, members of three important segments of the population of the area: Spanish Americans or Chicanos, Anglos, and blacks. We selected for the study three Spanish Americans (one female and two males), one black male, and one Anglo male. They were all between twenty and thirty-five years old; their median age was twenty-six. All interviews were recorded, transcribed, and published with their permission. Sessions lasted from two to four hours at a time. The study began in February 1972 and was completed in October 1972.

After determining typical patterns of property offenders' careers, through careful examinations of available data, I secured the invaluable participation of Nestor Baca, director of the Bernalillo County Juvenile Detention Home, to assist in selecting the subjects whose careers are described here, because of his familiarity with offenders who have been through the system.

Mr. Baca secured the subjects' cooperation for the study, assisted me with the interviewing, checked the transcription against the tapes to ensure fidelity, and provided me with translations of regional and subcultural expressions. He had known four of the subjects for several years, since at one time or another they were detained at the institution he directs. Only the Anglo subject began his juvenile offender career outside the state. Mr. Baca's participation was decisive, and without him the outcome of this research would have been, indeed, very different. For that, many thanks.

Once they understood the purpose of the research, the subjects were eager to help. Even though assured that their identities would not be disclosed, they did not attach much importance to the possibility that their names might be known. Their candid responses displayed confidence in my objective to use this project as a vehicle for helping others. All of them displayed an apparent genuine belief that they could help themselves and society if they could recall their experiences of crime as they actually took place.

We are confident that the subjects, to their best knowledge, however biased their conceptions may be, disclosed their sincere views of themselves, of crime, and of society.

The interviews were taped and transcribed without alterations or modification except as necessary to ensure anonymity, and in some cases to delete repetitious material because of limits on length. The names of persons and places, of course, have been changed.

The research was sponsored by the Criminal Justice Program of the University of New Mexico, with support of the Law Enforcement Assistance Administration (LEAA) under its grant (No. NI-71-050-6) to the program to provide research, evaluation, and planning related to the Pilot Cities Program in Albuquerque/Bernalillo County. However, the views expressed here by the persons studied in no way represent those of the Criminal Justice Program, the author, or the LEAA.

I wish to thank all of those whose cooperation and support made this research possible—especially the subjects themselves, all of whom expressed a strong desire to participate in the interest of preventing others from following in their paths.

The task of transcribing, translating, and typing was done with patience and efficiency by Ms. Millie Miller and Ms. Suzanne Miller, who deserve our gratitude.

Editorial assistance was generously given by Ms. Wanda Conger and Ms. Stephany Wilson.

Finally, and not least, thanks are due to Mr. William R. Partridge, Criminal Justice Program Director, and Mr. Fred Koehne, then Assistant Director, who provided support in helping to solve some of the administrative problems involved with this research.

Contents

EDITOR'S INTRODUCTION
On the Offender's Perspective

Integrative criminology requires a careful examination of the "official" view as well as the "outsider's" or "offender's" view as two sides of the same coin. Both are one-sided accounts of the same object—human conduct that at a given time and place is labeled a crime. Thus what "criminals" say is an essential part of the study of how the system operates, from the perspective of those who are self-committed for life to challenging the legal order.

Even if we are convinced that the criminal's perspective on the criminal justice system is distorted because of his values and norms, it is still very important to detect what these distortions are for each person and how society and legal institutions contributed to them. To place the criminal's rationalizations, ideologies, and social and cultural characteristics in the perspective of the overall social structure of a given place, time, and historical sequence is to search also for the "ills" of society and for the limitations of the official perspective. It has been said that "what distorts a recollection, constitutes, precisely, the 'sui-generis' nature of recollections. Recollections . . . independent in themselves from the present in which the recollection is made, are an abstraction."[1]

It is also important to point out the advantages and limitations of life histories in criminology. They give the researcher an opportunity to understand life as an ongoing process, in a fluid sequence of interrelated events. Thus, life histories offer the sequential dramatic qualities of the novel and of real existence. "The general point of view that is being propounded here is holistic rather than atomistic, dynamic rather than static, dynamic rather than causal, purposive than simple-mechanical."[2]

In addition, at a time when technological advances and cultural and social change are having an impact, not yet fully assessed, on the quality of life and on the traditional dilemmas facing human conduct,

1

life histories may help to detect, perhaps in surprising ways, the extent and scope of such transformations. From that perspective life histories may lead to more "objective" types of research.

Among the limitations of the approach is the inability to derive "rigorous generalizations" that can be "scientifically" demonstrated to cut across the entire spectrum of criminological theory and research. On the other hand, to require that the social sciences concentrate only on these types of generalizations is too narrow. There must be some way to take into account the fluid nature of human conduct, and life histories carefully reconstructed could be a step in that direction.

The interviews presented in this book were conducted in 1972 in Albuquerque, New Mexico, a city with a high rate of serious crime. The subjects, all of whom had begun committing crimes as children and eventually had served time in the state penitentiary, were selected to be as representative of the community as possible. They are: Jack, an "Anglo" male ("Anglo" is a term used in New Mexico to designate anyone who is neither Spanish American nor Indian—in this case, a Caucasian of European descent); Ralph, a black male; Modesto and Francisco, Spanish-American males; and Soledad, a Spanish-American female.

It should be noted that no effort was made during the study to check the truth of statements (especially accusations of harassment or maltreatment), since the main objective of the research was to obtain the stories of the subjects in their own words and from their own perspectives. However, we have strong reasons to believe that they expressed, to a large extent, what they believed to be true, based on their personal experiences with the criminal justice system and with society at large.

According to Hall,

> . . . we need to distinguish what "the common man" does and says about crime from what scholars say about crime. Viewed in broadest outline, the first enterprise, if assiduously prosecuted, would be a sort of chronicle, a history of conflicts and disputes, the pains and injuries human beings have inflicted on one another in connection therewith, and what reasons they gave to explain their conduct. This would include the action and talk of "offenders" (from society's viewpoint; oppressed, from their own) as well as those of pater, chieftain, official (oppressor or tyrant from

the offender's point of view). The second sort of enterprise would constitute analysis of the discussions of scholars, of theories of the above noted phenomena.[3]

While there is intensive criminological literature on "objective" appraisals of the criminal justice system, the literature focusing on the offender's point of view, while growing, still reflects serious omissions. We believe, with Albert Morris, that "even when they are lacking in penetration or sincerity, the verbalizations of criminals may have a diagnostic value as great as other overt behavior."[4] Clinard and Quinney elaborate on this point: "A final way of looking at the social nature of professional crime is through the language of the offender. . . . The argot used reflects the attitudes of the professional toward the law, himself, the victim, other criminals, and society in general."[5]

Since the interviews in this book represent life styles expressed in the criminals' own words, language patterns, and idioms, they were not changed except to alter names and places to ensure the anonymity of the subjects. In addition, some repetitious material was deleted because of constraints on length.

The study tried to capture, in its fullness and richness, the complex structure of meanings by which a burglar, like all the rest of us, experiences his world. Because of that, we reproduce here his living language, the ways in which he communicates with himself and others, his reflections, joy, grief, despair, and sometimes hope, all part of his "being in the world."

By doing so, we attempted to throw some light on the possibilities of a criminology in which meanings, as portrayed by actors from common-sense perspectives, become the essential concern of its concepts and conceptual constructions. From those "common-sense," primary interpretations of the actors, more refined conceptual analysis should follow as the task of the scientist. But such an endeavor, whatever its complexity, should not ignore life's basic meanings. In examining social phenomena, as Schutz points out, "we cannot understand otherwise than within the scheme of human motives, human means and ends; human planning, in short, within the categories of human action. The social scientist must therefore ask, or he must at least always be in a position to ask, what happens in the mind of an individual actor whose act has led to the phenomenon in question."[6]

In brief, we wanted to understand how our "subjects" view society, and especially law enforcement and judicial, correctional, and educational institutions, since most of their lives reflect a constant pattern of interaction with the law. And "to understand a problematic situation," in the words of Hall, "it is necessary to reconstruct and relive it with all the doubts, assurance, insights, sense of obligation, and aspirations experienced with the original actors in it."[7]

Even though we are very much aware of the risks involved in generalizations derived from selected cases, we believe these interviews reflect trends and situations relevant to the criminological literature of the United States and of other parts of the world. They are, of course, especially pertinent to significant problems in crime and law enforcement, judicial, and corrections efforts in New Mexico.

Criminological Implications

It seems plausible to infer from these interviews that property crime and drug addiction in Albuquerque are part of an established system of criminal behavior, if we take into account fencing activities and drug pushers.

It also seems plausible to believe that, from early childhood, there are few options open to children of broken homes, living in deprived neighborhoods with little parental supervision and with intensive associations with deviant peer groups (environments in which there is a basic breakdown of norms and values), other than to resort to criminal life patterns.

Crime is not an isolated phenomenon but an intrinsic part of the existing socioeconomic order of Albuquerque.

It is plain that, for the subjects interviewed, crime was a reality, however brutal, in their day-to-day lives. For some of them it was present in their homes, and for all of them it was an established pattern within their peer groups.

The presence of "fences," who provide the opportunity to dispose of stolen goods, is also well established. They are, indeed, an essential catalyst for property crime.

The cases described here show intense lack of stable and organized families. All the subjects except one came from less advantaged sections of society. As part of their socialization process, most of them were involved in deviant acts from early life. They were later caught in more severely punished crimes and, finally, were easy prey of the interrelations among drug addiction, burglaries, and other crimes, such as armed robberies.

It would be misleading to conclude, however, that their lives are merely the "product" of concrete, empirical circumstances, raw "facts." The subjects themselves have helped in the "co-creation" of their circumstances, by applying to their "world" selectives and distinct norms and values. Facts, values, and norms are not isolated events but are part of the unity of human existence and conduct. From the interplay of facts, values, and norms, the overall content of one's existence emerges. Biswanger says, "That we are lived by the forces of life is only one side of the truth—the other is that we determine these forces as our fate."[8]

The subjects were involved in what could be called "careers in crime." We prefer to speak of a life of crime—crime not only as a profession, but as a way of life.

The initial constellation of facts, values, and norms that resulted in the subjects' first conflicts with the law proved to be very stable and repetitive. Again and again, those initial offenders were dragged into situations in which defiance of the law was the result. As Jack says of juveniles, "Then once they get in trouble, most of them . . . continue getting in trouble until they wind up at the penitentiary. In my case that's what happened. I went from car stealing to burglary, to shoplifting, to armed robbery."

They are not isolated actors. As burglars, they were involved in a criminal "system" and operated with full knowledge of the opportunities and sanctions offered by society. Fences, pushers, policemen, neighbors, teachers, parents, grandparents, guards, probation officers, wardens, lawyers, judges, and many more are part of the plot.

The criminals form part of a structure of interrelated parts, a system of a kind, factual, normative, and valuational. The individual burglar is the "salient criminal actor"; he is often the tip of the iceberg of crime. Behind the burglar, supporting him, is the fence. Through him, stolen merchandise goes back to the market. The burglar is the external perpetrator of property crime. The fence is often the entrepreneur.

When property crime, as is often the case, is closely related to drug addiction, the structure of activities performed by the burglar is tied to the complex network of organized crime, as distributor or seller of drugs.

In the symphony of human actions and institutions of which the criminal is part, even his personal life becomes the history of society. Thus these accounts are part of the live drama of Albuquerque society today.

These are five portraits of bitter loneliness—of a search for meaning, for love, for belonging, for self-respect—taken from an endless road of self and social denial and destructiveness.[9] When Soledad del Valle talks about the birth of her illegitimate daughter, she says, "I was happy . . . I figured that finally I'm gonna have somebody that nobody can take away from me."

These stories could be challenged on the grounds that they may not be reliable. However, the principal assistant in the study had known all of the subjects except one for many years. He was aware not only of their records but also of many significant parts of their lives. Because of this, we had a good knowledge of their family life, school years, adolesence, early involvement in crime, crimes commit- ted, and circumstances of their detention and imprisonment, proba- tion, and parole. We are confident that in substance these are factual reflections of their experiences and perspectives.

The futility of the many efforts called "probation," some of the degrading features of correctional institutions, and the isolation of the "actors" of the legal process (judges, other court officers, and lawyers) from the "cases" they decide are all mentioned here.

The psychology of the burglar; his "intuition" for the right circumstance, time, and place; his profound knowledge of the prevailing mores and folkways that help provide anonymity for his wrongdoing; his relationships with the keystone of property crime, the fence; the interrelations between drugs and crime—all of these are vividly exposed. The burglar's rationalizations about the effects crime may have on his victims is expressed by Ralph: "I didn't mind too much about them. I figured all they have to do is call up the insurance man to get the money." They count, of course, on impunity, since only a small fraction of their crimes were ever detected.

As for probation and court proceedings, the subjects agreed on their lack of any deterrent effect. Jack summarizes their feelings about the courts: "I more or less thought it was a big joke. I'd say, 'They'll give me a chance this time.' " Finally, all of them gave detailed profiles of their experiences in the Santa Fe penitentiary.

At this point, it seems important to remark that orientation toward the future was largely absent in the subjects' lives. Modern psychotherapy has vigorously stated the importance of an orientation toward the future as a basic step toward spiritual and mental recovery. All those interviewed were rigidly crystallized into the present. A rational calculation of the risks involved in further criminal behavior appeared in varying degrees of intensity in all the cases. In the past, they had settled the issue in favor of committing crimes, minimizing the probability of being detected and prosecuted. Of course, they considered the intrinsic possibility that some day they would be discovered. But they regarded such an outcome as part of the balance between positive and negative sanctions upon which every human decision rests. Incentives for their criminal involvement existed in direct proportion to the probability that they could "beat the system," even to the degree of rationalizing the potential for harm to their victims: almost everybody, they said, is insured in today's society.

Common Patterns

Broken homes, criminal or deviant associations from early years, and even in some cases delinquent behavior at home characterized the childhoods of all of the subjects interviewed.

Soledad del Valle saw her mother become an alcoholic and then commit suicide after being divorced by her father. Ralph, raised by his grandmother in what he calls a "highly criminal environment," describes the illicit gambling operation conducted in her home. Jack remarks that his mother was divorced when he was three years old. Modesto was raised by his godparents. He never lived with his mother, and he doesn't remember when she married his stepfather. Francisco describes his father's alcoholism and how he was eventually found dead in a downtown Albuquerque parking lot after a drinking bout.

They were all left by themselves with no supervision or control. Their peers generally displayed a similar lack of parental control.

Schools seem to have played no significant role in the formation of their characters or moral values.

All of the subjects began their deviant behavior (including delinquent acts and, in some cases, drug use) early in life, some before they were teenagers. Modesto's friends introduced him to marijuana. He "graduated" to heroin at the age of seventeen. Modesto started shoplifting when he was thirteen. He was placed in the detention home many times and finally spent an extended stretch in a reformatory in Colorado. The first day he was released, he started smoking marijuana again. Jack also started shoplifting at an early age, although he was never drawn into the drug scene. The reaction of his friends to his first encounter with the juvenile court (at age twelve) was "No big deal." Ralph committed grand larceny at the age of seven and was in jail at the age of nine. Soledad went to live with her father and stepmother after her mother's suicide, but never overcame her bitterness toward them. Her rebelliousness finally led her to run away from home and to try heroin, at the age of fifteen. Early deviance as a factor of peer involvement was perhaps most graphic with Francisco, who describes it as a learning process: "The way it started out with me, I used to hang around with some older fellows. . . . I was learning a little more, you know, just a little more."

The successful burglar is an up-to-date urban social psychologist. He knows very well when and how to strike. All of the subjects stole regularly, some of them committing an average of three hundred burglaries a year. Jack and Ralph describe their craft with an aura of detached professionalism. For a residential burglary, Jack's technique is bold: "I would probably rob a place, if there's nobody there, in the daytime, in broad daylight, because the neighbors are not going to suspect anybody coming up there with a truck, in overalls that say ABC Furniture Company, coming in through the front door and moving the furniture out." Francisco also had a detailed methodology for selecting houses to burglarize.

All of the subjects reported strikingly high and relatively stable incomes from crime—far higher than they could expect to earn in the normal job market. Ralph, for example, said he averaged five hundred to five hundred and fifty dollars a week. Prior to their last conviction, Soledad and her husband, both addicts, stole four to five hundred dollars' worth of merchandise a day to support their habit. Their level of "success" in their chosen "profession," then, was far greater than any of them could have hoped to achieve in "straight" society.

There is once more, through the data collected, ample evidence of the direct reciprocal relationship between drug addiction and crime. Three of the subjects (Modesto, Soledad, and Francisco) were heroin addicts and relied on burglary and shoplifting to support their habits. Ralph admitted to popping pills, mainly amphetamines. Only Jack, who regarded himself as a professional thief, remained drug free. Soledad elaborates: "Every day we would have to steal. We'd have to steal at least three hundred dollars' worth of merchandise a day to support the habit we had. . . . Days that we would have good luck . . . and get a whole lot of money, you know, like people would think it would last us for a week but an addict isn't that way. The more money he has, the more he shoots, you know." Modesto and Francisco were very frank about their criminal activity in support of their heroin habits.

The burglar's reliance on the fence is well documented in all these accounts. Each of the subjects describes the integral relationship of fencing activity with burglary. Their dependence on the fence for quick conversion of stolen goods into money and for fast disposal of "hot" property to avoid arrest was a necessary component of their success and indicates that no city can sustain a consistently high burglary rate without well-established, sophisticated fencing operations.

"Most fences, you know," Ralph explains, "they'll come to you. They'll look through the records and say, like they'll go around town and check your record. . . . And if he feels like you're a pretty safe dude, he'll stop you one day and he might tell you, 'Well, I need a typewriter, an adding machine, stereo console,' or something like that. . . . he's the businessman type dude." Ralph, who sold his stolen goods at 75 percent of their price most of the time, said he always got almost full value. On the other hand, Modesto "never did get a good price," even though he was selling to individuals and not to fences. Fences, for him, were a last resort.

Impact of Police, Courts, and Correctional Institutions

The deterrent and rehabilitative impact of police, courts, and correctional institutions is generally described by the subjects as minimal, especially during the juvenile years, which are characterized by light treatment and short sentences. All the subjects seemed to feel that inequality in the system was more a factor of the income level of the offender than of his ethnic background—that society metes out harsher punishment to the poor. Their accounts seem to indicate that any deterrent effects of the system were more a function of the offender's desire to avoid further contact than of counseling, vocational training, and other "rehabilitative" programs offered by the system.

Modesto, talking about the courts, says, "It's not fair. . . . I could be caught with a TV in my hands and I couldn't get myself a lawyer or anything like that. I'd probably get sent up to [the penitentiary at] Santa Fe. The next guy could be caught with the same TV in his hands but with money in his pocket or his family with money in their pockets. He wouldn't go to Santa Fe." He comments on programs at the penitentiary: "They can show you all types of paper where it says 'We have this program and this program and this program.' It looks beautiful in writing, man, but in reality it's not what it says on that piece of paper. They do have a plumbing shop, electrical shop, all the vocational things, but what good if you go over there at eight o'clock in the morning and sit with a magazine?"

Jack talks of ethnic groups in the Santa Fe penitentiary, black cliques, Chicano cliques, and "gray" cliques (whites). All the subjects discuss the presence of illegal drugs in the penitentiary: heroin, pills, marijuana. The pervasive problem of homosexuality in the penitentiary is also discussed at length in several of the interviews.

The Conversion Process

Once in prison, most of the subjects reported a gradual change in attitudes, from great hostility and bitterness toward the "system" and its "perpetrators" (lawyers, judges, and, especially, prison officials and guards), through gradual acceptance of prison life, and finally to something that might be described as a "conversion" process or the desire to "go straight." In most cases, the onset of the conversion process seemed to coincide with the subject's ability to foresee the possibility of parole (that is, his having passed the midpoint of that portion of his sentence which must be served before he is eligible for parole). It was at that point that most of the subjects began to blame themselves more heavily than the system for their plight and began to take an active interest in various rehabilitative programs that might enhance their chances for parole. Jack describes the process for us: "I finally sat down and thought, 'What in the hell am I doing? If I want to get out of here I'd better straighten up and try to do something that will benefit myself instead of the other guy.' "

It is difficult to assess the longevity of the conversion process. Probably it varies considerably from individual to individual—ranging perhaps from months (or even weeks) to a lifetime. Soledad del Valle stayed out of prison only a few months, and Francisco, by his own admission after the taping sessions, appeared headed in that direction.

Perhaps Ralph states the problem most eloquently: "Like I've seen quite a few losers that won't ever come out and I've seen a lot of them return and I've tried to figure out why. I guess they say they get institutionalized, you know. Like they stay there so long that's all they know. When they're free, they can't face reality out here. It's supposed to be a cold dark world."

In this book we gain limited access to the world of the burglar—limited because we are forced to view the lives of the burglars through their own eyes and their own words. We do not have the sometimes more revealing insight of the participant observer, and we must recognize that we can never reproduce the unique experiences of the protagonists themselves. Nevertheless, these histories represent testimonies of our times and our lives worth considering.

There is no doubt that the world of the burglar is also part of our own society and its social institutions, our anxieties and our despair and hope. We have created the burglar; in turn, we are created by him. "We" and "they" are nothing but reciprocal dimensions of human society, of the "I" and the "thou." Our society, their society, cast them early in their lives into roles from which they may never escape. Just as they were cast as actors in certain roles, the society provided the necessary stage as the setting for their performances.

We have labeled them from the very beginning of their lives. We were preparing them, inventing them to be the propitiatory victims of the gods of our times: the unmitigated self-interest, indifference, and materialism for which this century is so distinguished.

Jack

Jack is the one person of the five interviewed who is not a native of New Mexico. He was born and raised in another part of the country and came into contact with the New Mexico criminal justice system as a result of only one crime—an armed robbery, for which he was sentenced to the state penitentiary.

When Jack came to the interview he was neatly dressed and gave an impression of self-assurance and confidence. He is well built, blond and blue eyed, and has rough hands and weathered skin—obviously a man who works outdoors. Throughout the interview Jack gave the impression of one who has committed himself to a plan of action, in terms of marriage, his job, and so forth. Of the persons interviewed, Jack can most truly be characterized as a professional criminal. All his crimes were deliberately planned and executed. Probably, also, if he returns to a life of crime, it will be a very deliberate act.

Q: What I'd like to do is go back as far as you can remember, when you were five, six years old.

A: When I first started going wrong?

Q: No, not necessarily, go back to your family situation as far as you can remember.

A: Okay. I was born and raised in a slum district of Chicago. My mother was divorced from my father when I was about three years old.

Q: Do you remember the divorce at all?

A: No, I don't. I lived with my mother. She worked nights as a waitress when I was a kid, which more or less put me on my own. I had a sister, an older sister. When I was say four, that would put her at twelve, she was boarded as a foster child. My mother was working nights and my sister was at the age where she needed someone to look after her. Mother figured it would be better just to board her out. So all those years I grew up on my own. When I was eight or nine, I would be hanging around with a . . . gang you might call it, kids nine, ten, eleven years old and no supervision, we were getting in trouble.

Q: What about school?

A: I was going to school, but maybe three days out of the week I wouldn't appear at school. The times I was there I did well, but I was always thinking about getting out of school and getting out on my own and when I reached sixteen they finally told me I wasn't eligible to be in school. Well, in between those times, I was constantly getting in trouble with the law.

Q: What kinds of friends did you have?

A: Well, the people I associated with were the kids in the neighborhood who were more or less in the same predicament I was; little supervision through their homes or their families, parents didn't care where they were. We would get home at eleven or twelve at night but during the day there was no supervision. They never asked you where you'd been or what you did, you know, and consequently we more or less roamed in a pack, thirteen, twenty kids.

Q: What about your mother?

A: She slept in the daytime and went to work at night. She'd go to work at five at night and get home maybe at two, three in the morning and sleep during the day. Like when she was sleeping, I was out, when I got home, she was going to work, which gave me the rest of the evening to myself. Well, being by myself, I wasn't going to stay in the house, of course, I was gonna go out, look for company.

Q: Did you have any relatives?

A: Yeah. I had a grandmother and several uncles and aunts. Once in a while I would go over and say hello but basically I used to stay on the street corner. We'd be outside, you know, and on the corner guys would ask, "What are we going to do tonight? Why don't we go down to the freight yards and bust into some cars and see if we can steal something," or "There's a dance down the street, let's go down there," or "Let's go steal a car to ride in."

Q: How young would you say you started getting in—

A: In trouble? Oh, probably ten years old.

Q: Until ten you were fairly straight?

A: Yeah, fairly straight because I wasn't aware of what was going on.

Q: Your dad, you never saw him during that time?

A: I might see him every two or three months. He lived in Chicago, by himself. We had a mutual understanding—"How are you? Everything is fine," you know, and that would be it. He didn't care, and I didn't really give much thought to him. My whole outlook at life at that time was, if you want something, go and get it. If you want to ride a bike, go out and steal it. When I was eleven or twelve years old if I didn't have the money I would go out and steal what I wanted. Sometimes we didn't have the rent or the food, see? We might go for three days without food so if we wanted to eat we had to go out and steal it.

Q: Was your mom aware of it when you started getting into things?

A: Yeah, she was, but like most slum families, if you stole something and got away with it, well, more power to you. It was something you brought home, something that you gained. You stole two or three dozen eggs and half a slab of meat, well, that's something more you had because you couldn't afford it otherwise. She might not have liked it but she'd never get down to where she'd give you a hard time about it. She might say, well, something was wrong, but still there it was.

We got along good. If I had a problem, I might come home and talk it over with her, you know, but usually she'd be gone. I'd be out in the daytime or in school, she'd be sleeping, I'd come home at night, she'd be getting ready to go to work and I might see her for a couple of hours out of the day. Back then most of them worked seven days a week, six at least. If she was off on a Sunday or a Saturday I was always outside anyway.

Q: Did she ever remarry?

A: Yeah, several times, and the last time she's been married thirteen years. But I haven't seen my mother now in ten years. I call her once in a while. She's in Chicago right now. And I'm out here. I figure the best way to start a new life and get away from it all would be to stay away from my immediate family, see, because she's very dominant. She wants things her way or not at all.

Q: So you had several stepfathers. How did you get along with them?

A: Most of them no good, because they had a lot of drinking in the house. Most of them wouldn't work, you know. It's just like any other slum family—most of them drank a lot, they were lazy, once in a while they worked, sometimes they didn't, and you didn't depend on anybody for anything, for your food or your clothes. If they bought you something, okay, they bought it for you. If they didn't, you didn't worry about it.

Q: Were you happier then when your mom was alone?

A: No, not really. I never really gave it much thought. I'd probably say, for any juvenile, eleven or twelve years old, most of them don't have enough supervision. They go out, the family never worries what they're doing or where they're going. They just don't care and they are probably the same as mine. My mother never knew where I was going or what I was doing or what I was going to do. I went out and did what I wanted. If a family doesn't have the time to take with their kids and ask 'em, "Where you been? What are you doing?" they're going to get in trouble. Any juvenile, I don't care who it is. Then once they get in trouble, most of them, unless they're pulled up right away, they continue getting in trouble until they wind up at the penitentiary. In my case that's what happened. I went from car stealing to burglary, to shoplifting, to armed robbery. I started out stealing groceries and shoplifting and from there stealing cars and from there into burglary and worked my way up to where I was up for armed robbery. I was sentenced to fifty years in the penitentiary, which I did only nine years.

Q: So when you were a kid, you were always with a group?

A: Yeah, you was always trying to outthink the other one. One guy would come up and say, "Let's steal these two dollars' worth of groceries." You might be trying to outthink the other guy and say, "No, I think I'll steal ten dollars' worth of groceries." But in the end you'd go together and do it and split it up and take it on home.

Q: Were the kids that you ran around with mostly your age?

A: Yeah, give or take a year.

Q: Were you organized into a gang? I mean, like did you have a leader?

A: You always get the toughest guy, he's going to be the leader. He'd say, "We're gonna do this," and if it sounded halfway decent we would do it. You might go six months and never be caught at doing nothing and all of a sudden get caught. They'd take you down to the police station, call your mother, say, "Well, we've got your son down here." She'd come and get you and they'd tell you, "You have to appear in juvenile court." The next day you'd appear in juvenile court and they'd send you to juvenile home for thirty days and let you out and you're right back in the same neighborhood, the same guys and everything.

Q: How old were you when you first got sent up to juvenile hall?

A: About twelve.

Q: For thirty days?

A: Yeah.

Q: Was that when you got caught the first time or did you have several chances?

A: I had several chances before that. The judge would tell me, "Well, okay. I'm gonna put you on six months probation" or "on ninety days probation," and let me go. Second time he'd tell me he was gonna put me on a year's probation this time, and let me go. After the third time he'd say, "I've given you two chances. Now we're going to send you to the detention home for thirty days." You go to the detention home for thirty days and come out and thirty days isn't really too long. You laugh at it and say, "Well, big deal." They didn't teach you nothin'. They told you to behave yourself and don't do it again. You don't have no training. You don't have no vocational training or no kind of rehabilitation, of course.

Q: What were your impressions of courts at that time?

A: At that time, I more or less thought it was a big joke. I'd say, "They'll give me a chance this time." I'd know I could do it and get away with it because if they caught me, so what? I'd go to court and say, "Well, I'm sorry. I didn't mean to do it," and get probation.

Q: During that first six months, what was your impression of probation?

A: I figured, if I get caught doing something else, they're gonna send me away. I figured I better be more careful.

Q: What kind of supervision did you have on probation?

A: Nothing, really. The court puts you on probation, you report to your probation officer once a week or once a month and he asks you, "How are you doing?" "Okay." "Are you staying out of trouble?" "Yeah." Most of the guys just tell a lie. They aren't staying out of trouble. And you'd be right back on the corner that night.

Q: What would you say the length of the interviews with your probation officer were?

A: Maybe five minutes. Just, "How are you doing?" "Okay." "Staying out of trouble?" "Yeah." "Fill out this form and I'll see you next month."

Q: Did he ever come to see you?

A: Oh, no. Chicago had about two thousand cases per probation officer. He doesn't have the time to go out and check or spend time with any individual, and it's the same way all over the country. A kid can see it. You could get arrested or go to court and come before him again and then he might do something, but if you can duck and dodge him for a month, you're all right.

Q: What was your experience, do you remember, in juvenile detention? Were you afraid when you went in?

A: Oh, yeah, I was a little nervous. After a day or two, it didn't bother me. I got to thinking, "Well, twenty-eight more days and I'll be out of this place." You started counting the days off. You went to school, but basically you didn't do too much of nothing. They'd talk to you once in a while about what could happen to you in the future if you kept on getting into trouble, but there wasn't really nothing that could help you put your mind on a different track.

Q: The experience didn't affect you either way?

A: No, not really. You got in trouble, you're up here for thirty days, you have to stay here, you do it the best way you can. If you're a tough guy, they're gonna make it rough on you; you wanna tend to your own business and you're all right.

Q: How large was the juvenile hall you were in?

A: Oh, about three hundred guys. It was a reformatory. They called it a detention home for kids from eight to fourteen or fifteen, and from fifteen to eighteen they sent you to the same building but a different wing in the building, and then from eighteen on you were sent to the state penitentiary.

Q: So you could stay there anywhere from a few days to several months?

A: You could stay there from a week, I guess, till your twenty-first birthday. And as you get older, they move you to different age groups, but basically they don't want to keep you there till you're twenty-one. But if you commit a crime serious enough, the judge can send you to the detention center till your eighteenth or your twenty-first birthday.

Q: The first time you went in, some of those kids that were there had already been there before?

A: Oh, yeah, you've got a great number of repeats. Probably from one-third to one-half come back. Some of them learn a lesson, some of them don't.

Q: How many times were you there?

A: I stayed twice overnight and got out the next day, and I was there for thirty days, and I was there for a week. Up around four different times in the detention center. And from the detention center

I went into the service and from the service I went to the penitentiary.

Q: Did the court send you to the service?

A: They caught me and they asked me—

Q: Where did they catch you?

A: Burglary—broke into a bar and they told me I could either go till I'm eighteen to the detention center or I could go to the service, and at that time, I just turned seventeen, I told them, "I'll just go in the service." I was in the service two years. I came out when I was nineteen, got an honorable discharge and came out.

Q: You did all right in the service?

A: Oh, yeah. I had no trouble at all. And I kept, you know, a pretty good record for two years and then when I came out, I was right back to the same neighborhood, the same people. I went back to Chicago and you got the same guys there, most of them. They were older, but their way of thinking was the same. So I went to Chicago, from Chicago I went to L.A., and I come out here and pulled an armed robbery.

Q: As a kid, before you were eighteen and got sent up here, what do you think would have been some of the things that really would have helped?

A: Well, when I was arrested and put on probation, close supervision for one thing. If your parents can't keep close track of you, the courts, the probation officer, could give you periodic checks, talk to you, give you counseling. They have boys' clubs all over the country. If you don't want to join a boys' club, at least get active in some young group. It's gonna help you out and I think that if that had happened, I probably would have went the straight way. If you don't have a trade, you need someone that can teach you a trade.

Q: Did you ever have any teachers that stand out in your mind as being either exceptionally good or exceptionally bad?

A: In grade school, all I can remember, to them it was just a job. When the bell rang at the end of the day, they went their way and you went yours. They weren't there. They never sat down and talked to you and told you, "Well, you're doing pretty good but you could do better," or "Let me show you what you're doing wrong," or "You're doing bad. Maybe I could help you out." I never can recall any teachers telling me that. They'd just come in the class and say, "This is your lesson for today." The class was over, they never said "hello," "goodbye," or nothin'. They just went.

I guess, when you figure if you don't have someone to just kind of pull you aside and tell you "You're doing pretty good but you're not quite doing good enough. Now let me show you what's wrong," then you're not going to give it much thought whether anybody cares for you or not. You're gonna say, "Well, I wish the bell would hurry up and ring so I could get out of here." And if you can, you might skip the last hour of class. Go home early.

Q: Do you remember in grade school, did you consider yourself one of the brighter students?

A: No, I wasn't one of the brighter students. I was probably about average. My grades were from a C plus to a B plus. Pretty good average student. And I never do recall too much homework but I showed no interest in school. All I did was think, "Well, I wish I could get to be sixteen and get out of here," and school was just something you had to do. You had to be there so most of the time you would be there. If you thought of a way to get sick or a way to get out of school, that's what you'd do.

Q: Didn't the school ever catch you for truancy?

A: Oh, yeah, they caught me several times and they'd say, "Well, you gotta bring your mother up here." I'd go home and tell my mother that I had skipped school and they wanted to see her at school. She'd bawl me out, tell me it wasn't right and don't do it no more and sometimes she'd go to school, sometimes call and say she had to go to work. She'd say, "Well, you're gonna have to be punished. You stay in tonight." But she went to work at five and I knew she wasn't gonna be home for another seven, eight hours so I'd go out anyway. I'd say it all comes down to supervision. When a kid has supervision, when they see him going astray to something that's not quite right, they give him closer supervision and sit down with him and explain what he's doing wrong and what could happen.

Q: Doesn't supervision actually imply caring somehow?

A: I'd say it's not only human beings. Hell, that goes for animals, too. And kids, they have to have someone be over them and tell them what to do and what not to do. If you go out and steal two dollars today and they don't tell you it's wrong, you say, "Well, this is easy. Watch, tomorrow I'll steal four dollars' worth." You might get away with it for a year. The longer you go the easier it gets and all of a sudden you get caught and you say, "Well, what happened?" But you appear before a judge in a juvenile court and he tells you, "You did something wrong and I'm gonna give you a sixty-day probation," and then turns you loose. You say, "Heck, they didn't do nothin' so I'll just continue doing it."

Q: Were you scared when you went to court, do you think?

A: The first time I was, and after that most of the kids would say, "They ain't gonna do nothin' noway and if they do they give you two weeks, thirty days. No big deal."

Q: Did you know that some states have closed down all of their juvenile institutions?

A: You take a kid eleven, twelve years old and word gets around there's no more juvenile homes. Now they know they're too young to be sent to a prison, so what are they going to do with them when they get in trouble? They're too young to send them to prison and yet they've committed an offense and they have to be punished.

Q: Are you saying, then, that they should keep the institutions open?

A: I think they should keep the institutions but I think, dealing with kids over the years—at Santa Fe when I was doing time up there, I'd come out into the town of Santa Fe in the schools and talk to different kids. They should have somebody. Well, they should have directors and the staff should be familiar with their way of thinking. Okay, say you've got a staff of ten or fifteen working for you. Out of ten or fifteen, you should have at least two or three men or women that have been there already, been in trouble, straightened up, living a straight life and want to, seriously want to help these kids get back on the right line. You might have fifteen on your staff; you have two or three ex-convicts. Now there is two or three states that do have ex-convict parole officers. They have them on the police force, the sheriff's department, and so forth. The average ex-convict could probably tell you more and help out more than the man on your staff that hasn't been there because he is looking at it from his viewpoint.

Q: But after a while, you quit being an ex-convict.

A: You quit being an ex-convict, but still, your way of thinking and knowing how these kids are thinking is still there because you've been through it yourself. The average man on your staff can't say, "Well, I've been there and I know how he's thinking," because he hasn't been there. The only thing he can do is guess what the other guy is thinking. He may have good ideas or his reasoning may be good but still, it may not be a hundred percent.

Q: So in other words, you're saying that we should keep institutions—

A: I would say, keep institutions but have the correct staff. In other words, don't just bring a person up off the streets and say, "Well, your qualifications are good. You've never been in trouble, you've got a Ph.D. in this and a master's degree in that," because all these degrees don't really mean nothing unless they can get down and circulate and be part of the group that they're trying to straighten out. You and I can walk into a group of kids, let's say twenty kids, and start rapping with them, talking with them, ask them what their problems are and tell them some of our experiences.

Or maybe that's just one of your staff here. That guy could be right out of college, four years of college, a young guy in the twenties. He could tell these guys what he thinks they ought to do and they'll probably listen to him, but while they're listening to him they're thinking, "This guy's a square," and the minute he walks out the door they've forgot all about him. I could walk in the same room, tell 'em my experiences and come right back in the same phase they're in now. In other words, I've been there and can tell them what they're doing and pretty close to what they're thinking. Bring them right to line with my experiences from juvenile to early till the late teens, till my early twenties into the penitentiary up until now, and tell them what would happen, what they can expect if they continue doing what they're doing and explain to them, "Here I am. I don't have no education, have no trade," this and that. I figure a guy with experience can probably bring them closer than a guy that is talking to them and not too much of an idea . . .

Q: Why does this need to be done in an institution? Why can't it be done on the streets?

A: It can, but you've got to have supervision.

Q: Well, that's what I'm saying, why can't you take that same staff and put them out on the streets?

A: If you have the staff to do it, but I've noticed this state, along with other states, is a very poor state because the legislature, your city and state government, won't give you the funds to hire the staff you need. You're understaffed in every institution I've seen in this state that deals with juveniles or adults and unless you have the right amount of people on your staff with the right qualifications and enough offered you can't do a good job anywhere. Now, if you're understaffed, you're just wasting your time. If your staff is up to par and you have enough men and people in the field that can go out and circulate with these kids that are getting constantly into trouble, then you can do your job. But till then, you have to fall back on your institutions because you've got two or three people in your institution herding over fifty kids there. But you put fifty kids on the street and three men can't go out and circulate· with them—they're too far spread out.

I've noticed in this state's parole system—you might call me an adviser to the parole system—this is something new they're trying out in the state. I meet with the parole officers in the state about once every month, since I've been out, and I talk to the parole officers and give them a few things that I know through experience—what to look for and what to expect and when a guy shoots you an answer, just how to answer him back. And I go to these parole meetings maybe once every three, four weeks and one of the parole officers asks me, "Well, what would happen if one of my clients asked me if I can get him a job or if he has a problem what should I say to him?" and I'll tell them from my experiences what would be a logical answer. Some of them they use, some of them they disregard.

Q: It's my impression that stealing is a fairly successful career in the sense that you succeed more often than you fail.

A: As a juvenile. As an adult, though, you don't, because as an adult, you're caught stealing, you go to the penitentiary for five, ten years. You come out and go for six months or a year or two, but then you're caught again, you go back up another time.

Q: I'm sure you have known people in the penitentiary that have stolen several hundred times and have gotten away with it.

A: Right. I've gone two and three years, consistently, week after week and never got caught. I pulled probably a hundred, hundred and fifty armed robberies before I was caught, which accumulated to quite a bit of money. I paid for my sister's house. Things were going pretty good; I like to have nice clothes, I had a new car, a nice apartment.

Q: Did you work?

A: Oh no, because stealing was so easy. You walk into a grocery store, near closing time, you tell 'em "This is a stickup," they give you fifteen hundred, two thousand and that's good for a month. The average working man does not spend two thousand a month. Well, when I was seventeen years old I was running two thousand a month. I was staying in Chicago but I would fly to California, Nevada, Seattle, and then I'd come back to Chicago. I'd go, make a score, and come back.

Q: Were you alone?

A: Several times I'd be with other people. I'd have a buddy, and say through the grapevine we'd hear, "There's a good payroll robbery in California," Sacramento. You'd just go out there and look at it. You might have five hundred dollars in your pocket, enough to last a couple of weeks. You'd look it over and if it looked good, you'd go ahead and get it.

Q: Was your thing mostly armed robberies?

A: From the time I was seventeen and up it was. Before that it was burglaries. I was burglarizing places for three, four hundred—restaurants, bars, offices. Mostly for money, not merchandise.

Q: So before you were seventeen, you spent most of your time in Chicago?

A: Right. Well, I'd say about eight months out of the year I'd be in Chicago. The rest of the time I'd be in Atlanta because when I was young my mother went to Atlanta and my sister stayed down there. She got married down there.

Q: When you were growing up did you see much of your sister?

A: No, but from the time I was about ten till the time I was sixteen I saw quite a bit of her. When I was younger, she was living in a foster home, and when she reached sixteen, she went back to my mother and my mother went to Atlanta for probably four months and when she left Atlanta to come back, my sister stayed there and got married.

Q: Did you stay in Chicago when your mother went to Atlanta?

A: No, I was down there with her. I stayed with her and when I went back with her to Chicago, my sister stayed down there. And after that, when I was about sixteen, I'd go to Atlanta by myself. I liked it down there so I would commute back and forth. And, like I say, when I reached seventeen, I was arrested and they gave me a choice of the service or the reformatory. I burglarized a restaurant. I spent two years in the service, and I was nineteen when I came out and for about eight or nine months after coming out I didn't work or anything like that. I got my hands on a pistol and started pulling armed robberies and the more I pulled, the easier it was.

But like I say, anybody that's been in crime all their life started from the time they were juveniles. That's where it stems from. You can never say a guy starts crime in his twenties. You might get one guy out of two or three thousand who's never had crime previously and he really did it because he got depressed or he's tight for money or something. But overall, it goes back to the time the kid is eight or nine years old.

Q: Would you consider yourself a professional criminal?

A: I was considered a professional armed robber because I specialized in supermarkets, payroll robberies—

Q: So they were pretty sizable?

A: Yeah. When I was arrested here, I robbed a supermarket. I got arrested four days later in a roadblock in Texas.

Q: How did you get away with it so long?

A: Stealing is, well, I guess you might say it's the element of surprise. You know what you're doing but the other person doesn't. Now you're robbing a place or burglarizing a place or whatever you're gonna do, the person on the street doesn't care what you're doing as long as you're not bothering him. Unless there's a police car right there while you're doing it you're not gonna get caught. When you pull an armed robbery, you walk in a place and you put a gun on somebody: "This is a stickup." You figure, what is the percentage of the police catching you? There might be a hundred police cars in the city. Half of them are on duty, half of them are off duty. Now what's the percentage of one of them being outside the store in a large city? Because in too many places they have beats and when criminals are there they're not going to be around. You're only gonna be there three, five minutes. Very slim odds that you're gonna get caught.

Q: How do you select the place?

A: Well, usually you look at it for a couple of days. You might see a place you think has some money in it, you might look at it for a couple of days, a week, two weeks, see what their routine is, how many people are in the store at a certain time of the day, maybe five at night when they're getting ready to close there might be only three people there, where at four o'clock there are twenty. You watch the place for a period of time and you can more or less tell the routine every day. People, especially in this country, are basically in a routine. They go to bed at a certain hour of the night, they get up at a certain hour, they work a certain hour, they open a place of business and they close it at a certain time. There's usually a slow period during the day and there's a busy period. Usually two or three o'clock in the afternoon is slow whereas eleven, twelve o'clock in the morning is busy. The actual person that's criminally inclined and looking for something to steal or rob, he spots this. There's a routine and if a person wants to do something wrong, just by watching for one week he can more or less tell what to expect. At the weakest point, which might be the slowest time of the day, that's when he'll rob. The same way with a person that robs a bank; the average bank robber robs a bank between three o'clock in the afternoon and eight o'clock in the morning because the bank is not busy then. If it opens at eight o'clock in the morning, there aren't too many people there. The less people you have to put up with, the easier it's gonna be to steal something. That's why most burglars rob at night, because in the dark the less the chances are of someone seeing 'em, plus the business is closed. The average burglar in this city right now strikes probably from eleven at night to one in the morning.

Q: You mean in a business?

A: Right.

Q: How about in a residence?

A: Well, if the person is on vacation you can spot that right away. You walk up to the door, you ring the doorbell—you're a salesman looking for someone, a fictitious name. Nobody answers. You know there's nobody home. You're parked around the corner. What's the chances someone's gonna be home in fifteen minutes? You go ahead and pull the job. The person that burglarizes at night is normally gonna get a house at the wee hours, say at two or three in the morning. That's when the average person is in the deepest sleep, at three in the morning.

Q: So they do it either in the afternoon or—

A: Early in the morning. If a person is going to rob you . . . well, if I was going to go back into burglarizing right now, I would probably rob a place, if there's nobody there, in the daytime, in broad daylight, because the neighbors are not going to suspect anybody coming up there with a truck, in overalls that say ABC Furniture Company, coming in through the front door and moving the furniture out. They're not gonna pay no attention. They may even want to come over and help. A police car comes up, you're blocking the traffic, he may get out and direct the traffic around your truck. He's not gonna think nothing of it.

Q: Did you ever do anything like that?

A: Oh, yeah. When I was a kid, I worked with older people. They'd say, "Now we're gonna go into the house over here. They're on vacation. They got a good dining room set, TV set, good bedroom set, refrigerator . . ." They'd move up a bobtail truck, get a sign put on the side, "Moving Company." Most locks on doors are simple—bust it with a screwdriver or a hammer and just open the door and, if you know no one's gonna be there or you don't think there's gonna be anyone there, you can clean the whole house out in thirty minutes. And I'd say the average burglar is hitting this time of day, right now, in the afternoon.

Q: There's probably not too much on weekends, though.

A: Well, usually on weekends you don't get a burglar, not in cleaning out a house, just during the week because the man of the family is working. The kids are gone to school, of course. A housewife is not gonna pay no attention to what's going on next door or across the street unless it's a personal friend. Then a moving truck comes up with a sign "Moving Company" on it and they still won't think too much of it. They say, well, Mary or Alice, she's having her furniture moved or they're repossessing it or something like that. But the average neighbor don't care what's happening in your house. If a fellow starts coming in and busting all the windows and sets the place on fire, they may call the police, but when a truck comes up and starts moving furniture, they're not gonna think nothing of it.

I had a load of TV sets and recorders, tape recorders, that we took out of an appliance store. We took them out right after the place closed at five o'clock in the afternoon. We parked across the street in the truck, we waited for the people to lock up and leave about ten minutes past five. All right, at a quarter past five I was at the rear entrance, opened the door, went in. I got the cash drawer, had maybe a hundred and fifty dollars in it, petty cash, we took that, we took ten TV sets and the same number of tape recorders in a small pickup. When we come out of the alley and hit the main street, the truck stalled right in the street. Had a whole load of hot goods in the back of the truck. A police car pulled up behind us.

"What's the problem?"

"We gotta make a late delivery and the truck's stalled." The cop came out and helped us push it to the curb and then he directed traffic around the truck. He directed traffic until we got the truck started. We said, "Thanks a lot." He said, "Okay," and we went on about our business.

Q: Were the guys wearing uniforms?

A: No, I had a pair of khakis on and a plaid shirt that said "AP Appliance" or something like that. Other times when we got TV sets we were TV repairmen. You go into any secondhand store and get a khaki shirt and khaki pants, you know.

Out at some of these construction sites where they're putting up new apartment houses, along there, there are already appliances in them like sinks, air conditioners, and so forth, just sitting there. You pull up with a truck. You have maybe a fence in town, a guy who'll say, "You give me fifteen air conditioners and I'll pay you so much for them." Okay, you just happen to know a housing project five miles out of town that's got fifteen air conditioners. You've been out during the day to look it over. So they shut down a job say at three, four in the afternoon. You're right there loading up the truck. You may have on your shirt "Air Conditioning Company" or something like that and nobody's gonna pay no attention as you load up, and if a police car comes in the neighborhood, if you're cool, you're not gonna break and run. You flag the cop down and ask for directions. Well, he's not gonna wonder what you're doing here at this time of day with a load of supplies. You see a cop coming down the street, the truck already loaded and ready to go just as he pulls up.

You wave him down and say, "I'm looking for Ajax Construction. I've got a load of supplies here."

He won't know what's going on in a construction project. "Well, no. You could check around the corner. Check down the street," you know.

You raise a little hell, say "I gotta get this delivered and get home. My old lady's waiting on me. If I drop them here will you keep your eye on 'em?"

He ain't gonna keep his eye on 'em. "No, you can't leave them here. You better take 'em back to your shop." You just cuss him out, get a little belligerent with him. You throw their whole way of thinking off. This is your professional thief. A lot of times a cop will say, "Well, you can't leave 'em here. Now get 'em out of here."

"All right, if you're gonna be that way about it, I'll report you. What's your badge number?"

Q: On commercial burglaries did you ever go into a lot of detailed planning or was it a spur-of-the-moment thing?

A: Well, in any large city there's always a fence system. If you're raised in a city, just through the grapevine or being associated with different thieves, you're gonna meet the fences. Like I've been in this town now for five months and I'm not stealing. I've been straight since I've been out but I know of two fences who'll buy anything you want to sell 'em right now. And I've had no dealings with them but yet if I have a load of refrigerators I know where I can dump them right now. Or, if I wanted to buy something hot for a cheap price, I'd know where to go. I've had no dealings with them at all, but still I can go down here on First Street and dump my load.

Q: And most straight people are not aware of that kind of thing.

A: That's right because their way of thinking is not even into that field. A straight person thinks, "Well, I've got three hundred dollars' worth of bills coming up the first of the month. Now, how can I get some overtime in to pay the bills? I've gotta ask the boss for a raise or get some extra hours." When a thief will say, "I owe three hundred dollars, but if I go out and steal a thousand dollars' worth of merchandise and sell it, I can pay my bills and have something left over." And his whole concept of thinking is on that basis.

Q: If you steal something, you get about a fourth, a third of what it's worth?

A: Say you steal a tape recorder which sells for two hundred and twenty-five dollars. You might get seventy-five for it brand new, which is a third. But you're not thinking "This guy is sure beating me down, only giving me seventy-five dollars for it." You're thinking, "If I can get seventy-five for one, if I bring him ten, that's seven hundred and fifty." So you're gonna try and get as many as you can. You're thinking about what he's gonna pay you per item and how many he can take off your hands and if he says, "Go out and get as many as you can," then you're gonna steal twenty or thirty. You'll say, "Well, I made a good day's pay." You're downtown in a bar or at a club somewhere having a good time and when your money runs low you think, "I'll look again." And that's your average thief.

I've known guys that have stolen and done real good and gone into business for themselves. Now, if you was to mention that something was hot, they would call the police on you because they've made theirs and gotten away with it, now they're successful businessmen and they don't want nothing to do with somebody that's stealing. Now, here's the difference. Some guys steal because that's all they want to do. Some guys make it real good and say, "I'm gonna quit and put my money into something and make an honest living." You don't find too many of them like that, but there is some around and I know some of them. They've got good businesses. When they were younger, they went out and stole, they accumulated enough money without getting caught that they put it down in a business.

Q: When you were living in Chicago and flying all over the country, say you were going to San Jose or somewhere to pull a burglary or armed robbery, what would be the process in planning? How would you find out about the place?

A: Well, a guy, just a straight guy, maybe out in Atlanta, might say, "I work for Gillette Razor Blade Company in Albany." In a week or two he'll be telling you, "Well, I worked for Gillette Razor Blade Company and I got fired. They pay out there every week and they got a fifty-thousand-dollar payroll every week." Right away, your ears are gonna pick up "fifty thousand dollars."

"Oh yeah?" and you ask this guy some questions like, "What is the security there?" or "What kind of guards do they have?"

He says, "They got one guy with a gun when they're paying out but he's an old man."

Maybe the two or three guys that are with you say, "This sounds pretty good," and you have the money, you're not doing nothing, so you fly to Albany and check it out. You get to Albany and you can't really get in and see what's going on, so you tell one guy, "Go up there and apply for a job. Say, work a week in a warehouse, as a janitor or anything just to get inside the building to see what the security is." The guy goes to work for a week, he finds out what the security is. As I said, everybody has a routine. So their routine is: The guard gets here at eight-thirty in the morning, goes to lunch at eleven, comes back at twelve, he makes the rounds, you know, and he more or less knows what's going on inside. He goes to lunch at eleven and you get there at ten past eleven and he's downstairs four or five floors eating his lunch.

I'd say it all falls back on routine. That's a bad habit people have. If they'd shift around every day, there would be a lot less criminal activity. I can probably go out downtown right now and come back Monday and tell you the routine of a place and you can go back and check me and I'll be right. The same routine. That's your criminal's way. He goes by a person's routine on your payroll robberies, your bank robberies, your armored cars, your supermarkets. Your professional crook is not gonna go down here and rob a gas station.

When you have a gas station or a Circle K being robbed, you say, "Well, there goes a guy that's not making it and he needs the money." That's not your professional thief, because a professional crook is not gonna go rob a gas station for sixty dollars. He can go down the street and get six thousand. If he gets caught, the penalty is the same, but yet all the time gas stations are getting robbed, cab drivers getting held up.

Q: What does that indicate to you?

A: Teenagers or youngsters in their early twenties. Guys that are bumming around. They don't have a job, most of them are youngsters. As a matter of fact, if you listen to descriptions on your armed robberies here, like I say, gas stations and cab drivers, "two guys in their early twenties or late teens," that's the description. Very seldom do you hear of a guy, "five foot ten, forty years old," stuck up a cab driver. If he's forty years old, he's been around. He'd never rob a cab driver. He'd say, "Why rob a cab for forty bucks when I can go next door and get four thousand?"

Q: What's the largest robbery you ever pulled?
A: The one in this supermarket. It was over fifteen thousand. The money was never recovered and that's one reason why I did so much time. They were constantly asking me where the money was. I never got the money because, well, there were two other people involved, two guys that I ran into in Reno, Nevada, that was out on bond pending another robbery in Reno, and their lawyer wanted five thousand dollars to get the charges dropped on them. I was with them but I wasn't arrested up there. And being in Reno, there was a lot of heat out there. Not working, I was constantly hanging around town. They come to know your face and they start picking you up. I was picked up on suspicion four or five times. Never booked because they had nothing on me.

But one of the guys was from New Mexico and we had talked about it earlier, that if somebody got busted and we needed some money, there was a good robbery in Hobbs. One guy knew the layout because his brother-in-law was the manager of the place at one time. So when they got arrested and got out on bond, the lawyer wanted the money and they couldn't leave town. They were constantly under surveillance.

I thought, "Well, hell. I'll go and get it myself." So I left Reno and came here to Hobbs and got in touch with this guy's brother-in-law and told him what I was there for. He agreed to take me to the place and pick me up after the robbery and get me back to Reno for a percentage of the money. For a thousand dollars he was gonna take me there, get me after the robbery, and get me back to Reno. Well, I grabbed the manager in his car when he was coming out of the store, brought him back, and got him to take the day's receipts out of the safe. Had to tie him up and his assistant manager and there was two or three stock boys in the store working. Took them to the back and locked them up. So I got the money in a big paper sack and the fellow picked me up and I had a place to stay that night. I knew within thirty minutes to an hour when they would have roadblocks set up. So the plan was that he was to drop me off for the night here in the town, circulate around the town, go out to the edge of town and watch the roadblocks. And, within twelve hours, when the roadblocks were put down, come and get me.

Well, he had an old lady that was working at one of the cafes on the edge of town and he wasn't doing too good with her so he said, "Give me three hundred dollars, I'll go and give it to my old lady and tell her I'll be back in town within a week. Take you to Reno." So I gave him three hundred. Instead of him going out and giving it to his old lady and leaving there, he got to drinking and talking to an oil rigger. Well, this guy that was with me was a little bit tougher and they got in a fight. The guy knocked him down. He pulled a gun to kill him but by then the owner of the cafe had called the police and the sheriff come out there and arrested both of them.

So the next day no one shows up and I'm stuck. Well, this guy that was arrested in Reno, he has people from Hobbs and I went and contacted his people and told them the situation and they put me up in a motel on the Texas–New Mexico state line, and I stayed there for a day and a half and the day after that, I tried to get out of town and I had a pickup truck, belonged to the family.

I gave one of the sisters the money. I kept just enough on me for my personal needs. I said, "Take the money, get it back to Reno, get them out and if I get out there all right, everything will be okay. Just get the money out there to the lawyer. If I get arrested, get them out and tell them to come get me out cause there's enough money." Then I was arrested in a roadblock.

Q: They were still looking for you?

A: Oh, yeah. One of the employees was shot in the robbery. I shot him in the robbery and it was pretty hard on my case. They had roadblocks strung sixty, seventy miles out. The state police had road-blocks up and they didn't think I had gotten through them, which they were right.

They finally got me at a roadblock from my description. It fit pretty close. I had no mask or anything. I had planned on coming into town, robbing the place, and getting out. So the description fit pretty close and I hit the roadblock. They spotted me and they said, "We don't know if you're the guy or not but it will only be a few minutes out of your way. Why don't you come down to the police station?" and I told them, "All right." My intention was getting back to the town and running, because I figured they had me.

Well, one of the deputy sheriffs spotted me and he could see where I had my mind. He said, "Don't run, I'll kill you." So I went back to the police station and he brought the manager and two of the stock boys and another person from the store out there and they said, "Yeah, that's him." And I went to court and they had four or five charges of armed robbery, kidnapping, theft of over twenty-five hundred dollars, assault with intent to kill, and they said they were going to prosecute me on all the charges but if I pleaded guilty they would drop all the charges except armed robbery. So I pleaded guilty. I got fifty years for armed robbery. I didn't think anybody could get fifty years for armed robbery.

Q: You had never done time as an adult?

A: Yeah, I'd done a year and I'd done six months for burglary, carrying a pistol, and I had discharged a firearm right downtown in Chicago and got six months for that. I thought I was really doing a lot of time then, six months, a year is a lot of time. So when I was arrested here for armed robbery I said, "They're probably gonna give me two or three years." I was really sweating it.

"How am I gonna do three years?" I asked them. "What does the penalty call for for armed robbery?" and one of the cops told me, "Well, you'll probably have to do three or four years." I thought that's what the sentence was, three or four years and I was really sweating it out.

I went down before the judge and he said, "How do you plead?" and I told him, "Guilty." He says, "I'm gonna have to sentence you to ten to fifty years." Boy, I sure did get sick. Boy, I felt weak in the knees.

Q: Didn't these people ever come back to try to help you out?

A: No, they just went their merry way with all the money. Everyone asked me what happened to the money. I told them I had dumped it out. For about a year I was really expecting these guys to get me a lawyer, post bond . . . I was gonna appeal my case, you know.

As time went by, I realized they weren't coming back. I guess it was after about fourteen months people quit bothering me, quit asking questions, and that's how I did my time.

Q: So they never found out that these people had taken the money?

A: Yeah, they found out about, oh, probably two years ago. I went before the parole board. They asked me about it and I told them what happened to the money. After seven years it's too late, even in this state, they go seven years and you can't touch them. Well, I'll take that back, after three years, seven years is on murder, the statute of limitations on murder. Three years is armed robbery; I think burglary is fifteen months. It depends on the crime. You figure, for stealing, armed robbery is your major crime. You're stealing with a deadly weapon—in other words, you're using force. A burglar is burglarizing with intentions of no one being there on the premises. A check writer is not dangerous.

Q: Did you ever do that?

A: Write checks? I have several times but I didn't see no money in it. I wasn't very good at it. I couldn't even walk up with a straight face and say, "I want to cash a hundred-dollar check." I was kind of young and the other person see me standing there, a kid seventeen, "What's he doing with a hundred-dollar check?" If you write one for twenty, you're wasting your time. I did write several bad checks but I didn't see no future in it so I just passed on.

Q: Were you ever involved with drugs at all?

A: No. That's one thing I never used. I've seen quite a bit of them on the street and in the penitentiary, drugs, and as a kid I never had any desire to get high or smoke weed or pop pills or shoot heroin. Most thieves won't mess with drugs. Now, two classes: If a guy is addicted, he has to steal to take care of his habit. Then there's the regular thief, stealing for money. And I never was addicted or never did use the stuff. I tried smoking weed one time in the penitentiary and I got a good headache out of it. It didn't do anything for me so I eliminated it.

Weed, now, if it's under two ounces, it's considered a misdemeanor. But they've got a ten-dollar bag which I think is two or three ounces of weed. I'd see it every day. Guys all over town smoking it, but it never entered my mind, "Well, I think I'll get high." What I call getting high is going out to a club and drinking a few beers and getting high and going home and sleeping it off and getting up the next day and going to work.

As I say, I've been around it quite a bit. I've seen a lot of it, especially in your teenagers and your juveniles. A lot of them will be dropping pills or smoking weed. Even some of them will go on the hard stuff. Somebody will come along and get 'em high on pills and come around and say, "How does it feel?" And they'll say, "Well, it feels real good." Then he'll say, "I've got some heroin here. It's even better than the pills," and they'll say, "Let's try it." And pretty soon you've got an addict. Somebody will come and turn these kids on, and they like the feeling of being high; then before long, they get strung out.

Q: I'd like to back up a little now. How long did you live in Reno?

A: I'd say around a year.

Q: It was mostly Chicago that you've lived in?

A: Yeah, Chicago and Atlanta.

Q: When you were in Atlanta, were you living with your sister or by yourself?

A: At first I went down to stay with my sister.

Q: Was she married?

A: Yeah, she was married at sixteen. She and I went separate directions. She went the good way, I went the bad way. You know, her old man was straight. They got their own business down there now.

Q: Did she ever question where you got your money?

A: Oh, yeah. She'd think I was doing something against the law. She'd say, "Don't come around the house." Her husband was a deputy sheriff so I kind of shied away from them after a while.

Q: You mentioned that you'd bought your sister a house.

A: Yeah. Well, when they first got married, I was stealing then, and her old man was a deputy sheriff and got sixty dollars a week. They was just kind of making ends meet. All right, they turn up and bought a house for four thousand. That was in—well, in the early fifties, middle fifties, and over a period of a year I probably gave my sister about three thousand dollars, which helped pay off the house. Then, after they got on their feet, my sister asked me, "Where did you get the money?" Well, I told her and she said, "You better not let Sam know about it," that was her husband, "because he's in the police department and he'll get you in trouble."

And I'd come over there and he'd say, "Where are you working?" and I'd say, "Well, I'm not working."

"Where do you get your money at?"

"Here and there."

"I think you're stealing and if I ever catch you I'll lock you up."

Things were getting better for them at that time. They were beginning to see a little daylight so he started tightening down and he told me, "You better not come around the house," and so forth. The first year they were married, my sister never questioned me where I got it. She kind of knew. She was glad to see the money because things were tight for 'em, but after things started looking better for them, then she started asking.

Q: You must have been what, thirteen, fourteen years old?

A: I was probably fourteen, fifteen and she's several years older than I am. I would come over to their apartment and it would be nothing for her to say, "You got ten dollars, twenty dollars?" And I'd say, "Yeah, I got twenty," or, "See me tomorrow night," and I might go out and pull a burglary or something. I pulled an awful lot of burglaries in Atlanta. There's a main street in Atlanta and there's probably fifty bars on that one street and I've probably burglarized two-thirds of them.

Q: That wasn't armed robberies?

A: No, that was burglaries. I got to armed robberies when I come out of the service.

Q: Were you an armed robber before you went into the service?

A: Yeah, but I wasn't what you might call a compulsive armed robber. I was doing anything I could make money at. I'd pull burglaries, armed robberies. I'd go break into an applicance store and steal a lot of goods, anything I could make money at. But after I came out of the service and started doing armed robberies, I had it in my mind I wanted to be a professional thief and I'd never get caught. I was too smart for the police. So I started pulling armed robberies.

Q: How many did you pull before you got caught?

A: I don't know. I'd say quite a few. The average armed robber usually gets away with fifteen armed robberies before he's caught. That's what the statistics are. You can pull fifteen armed robberies before you get caught. Some of them get caught sooner, some of them get caught later. I probably pulled twenty or thirty before I was caught. I was going pretty strong. The first time I was ever caught for armed robbery I went to the penitentiary in Santa Fe. I had pulled armed robberies prior to that but I was never caught at an armed robbery. And, well, with the arrests, especially as a kid, detention center, it was for breaking and entering. I stole a car another time and then one time I had a master key to the city parking meters and I was opening up the parking meters at night.

Q: What's been your experience with the police?

A: They're after one thing. If you did something wrong, they want to catch you and prosecute you. I've never heard one say, "You shouldn't do it," or ask you what your problems are, you know. They say, like, "I know you did it and we want a confession. Who are your accomplices?" Most of them will try to use force to scare you. "You either tell or we're gonna take you in the back room and beat your brains out."

Q: Did that ever happen?

A: Beat my brains out? Yeah, they worked me over a couple of times and in Atlanta they took me and worked me over there and they'd hold me twenty-four hours or forty-eight hours and then turn me loose. When I was arrested here, the deputy sheriff cocked a shotgun at my head and told me he was gonna kill me. Kept telling me "Go ahead and run. Go ahead and run. I'll give you a chance."

I told him, "I ain't nuts. I ain't gonna run." There was an FBI man there and I told him, "This guy's crazy. He's going to kill me. Stay here with me." So after that he was all right. That guy might have, too, you know, cause most of them, well not most of them, but a lot of them, are pretty trigger-happy.

But I have been worked over by the police. You know, take you downstairs to one of the cells or to one of the detention homes and they really work you over.

Q: You've been in jail several times?

A: Oh, yeah. I've been arrested on suspicion a number of times. I've been convicted once for armed robbery and twice for burglary. Once I got six months, I got eighteen months, and a lot of probations. I did time for the first time I was arrested in a detention center, and I got arrested again and they put me on probation or I could go into the service, and prior to that I was arrested in Chicago and they gave me six months but I only did four and a half months out of the six.

Q: Where were you?

A: On Gull Island—it's something like a reformatory.

Q: What were your experiences at the reformatory?

A: Working. You put in six days a week working. I was working in textiles and making blankets and weaving. They had a furniture shop, a textile shop, a large kitchen. They try to keep you busy but that don't reform you. They don't say, "Well, we're gonna give you a trade" or—

Q: Didn't that give you a trade—working in the textile shop?

A: It depends on what you call a trade. When you make blankets or build furniture for the state, or metal cabinets, put desks together, it's not too much of a trade. They may say, "You're here for a six-month sentence. You're gonna be here five months. Behave yourself and you'll be out in four." You fasten legs on metal desks every day. You really don't learn. You just gotta keep up with the furniture coming through and at the end of the day you say, "Well, I'm going back to my dormitory, eat supper" and that's it.

Q: Did they treat you well there?

A: Yeah, they never harassed you unless you gave them cause to. You step out of line, they get on your case, but basically if you were minding your own business, they'd leave you alone. Same way in Santa Fe, you know. You get out of line and they get on your case but if you're minding your own business they don't bother you. Give them some lip, they'll just show you they're a little stronger than you. If you went along with the rules and did what they told you, they wouldn't bother you. As I say, that's what kept me in Santa Fe for so long, because for the first five years up there I was considered a troublemaker. I was constantly in and out of solitary confinement and after I was there for about six years I got to thinking, "I'm a damn fool for trying to be a tough guy." I settled down, I got out.

Q: What was your inital impression and some of your experiences in Santa Fe?
A: Well, in Santa Fe . . .
Q: You were about twenty then?
A: Yeah, I was about nineteen. The average age group in Santa Fe is probably twenty. You got older guys like sixty, seventy years old but the population is seven hundred and I would say two-thirds are in their early twenties. Well, probably not quite two-thirds, maybe another third would be sixteen to eighteen and another group would be forty up.
Q: Did the age groups generally stick together?
A: Most of them do. The younger guys stick to themselves, the older men have what they call an old man's dormitory in Santa Fe and they stay together, the young kids who are sixteen to nineteen, they have a separate unit for them. From nineteen to thirty is where the regular housing is and usually everybody sticks to their own age group, more or less two or three years apart. Up there in Santa Fe there is mostly cliques and only the strong survive because there are constantly fights up there. You have your black cliques, you have your Chicano cliques, then you have your gray cliques—whites. Your whites and Chicanos mostly got along. The blacks didn't get along with nobody. They were constantly at war with everybody, anybody that wasn't black just didn't fit.
Q: Are there quite a few blacks in Santa Fe?
A: Probably two hundred. When I went up there, there was about forty, maybe forty-five. When I got out of there this past year, there was probably about two hundred, two hundred and twenty-five blacks. You might say there's racial conflict up there all the time.

Q: The whites and the Chicanos stuck together?

A: Basically they did. They had their own little group, you know, what they call Chicano Power, then they had Black Power, and I don't think the whites had any kind of power. They just—

Q: How many whites are there in Santa Fe?

A: In Santa Fe? Probably a hundred and fifty. I'd say there's probably a hundred and fifty whites, maybe two hundred blacks, that's three hundred and fifty, and probably another three hundred and fifty or four hundred Chicanos. You got to stick together or get run over.

Q: What happens to the ones that refuse to stick together?

A: They get harassed, they get beat up, stabbed, you know, and they wind up in confinement, protection. Some of them are sent to the farm, somewhere where they don't have too much trouble. But it's like anything else, you've got the younger kids up there that can't stick up for themselves in trouble.

Q: What kind of trouble?

A: Well, you've got a lot of rapes on the young kids up there. You get a kid sixteen years old in there, kind of weak, he gets raped. And if a guy is a known informer or something like that, then they'll give him a pretty bad time. Most of them went right to lockup, or they went to the farm.

Q: So a lot of them at the farm are known informers or—

A: People that couldn't make it in the walls.

Q: They're moved for their own protection?

A: Yeah. There are a lot of stabbings up there, a lot of people get hit with clubs and pipes. Everybody up there has a weapon—a knife or a straight razor or something, and I have seen a pistol up there in the penitentiary.

Q: Homemade or—

A: It was a .32 automatic. There's a lot of narcotics up there, too. A lot of guys getting high all the time, on the weekends especially.

Q: How do they get the stuff?

A: Well, some of it comes in through the guards. Probably the rest comes in through the visiting room. Up to when I got out, visiting wasn't really what you'd call tight security. You may get a girlfriend or a wife coming up to visit with a guy. If she's bringing in heroin, she'll bring it in a balloon, put it in her mouth and when he comes to visit there's no screen, just a table and a seat. When the guy's girlfriend or wife gets ready to go, she kisses him goodbye and passes it off through the mouth.

Then there are restrooms for visitors to use. They drop it off at the restroom and one of the trustees helps there, cleans up outside. You tell him, "My old lady is dropping off four bags of weed in the restroom," in the garbage or trash or in a pipe or something. So Saturday afternoon he's out there sweeping the hall, watching for the person. The person goes in, comes out, and the trustee goes right in behind her. No guards there, he picks it up, puts it in his belongings, comes through from the visitors' room to the main institution. He gets shook down (shakedown is just one of these top deals, you know), and goes right on through with it and drops it off. There's a lot of cash money up there. It's all commissary, you know, cigarettes . . . and a ten-dollar bill up there will go for fifteen dollars' worth of canteen. There's a lot of green money up there.

Q: How do they get it?

A: Same way, from visitors, guards, through the farm. There's people on the farm that are up there for a short time. Everybody knows everybody, just about. You might get a guy that's working all day at the farm and might come in one or two days from the farm making deliveries. Anybody can go from downtown Albuquerque to the farm. Say they have a hundred dollars in twenty-dollar bills, they drop it off at the farm. If somebody on the farm knows where it's being dropped off, then they just have to watch for them and pick it up. There's no security there, really.

Q: Have you been at the farm?

A: No, but I know what it is, though. Other guys, when they leave the farm, drive up to the main institution, walk to the gate, and sign in. Sometimes there's a shakedown coming in, sometimes there's not, but five twenty-dollar bills stuck down in a jock strap or in your shoes aren't that bulky. He gets searched, nothing's found and he walks right into the institution, into the main population. If he's got twenties going to another inmate, he finds out where he's at and passes it on. Happens all the time.

Q: So money among the inmates is used to purchase illegitimate—

A: Well, more specifically, it's used to buy narcotics. I'd say, in a week up there, you'd probably get fifty caps of heroin, maybe a pound of marijuana, maybe a thousand pills. The only way you can buy narcotics up there is with green money. A cap of heroin will sell for ten dollars, for five you can buy four sticks of marijuana or maybe five pills.

Q: What happens if you get busted?

A: Automatically, if you get busted with narcotics or with green money they lock you up in segregation. They'll ask you where you got it and you tell 'em, "I can't tell." They don't press it because they know that if a guy squeals, his life is in danger. They let it drop. All right, you go to what they call a court. It's conducted by two W-1s and a classification officer and a captain. They'll take away some of your good time. Like they'll take away twenty days good time or ten days good time and that's it—put you back in population. If they ever catch money, they confiscate it, of course. It goes on your record for the parole board. There's a mark on your record. Outside of that, that's all there is to it.

Q: How often do they catch someone?

A: Probably once or twice a month. But you figure two guys out of about two hundred is a pretty low average. The odds are pretty good that you're not gonna get caught. I've known some guys that have been bringing narcotics in for six, seven years and they've never been caught and probably never will get caught.

Q: Are there pushers in there?

A: Oh, yeah. They get a load of stuff in and they push it. Maybe one guy will get in a thousand pills. He'll have two or three guys selling for him. He'll be out of the picture altogether. He just plans for the pushers and they sell it and get their little percentage and the guy, he gets the main bundle. He may invest fifty dollars for a load of pills and from that fifty dollars, he'll get back five hundred.

Q: What does he do with his money?

A: Well, usually he'll send it back out to a relative or a friend, or he can give it to a guard and tell him, "Here's five hundred dollars. Now, I'm gonna give you ten bucks. You take it and go downtown and make out a money order in my name. Use my sister's return address and send it back to me." The money comes right back into the institution and is placed in his account. So some guys got a pretty good-size bank account by the time they get out.

Q: You know this yourself? You're personally familiar with some of the guards that do it?

A: Oh, yeah. I know probably eight or nine different guards that have brought stuff in. Usually they'll last six months before they're fired, till the word gets out and gets back to the warden. In fact, if you look at my record, one of them did approach me. Wanted to bring some stuff in, not to me, but to somebody else. The way he got fired was, during the pro football game the year before last, I made a twenty-five-dollar bet with him, cigarettes against green money, and I won the bet. He paid me off with a twenty-dollar bill and a five-dollar bill.

That afternoon I was in the restricted area of the institution and a captain and a lieutenant and three guards stopped me in the hall and shook me down, gave me a strip shakedown because I was a troublemaker. I had the money in my boot, in my sock, and they found it. Now, a guard can take a bill, say a fifty, out to the information booth and get change for it. This guard had cashed a fifty-dollar bill at the information booth and when they gave him change they took the numbers off the bills that they gave him.

Q: They already suspected him, then?

A: Yeah. He gave me the twenty-five dollars and when they caught me with it, through a routine on the bills, they found that, sure enough, the guy named Delgado had received the money that same day and there I was with it. So they called me up and they said, "Well, we know Delgado gave you the money." Then the warden called me up and he had information about Delgado that I didn't know. He said, "We know this guy's bringing in pills. He's bringing in marijuana. We know he's bringing in hard liquor and we know he's gambling. We know he gave you the money because we have the numbers on it."

So I told them yeah, Delgado had given it to me. Then they went and got Delgado. He was a steward in the kitchen. They confronted him with it. Well, he denied it. So then they went out and got about ten other guys that he had brought stuff in to. They had one guy they had caught with ten or fifteen bennies. So they really put it to that guy, because he only had about six months to go and he had about three years good time. They said they were gonna take away his three years good time unless he copped out and got this settled and Delgado out of the institution. He's thinking, "Well, what's worth it, Delgado's job or my three years of freedom?" So the guys said, "Yeah, Delgado was the one."

They couldn't get enough evidence to prosecute him because they never really caught him. They couldn't prosecute through hearsay, but they knew he was the one. So the warden told him in the morning, "You're fired. If you come back on these premises, I'll have you arrested," and they run him off. That's usually about all they can do when they find out.

Q: Was this acceptable with all of the guys, that you ten fingered Delgado?

A: It is when it comes down to whether it's you or him.

Q: But it's not acceptable one prisoner against the other, is it?

A: No. One prisoner against another, you're supposed to take what's coming to you. To me, there's no sense in the convict code because I seen it during the riots up there. So many people implicated other people trying to save themsleves, and to me that terminated the convict code. But in prison and even in juvenile hall there's a convict code. I can't squeal on him because the rest of the guys will be after me. But in any institution you go to, no matter where it is, you have your informers. Anywhere. You can't run an institution without informers, whether it's through throwing notes or guys stepping around the corner whispering in your ear or what.

Q: How long are you on parole for?

A: Five years and I'll probably be off in about three, two and a half and get discharged. But you get to thinking as you get older, you get wiser. You get to thinking there's no percentage in stealing because you can't constantly keep it up without getting caught and if you get caught, you're right back in the penitentiary. And who wants to go back for five more years?

Q: Well, if you go out and you pull ten armed robberies and you accumulate a hundred thousand dollars—

A: But you can't go out and pull ten armed robberies and accumulate a hundred thousand dollars because there aren't that many places that have ten thousand apiece. The average armed robbery, if you get five thousand, you got a pretty good score. If you get twenty-five or thirty thousand it's exceptionally good. Your average bank robber these days gets fifteen, ten thousand or less. Where else can you find money but in a bank? Banks are where all the money is and if you can't get more than ten thousand in a bank, you can't go into a local supermarket and get—

Q: Then it's not really worth it—

A: A hundred thousand dollars isn't worth ten years of your life. You can say, "Well, I'll go in the penitentiary for a hundred thousand dollars. That's ten thousand a year or two hundred a week." But if you spend ten years of your life behind bars for that amount of money . . . For me, when I was younger, I'd say, "Yeah. It sounds like a good deal." But now no amount of money is worth my freedom because too many things can happen, plus you're losing all the luxury of being free. You're locked up. You can't say, "I'm going out to dinner, go to a movie and go on a date," or, "I'm going driving." You say, "I'm going to my cell block, to my job, and back again." You're in a small confinement, you're told to do this, do that, don't do this, don't do that, and throughout the years it becomes pretty tough. That's why a man coming out of the penitentiary is placed on parole, because he gets to the point where he needs to be guided and told what to do. You get into a rut in the penitentiary. Some people come out faster than others and don't need parole but basically everybody needs supervision that's been locked up because if you have a problem, at least you have someone you can sit down and talk it over with.

Q: Are you under close supervision now?

A: No, I'm under what they call minimum supervision.

Q: Why?

A: I don't know. Probably just my attitude, the way I've been progressing since I've been out. Some people come out and they lay around for a month before they get a job. Once they get a job they stay there for a week, they get fired or they quit, you know. I came out, got a job the same day I got out, and I'm still on the same job.

Q: What are you doing?

A: I'm doing construction work. The wages are pretty decent. I'd rather make five hundred a month than maybe make ten thousand a month and be caught.

Q: Are you married?

A: Yeah, I'm married. I got married about four months ago.

Q: Shortly after you got out?

A: Yeah. I was married before I went in the penitentiary, too.

Q: Where was your wife?

A: My wife's home was in North Carolina.

Q: She was staying in North Carolina and you were staying in Reno?

A: Reno and Chicago; I might see her two days out of the month.

Q: Did you have any children?

A: I had two.

Q: By your first wife?

A: Yeah. When you're not home, it just can't work out. When I went to the penitentiary, that ended.

Q: How long were you married?

A: I got married ten years ago but actually I didn't stay with her that long, maybe a year and it was nothing stable because, like I say, I was never home that long. I might drop in, say "Hello, how you doing?," stay two days, and leave again. Her home was in North Carolina and that's where she wanted to stay.

Q: How old are your kids?

A: Oh, let's see, one is ten now, one is eleven. I haven't seen them in nine years.

Q: Did you go with your wife before you got married?

A: About two weeks.

Q: Did she know what she was getting into?

A: Probably, but she was too young and to her, at the time, it sounded like a good deal. Here was a guy with a little money in his pocket. I was showing her a good time but it's like anything else—that gets old too, you know. So when I went to the penitentiary she said, "Well, it's not gonna work out," and I said, "No kiddin'?" I got fifty years locked up and she's out there. So I told her to get a divorce through welfare.

Q: So you haven't seen her or your kids since you got sent up?

A: No, I just put them out of my mind.

Q: Did she remarry?

A: I don't know. She probably has.

Q: I suppose in the penitentiary you get a reputation among the guys for whatever—

A: Yeah. They always know your business. There's no secrets in the penitentiary. No matter what you do or who you are, what are your causes for being there, they always know. They can tell you what you're there for, how long your sentence is, what kind of guy you are. Especially in this state, the penitentiary is so small. The average penitentiary, they've got twenty-five hundred people. Here, it's only several hundred. Everybody knows your business.

There's always guys that will go up and try to pretend they're something they're not, but they get straightened out pretty quick. No matter what you do, why you're there or what you've done before you got there, they know. The convicts have access to your records. It's nothing for a convict to bring up your jacket, look at it, see what your charges are, see what you've done.

Q: Who are the guys that are looked down on there? What kinds of offenses?

A: Well, mostly your sex crimes are looked down on. Those guys are given a pretty rough time up there. You've got a lot of guys that are married and have kids of their own. Well, you get a guy up there for assault on a young boy or a young girl and right away they start thinking, "It could have been my kid." And then the other guy who is looked down on is the habitual snitch. Whatever he sees, he's got to run and tell one of the officers. Most of the guys in the penitentiary have something illegal going on and they say, "This guy is peeking around. If he sees something, he's going to get me in trouble." So they try to eliminate him, usually by giving him a hard time or putting him in the hospital or something like that. But that's about the only two people that really get a bad time.

If you mind your own business up there, generally you get along. You have all these young guys up there that try to make names for themselves and they'll give a new guy a hard time. The strong take over. It's a jungle, that's what it is. The strong survive, the weak don't. If you're weak, or weak minded, you might as well forget about it. You've got trouble. This is true in any category in any institution—if you're weak, the stronger ones are gonna ride over you.

Q: But they do have a protection system, don't they?

A: Yeah, but not very good. Your protection system is being locked in confinement.

Q: That's the legitimate protection. How about the illegitimate protection system?

A: You can't really call it a protection system. You get a lot of these kids up there, really scared and maybe some bigger guy will walk up to him and say, "Give me ten dollars a week and I'll protect you." Once you do that then the rest of the time you're there, you gotta pay through the nose, and who wants to give up everything you've got to have someone protect you? If you're strong minded you don't need protection. You can protect yourself. The other guys can protect themselves, why do you need to pay for protection? Once you pay the first time, then you're constantly paying. If you establish yourself right away, well . . . You have a problem with a guy and whether you get beat up or whether you don't, it's worth taking that risk just to get him off your back. What I'm saying is, if a guy is picking on me and he beats me up and I'm constantly fighting back at him, he's gonna get tired of it and say, "One of these days this guy's gonna get me. I'll leave him alone and I'll look for somebody else this week." But if you find a guy that's gonna bow down right away and say, "If you don't hit me, I'll give you five dollars a week," once a week he's gonna come and say, "Give me five dollars. If you don't have it we're gonna beat you up," and you've got to go out and get it. But it's a jungle, that's what it is.

Q: Isn't there also a protection system where if a guy will go down for another guy he'll protect him?

A: Yeah, it's the old thing to fall back on. I may protect this guy—if two of us get caught doing something, and they catch me but they don't catch the other guy, I'll take the rap. But you go before a deputy warden and he tells you, "Well, you have a ten-year sentence and you've got four years of good time. Now, if you don't tell us what happened, we're gonna take that four years." What's worth it more—your four years or the other guy? So I say the convict code is not really what you'd call a code. It sounds good—a solid convict code, nobody snitches on nobody. But when it gets down to you or the other guy, then the tune changes a little bit.

Be the same thing if you got two guys at the detention home and you've got them both in your office and you say, "We know that you all were gambling. We caught Joe but we didn't catch Bill. Joe, if you don't tell us that Bill was gambling, we're gonna keep you here for thirty days more." The odds are that Joe will say, "Yeah, Bill was the one that started the poker game."

Q: Is Bill going to be after Joe?

A: Yeah, probably. But if you've got a guy who's got the nerve to implicate the other guy and he's strong enough to take care of himself later—in other words, if he implicates one guy and the guy comes up and says, "You snitched on me," he can say, "Wait a minute, man. I might have snitched on you but what's more important—my two years and six months or you? And if you're man enough, you're not gonna let me lose my two years and six months. You're gonna go up there and admit it yourself. If you don't care for me, why should I care for you?"

So what it breaks down to is self-preservation. You look out for yourself. What do I care about the other guy? When I first went there, I did. I'd get caught shooting dice or playing poker or drinking homemade beer or something, and they'd say, "We know this guy was the one that sold it to you," or "He's the one that made the beer," or "He was in the game, now are you gonna tell us about it?"

"I ain't telling you nothing," I'd say. So I had to go to solitary for thirty days. But as time went by, I got to thinking, "I'm a damn fool for taking his raps for him while he's out there enjoying himself and I'm in here. Because if he cared for me, he would have gone and told the deputy warden, 'Wait a minute. He had nothing to do with it. I'm the one that did it,' but if the man can't do that, he don't care for me. So why should I care for him?"

And especially if you get a guy that's doing a lot of time in the penitentiary. The average guy has ten to fifty years—that's the average sentence and that's a lot of time. On a fifty-year sentence you've got twenty-six years good time, and they can take twenty-six years good time away from you if they want to. I never heard of nobody losing twenty-six years but they do take away two or three years at a whack. And is three years of your freedom worth this other guy not taking the rap for something he did or is his little freedom worth your three years? That's the way you look at it. Do you want to spend three years for another guy's doings or do you want to get out?

Myself, I don't want to spend time for nobody. What I do and get caught for, that's my consequences. I have to pay for it. Why should I do time and be confined for another guy? I'm doing time and he's out there and everybody's saying, "Well, look at that fool. He sure is a sucker," you know. That's what they say. I told a lot of them the last year I was up there even when the riot came on, they'd tell me, "Come on. You gotta participate in the riot." Well, the first day they had a strike, nobody goes to work.

Q: How did it start?

A: It started with two powers, from what I understand. Martinez was one of your main persons. He was the outside agitator. They was trying to get the administration that is in there, out, and I think there was outside agitation through your Black Berets and your Brown Berets here in Albuquerque because there was lawyers from these different organizations seeing leaders through visiting privileges. They'd bring information in, "This is what we're gonna do today. This is what we're gonna do tomorrow." Well, they called for everybody to sit down, nobody to go to work Thursday morning.

Q: Why did it start?

A: Well, every excuse. They wanted better working conditions, more privileges, you know, usually a lot of grievances in a penitentiary. No matter what they got, they want more. Anybody with a strong mind can probably lead the rest of them around because the other guys have been locked up. They're just like sheep; if it sounds good to them, they're gonna follow. Some of them do it because they think, what is their friend gonna think if they don't follow? They don't have a mind of their own, really. They called for a general sit-down strike for better working conditions and they wanted pay for all their jobs, you know. And anybody who goes to work is a no-good bastard and maybe gets hurt.

All right, I'm going to parole board the next month. So Wednesday night they spread the word around: Nobody goes to work the next morning. Out of several hundred people when they called work call, about thirty of them were ready to go to work. I was one of

them. I had my jacket on, I was going out the door, going to work.
"Hey Jack, you can't go to work, you sorry bastard." I told him, "You
do your time, I'll do mine. I've been here nine years, how long you
been here?" A lot of them just been there six months, a year, two
years, the majority of them. When you've done nine years, you've
done a lot of time. Two or three years is nothing. I said, "You all have
been here a short time. I've been here a long time. You do your time
and I'll do mine," and I went to work. Out of a population of seven
hundred, I'd say maybe thirty of them went to work, the rest of them
laid in. I come back from work and I got a few "boos," you know, but
nobody did nothing physically.

"How come you went to work?"

"Well, I'm going to the parole board and I want to go home. You
do what you want and I'll do what I want."

They had another meeting that night and passed the word
around the penitentiary. They gave the warden an ultimatum; he had
to come up with their agreements by the next day at noon or they're
gonna riot. The warden told them, "No, we can't go along with your
agreements," so they rioted and they tore the place to pieces. They
busted every window in there, ripped up all the mattresses, and so
forth, you know.

Well, when it started, they had the local National Guard on call,
they had the State Police outside the fence with rifles, plus they had
probably two hundred and fifty hired personnel working in the
penitentiary on alert. They started with tear gas, tear gas and night
sticks. It took them probably thirty minutes to put the whole thing
down. Came in and shot tear gas in and if you didn't get in your cell,
they'd put you in a cell. That was the end of the riot and during that
thirty minutes they'd done quite a bit of damage. An awful lot of
damage, as a matter of fact. There was a couple of hard cases that still
wanted to continue with the riot and consequently they got a little
knot in the head or pushed around a bit heavy, you know. You can't
treat a wild man with a kid glove. You can't tell him, "Please get in
your cell," when he's already done two hundred thousand dollars'
worth of damage.

Q: Where were you when the riot started?

A: I was in what they call Cell House Number Two—it's one of
the three cell houses in the institution, the rest of them are
dormitories. There were people running all around me, some of them
starting fires. Probably, out of a population of seven hundred, only two
hundred participated in the riot. The rest of us stood around and

watched it. I'd say actually about six hundred were hurt by the riot because, while only the original two hundred participated, the rest of the population got punished because they never knew for sure just who was in it and who wasn't in it.

But once it started I made it very clear to the deputy warden who was in our hallway leading to our cell block. I stood up and I told him, "Say," I says, "what they're doing right now, they're doing it," I says, "you remember in the future I had nothing to do with it." I stood right there and watched them and the next day the deputy warden come around and he said, "Well, I remember what you said yesterday. You want to go to work? Everybody's locked up," and while everybody's locked up I was working.

The following month I went to the parole board. It was brought to the parole board's attention that I had nothing to do with the riot and they gave me parole. There was a lot of guys due for parole at the same time but they weren't sure whether or not they were in the riot and a lot of them got denied on the parole board. The guilty and the innocent both got punished.

Q: How long did you stay after the parole board hearing?
A: About three weeks.
Q: Did the situation improve any?
A: No, because during that period everybody was locked up and I think there's still quite a few locked up. They've been there for five months. They let quite a few of them out of segregation, but still—
Q: The riot was in October?
A: October. Six months, and I'd say there are probably . . . well, when I got released, there was about a hundred and fifty of them turned loose into the population, which left about five hundred and fifty still locked up. They'll screen them and every day let about twenty or thirty of them out. See who had anything to do with the riot, you know. What they're trying to do is weed out the trouble-makers because, like I say, up till then the convict code was real solid, you know, but when they seen that they were in a bind, everybody started talking and the convict code went to pieces. It's the same in any institution. You can get a bunch of guys in a squeeze and they're gonna tell you what's happening. You might get one out of fifty who's gonna be a tough guy and tell you nothing, but if you keep on working on him, he's gonna tell you eventually.

But there is no such thing as a convict code. There is no such thing. It's self-preservation. Why should I take the other guy's rap? I know myself I'm not gonna take that other guy's rap. If they pick me up on a sidewalk cause the place next door was robbed and I was in the vicinity, and now they think I did it and I know that somebody else did it, and they're gonna send me away, now wait a minute—

Q: You took somebody else's rap before?

A: That was before I got to really thinking. That's when I was a little bit younger. I thought I was a little bit tougher but there's no such thing as a tough guy because you take another guy's rap, you're just a damn fool. Like I say, is your freedom worth somebody else's pleasure? My freedom ain't worth nobody else's pleasure. I made that very clear in the penitentiary and I wasn't considered a rat or anything else, I was considered an old-timer up there and that's all there was to it. I made parole in October and at the time I was discharged nobody ever got in my face or gave me a hard time, but nobody ever did anything in front of me neither. They just figured, "Jack isn't gonna take the rap for nobody so if you got something going on, don't do it in front of him, cause if it comes down to you or him, it's gonna be you."

Q: How did you feel about some of the demands that the rioters were making?

A: They're kind of ridiculous from my point of view. The working conditions weren't hard—you work five days a week which the normal citizen does. The average citizen works eight hours and you was only working six up there, not hard.

Q: Were all of them working?

A: Probably about ninety-five percent of them were assigned to one job or another and basically they had a good program for education—school, high school, college and vocational trades. They had the DVR program up there—carpentry, electricity, masonry work, plumbing, welding. Division of Vocational Rehabilitation.

Q: Did you select the program you wanted to go into?

A: Oh, yeah. I decided to go into carpentry or construction and I got four hundred and fifty dollars when I graduated. I also got my GED up there—high school equivalency. When I went up there, I had something like a seventh-grade education and I got my GED, which has helped me. My education is basic education. It was nothing when I went up there and I learned quite a bit.

Q: Did you do this all the time you were there or just during the last few years?

A: I'd say probably the last couple of years. I finally sat down and thought, "What in the hell am I doing? If I want to get out of here

I'd better straighten up and try to do something that will benefit myself instead of the other guy."

Q: What kinds of things did you get involved in before, when you were known as a screw-up?

A: I'd say probably bucking of authority. They'd say, "You have to do this," and I'd say, "I don't have to do it," then do just the opposite. They'd say, "You have to be to work at eight in the morning," and at nine-thirty I'd show up. They'd say, "Where have you been?" I'd say, "I was down at the hospital," usually goofing off. They'd say, "You're not supposed to gamble," and I would gamble. They'd say, "You're supposed to be in bed at ten at night, TV goes off at nine." At ten they count, I'd be in bed for count and then get up to watch TV or gamble.

Q: Where did you get money to gamble with?

A: Well, everything is a hustle up there. For a long time I was working in the gym or the kitchen. In the kitchen I was selling sandwiches. A guy would want a sandwich at night. It would cost him a pack of cigarettes. I'd sell maybe twenty sandwiches a day, that's twenty packs of cigarettes—two cartons. Up there, cigarettes were worth money and the more cigarettes you had, the more money you had.

Q: Besides that, cigarettes were legitimate.

A: Yeah. The canteen was there. They had 'em so they were worth cash.

If you work in the laundry, you can press clothes. They don't press your clothes for you and if a guy wants you to press his clothes you charge a pack of cigarettes to press his clothes. No matter where you went, they were hustling. The school building—the guy had india ink for tattoos and could make a lot of money. You could sell anything. It was strictly against regulations, you know. If you were working in the appliance shop and you wanted something special for your cell, a light fixture or a new faucet for your sink, you tell a plumber you will give a carton of cigarettes for a work request and they come and take care of it. Some guys had money from home. They're too lazy to clean up their cell. They hire another guy to clean up their cell for two bucks a week. One guy had ten guys a week cleaning up his cell, two bucks apiece, twenty bucks a week. Twenty dollars a week is a lot of money, might be like two or three hundred out here. And anything up there was worth a hustle. I don't care what you did. Wherever you're working, you can hustle money.

Q: Where there male prostitutes?

A: Male prostitutes? No, there's a lot of homosexuals up there. Most of them are younger kids and then they got a lot of plain homosexuals you know, off the street. And up there they call it . . . a guy would have an "old lady." If he had an old lady, let's say he was a homosexual off the street, had an old lady, nobody would bother him. He was going with somebody. If they did it was grounds for killing them. This used to cause a lot of trouble. You've got a lot of young kids sixteen years old that come in there, seventeen, and up to twenty-one, twenty-five even. They're real scared or real timid or if they show any feminine ways about them, the older guys sound them out and if they show any weakness at all, they're in trouble.

But as far as male prostitution, there wasn't any because there's too many homosexuals up there. You got a population of seven hundred and there are probably about a hundred and fifty homosexuals up there—free-world homosexuals and penitentiary homosexuals. You probably figure out of the other five hundred and fifty, maybe a hundred and fifty, two hundred of them mess around with kids. The rest of them just ignore it.

The officials of the penitentiary see what's going on and, as long as it's not causing any trouble, they just leave it alone. They never harass them or bother them. Most of the kids in there had girl names—those that were indulging in homosexual activities—like Joe Brown might be called "Maxine." One kid they called "Princess," another one the "Queen," and they stayed in their cliques, called girl-boy cliques. The guards would come down the hallway and a guy would be in the hallway and the guards would say, "Hey, what's going on there, Princess?" They never call them by their real names. They call them by their nicknames and they never went out of their way to harass them. They never said, "You're doing wrong, you better stop it." It's going on and they know it. Every institution's got it and most of your wardens allow it because it stops a lot of trouble. If the person wants to participate in it, they don't bother them. It's only when somebody's trying to force somebody, they'll step in and do something.

Q: But aren't the younger kids forced into it?

A: Yeah, most of them are scared into it and once they're scared into it they get a name and then after that they can't get out of it. And then wherever they go they have pressure from the other guys, so they accept it and go about their way.

Q: Were there fights over them?

A: Oh, yeah, most of your fights come along with your free-world homosexuals. They come in there and get hung up with a guy in there and two months later they see another guy they like even better so they decide to go to the other guy. Well, the first guy doesn't want to go along with it. "Wait a minute. You can't leave me. You're mine," and pretty soon one guy is fighting the other guy over it to see who gets the kid. All your homosexuals up there are not kids. Some of them are almost fifty years old, sixty years old.

Q: Were most of these guys married or single?

A: The ones that were indulging? Some of the girl-boys were married. Heck, I used to see them a lot of times. "My wife is coming to see me this Saturday." They would get all dressed up and go to the visiting room, you know. "Hurry up, come on back."

Q: How about the guys they were using?

A: Some of them were married. I'd probably say half of them.

Q: So possibly the problem could be alleviated by conjugal visits with their wives?

A: I'd say yeah. That would probably stop about eighty percent of it. Now, you're always gonna have some who are gonna want to play—

Q: But it seems to me it might be the one that is the real homosexual rather than the one that's in a situation—

A: Right. Most places except Santa Fe will weed them out and put them in a separate unit, but here they don't have the housing space for them.

Q: If they have a hundred and fifty—

A: If you have a hundred and fifty, maybe fifty are willing and the other hundred are forced into it when they first get there. But they don't have the facilities or staff. They've only got three housing units, three cell blocks, the rest of them are dormitories, fifty, sixty guys to a unit, shut the lights out at ten o'clock and there's no guard inside a unit. You're there by yourself with all the rest of the guys. It's all one big dormitory and what's to prevent one of the young kids from getting raped? If he yells out he's just encouraging getting beat in the head or really getting hurt. No adequate staff so there's just not that close supervision.

If they had a guard assigned inside a dormitory at night, then there wouldn't be any problem because everybody would be afraid of the guard seeing them—the dormitories aren't that big. A single-floor dormitory . . . probably sixty, seventy feet long, thirty, forty feet wide. Bunks are pretty close together, four rows of them, fifteen to a room. Now if you had a guard inside who was there all night, they wouldn't do all this.

In the cell block you can't go out at night because you're locked up. You don't have to worry about it. They're one-man cells. But being in a cell block is a privilege. You've got to work your way into it. Once in a while you get a homosexual off the street, especially a young one, seventeen or eighteen, that has it on his record and he'll come in and they'll segregate him right away. They'll put him in a cell. Or once in a while you'll get one that comes in there a real Nellie. You'll see him coming in with this long hair and "yoo-hoo." In ten minutes he's whistling at all the guys. The warden sees him and says, "Oh-oh, get him out of here because he's gonna cause trouble." You might get fifty guys fighting to see who gets him. You know what I mean? So they segregate him.

The rest of them, they put in the dormitory and the weak don't make it, the strong survive. It's a jungle, that's what it is. You're in two different worlds. You've got your outside world and you've got your world in there.

Q: How do you change the whole thing?
A: The way of living?
Q: Within the institution.
A: How do you change yourself or what?
Q: No, the culture that occurs in the institution.
A: Well, after a psychologist, a psychiatrist all started to probe into it, I really haven't seen anybody come up with an answer. For one thing, you gotta have close supervision. You have to weed out the ones that you know will cause trouble. Out of every group of a hundred you have one or two leaders and if you can get the leaders out and segregate them from the other ninety-eight, chances are you'll have yourselves a pretty good bunch of guys. But it just takes one or two guys to cause the rest of them to go wrong, to follow them. You got a guy who's gonna jump up and say, "Now we're gonna do this," and if somebody in that group is afraid to do it, they're gonna do it anyway thinking, "Well, if I don't do it I'm afraid these tough guys will get on me about it." But if you get your leaders out and segregate them, then somebody from administration can step in and talk. Then you'll probably have a pretty good bunch of guys. Usually you're gonna have your troublemakers in a group. You set up some kind of council, an inmate council or a group within the crowd . . .
Q: Do they have any?

A: The older guys, most of them, they have group councils, you know, but they don't weed out the troublemakers from the rest of them. Some guys, their minds are strong enough to rebel against somebody that wants to cause trouble. Some of them aren't. Usually your older guys or your guys that have been there a while know the consequences, what's gonna happen if they do something wrong, and tell the tough guys or the one who's trying to cause the trouble, "Well, stay away from me," or "Go see somebody else." And usually they do—they'll walk away from you and they go find somebody else that's weaker or somebody that's trying to get a name for themself, to go jumping on some guy: "Let's jump on him and whip him." Some of the guys they pick on are kind of tough themselves. They tell them to clear it, "You get out of my place or pay the consequences," and usually the guy making all the noise is not tough, he just wants to be heard. If somebody goes against him, he gets a little nervous: "Now why should he tell me to get away? He must be pretty tough, so I better leave him alone and look for a guy that'll buckle." I've seen it happen every day, you know—a guy will walk up and tell a guy, "I want you to get over there and watch Joe because I'm going to stab him." And the guy tells him, "Well, you better go find somebody else, because you get me involved and I'll beat your brains out." The first guy gets nervous, you know, so he goes and tells someone else and he says, "Yeah, yeah, I'll watch." The strong guys run their own life, the weak guys, somebody else runs it for them.

Q: Were you considered a leader?

A: I was until I finally decided to cut them all loose. I had a lot of influence with the white guys up there. When the riot started in my hall I probably kept about twenty, thirty of them out of it. That's one of the reasons they let me out.

Q: I think I may have seen you there.

A: You probably did. Had my own private cell, Cell Block Number Two, pretty good deal. And generally, you know, I could persuade for or against the administration by the type of guy I was. I got along pretty good with most of the guys and about a couple of years ago, I started going along with the administration and I could get guys to cool it, you know. Because for a while I was real rebellious against anything they come up with. I thought it was wrong—the administration. And after a while I started to think, "Well, I'm wrong because they're out there and I'm in here so I have to be wrong," and after that I seen the light. A lot of guys go up there, they're real nervous when they first come in. They're going into a strange environment, strange group of guys, and they figure, "Well, I gotta let them know I'm no weakling or show 'em I'm a tough guy or I'll get in trouble." So they come in and try to act tough. Some of them don't. Some of them come in real meek and mild-mannered and when someone jumps on them they're yellow and it's up to you to do something with them. But everybody that comes into that institution comes in scared. Even your real tough guys come in nervous.

Q: It's easier the second or third time, isn't it?

A: Yeah, if they're going back to the same place. If they're going to another penitentiary or institution it's like going in for the first time.

Q: Is this pen any different from others?

A: Oh, well, you've got your different faces of course, until the guys get to know you.

Q: But the culture within the pen?

A: No, they're all the same—you get the same codes, somebody's doing something wrong, you keep your mouth shut, don't tell the administration. They're basically all the same, always somebody in the penitentiary is doing something wrong, selling clothes, making beer, selling drugs.

Q: Are most of the guys aware of it?

A: What's going on there? Probably ninety-nine percent know what's going on. The other one percent just don't care to—to get involved, whereas the others just ignore it and keep on going. Usually the administration knows what's going on because, like I say, they have informers. I know from fact, through talking with the warden, the associate warden, and so forth, that you get some of your leaders who get caught at different things and the warden will get them and say, "You're either going to cooperate with me or I'm gonna lock you up for two years in solitary," that's segregation. "If you cooperate with me you can go right back and continue the way I tell you to. If you let me know what everybody else is doing, I won't bother you."

"Yeah, that sounds like a pretty good deal." So he comes back out, his poker game continues or his brew-making continues but everybody else around him is getting busted because he knows what is going on. But you don't have one, you have a number of guys like him. Then you have your habitual snitches. They go around trying to find out what's going on so they can turn you in to the warden. Maybe they're trying to get points or a special favor or something, you know.

Q: And do they get it?

A: Some of them, until the warden gets tired of using them and they're locked up in segregation or a guard maybe, a crooked guard may find out and pass the word on to the population. Once in a while someone will make a mistake and pass a guard a note and the guard just may be somebody that's on the take. So he'll turn around and pass the note on to the guy that's being snitched on, say, "He gave me a note and it's got your name on it," and then pass it on to the warden. But the guy that's passing the note is in trouble then. He may be asleep and a chair or a set of lights or something drops on top of his head. He's seriously hurt and they have to take him out and lock him up in segregation.

I'd say they probably keep forty or fifty guys in segregation all the time. Some of them for their own protection, some of them for protection against someone in the population. Might be hot blood between two guys and the one that's at fault, they'll lock him up and keep him segregated from the other guy. Some of the guys are just too scared, they lock them up.

But you could go on and on about the institution up there. There's so many things. It's kind of hard to visualize it. I guess the only way you could really see it is to spend some time there yourself. You go up there on a tour, you see everything looks real dandy. Say, "You guys got it made. You're in prison but still you're doing pretty good." But when you live there with the guys you see things that you don't normally see on a tour. You go up there and the warden tells you about what's happening, or a captain or a lieutenant. They don't tell you, "This guy just got through beating this guy on the head because he owed him two bucks." They tell you about the appliance school and this college program and the IBM computer hookup that's turning out ten thousand car licenses a day. They tell you the fine points of the penitentiary but they're not gonna tell you the other side because if you've never been there it's hard to believe. The place is a jungle.

Q: I wonder why people continue going back.

A: I really think that some guys can't make it outside, so they'll want to go back, especially if they've been in prison all their life. It's like a magnet, just draws them back. Some guys actually want to get caught, so they take chances that the average person wouldn't normally take and if they get away with it, well, that's to their benefit. If they get caught, at least they're going back where they've got a pretty good bed, food, they don't have to tire themselves for anything. I've seen guys come back time and time again.

Some guys have a status up there that would be nothing out here, and I would say that a person that would think that way is not a normal person. A person like that needs help and in this state they don't have the help to give him. They need a hospital or a separate institution where they separate these guys and weed them out and give them the therapy they need. They don't do it, of course. Take one guy that's trying to make it, another guy is trying to start trouble. Put them together and then you have a clash. One guy just don't care what happens because he likes it there. The more trouble he causes the more people look at him and say, "Wow, that's a tough guy. He causes trouble." The other guy might be even tougher but he don't want no trouble. He wants to get out, and lets the other guy give him a hard time. As long as it doesn't get out of hand, he'll just go along with him, just to avoid trouble. But they should have these guys separated and they don't do it. They don't have the staff or supervision to do it. They got two hundred guys assigned to the state institution, they have three shifts. Where they have two hundred people they should have four hundred and then they might not be able to completely supervise it. It all breaks down to supervision and counseling and they don't have it.

Q: Do most inmates go through therapy?

A: The ones that want to can ask for it.

Q: That's a good way to get out, isn't it?

A: No, not necessarily. This guy had a life sentence, requested it, he wasn't eligible for the parole board for ten years. Other guys go up with a year and ask for it.

Q: What's the advantage in going?

A: If you have a problem where you can't get adjusted to the penitentiary life or maybe some of your family matters are really bothering you and you can't get to it but it bothers you, you go to therapy meetings and talk it over. Something—it relaxes your mind if nothing else. But it really did help me. It took the edge off. I was really at a point where I didn't trust nobody. As I recall, it took the edge off me because I settled down a lot.

Q: When you came out you said you got a job the same day—

A: Yeah, I got a job the same day.

Q: Did you get the job on your own—

A: I came out and got my own.

Q: I thought you had to have a job to get out?

A: I was paroled to the halfway house. It's good for guys that don't have jobs—a big help.

Q: How long did you stay there?

A: Fifteen days, until I got my first paycheck.

Q: Does your boss know that you've been in prison?

A: Oh, yeah. I told him right away. He asked me, "What experience do you have?" I told him, "Nine years in the penitentiary. I just come out." He said, "That's good enough. If you don't know it, you can learn it," and he put me to work. Not every boss takes the same attitude but this guy did. Of course this is a construction job. It's not a government or a bonded job.

Q: Yeah, but a lot of these construction companies won't hire ex-convicts.

A: I'd say about a third of your construction help are ex-convicts—somewhere along the line they've been in trouble. Most of them are pretty hard guys. You have to be truthful at the start. If they find out later, they're gonna say you lied and we're gonna have to let you go. But if they hire you knowing what you've done they can't fire you for that reason. So I say, let them know. That way, if something happens in the future it won't be because of prison. And a job like that, most guys, they give you a chance.

The city of Albuquerque, in the Albuquerque schools they're hiring ex-convicts. Springer Corporation—they're hiring ex-convicts. As a matter of fact, the assistant manager of Springer, I was in to see him not too long ago and he asked me, "Have you ever been in trouble?" I say, "Yeah, I just got through doing nine years." He says, "You want a job?" When I was first introduced to him he puts me down as being just another guy. There were three of us together and he asks me, "Have you ever been in trouble?" and I say, "Yeah, I just did nine years in the penitentiary." He says, "Well, what happened in the past is past." He says, "You need a job?" I told him no, I had one. He said, "If you need a job in the future, come over and see me." Not every person is gonna have that attitude. Springer is a pretty good-size operation in this town. The assistant manager, he's the vice-president I guess, says, "Well, what happened in the past happened" and would take me in.

Q: What were some of the things you were nervous about in coming out for the first few weeks?

A: Well, the first week I was out I had the, you might call it a schizophrenia complex—people staring at me, you know, they all know I was in the penitentiary. The people I met were strange, because you're not used to talking to somebody that is straight, and just talking to them made me feel uneasy. Then you always have the feeling they're gonna find out you were in the penitentiary and put you down for it. And generally just getting used to being free again, you know. You want to go to a restaurant and have a cup of coffee, you just go. You don't have to ask, you just get up and go. You feel yourself looking around to ask somebody can you go. And you don't really have to do it. You're not really used to it.

I'd say it takes probably two years to really get adjusted. Right now I feel like I'm adjusted but I'm probably not because a lot of my old ways are still there, especially my speech or my actions. I might be sitting down and if someone comes up behind me I get real nervous and I look around to see who it is. In the penitentiary you have to, you have to know who's behind you. But out here you don't have to have that feeling. Somebody's behind you—you shouldn't think nothing of it, whereas if you're in the penitentiary and someone steps up behind you, you dive for the floor because you don't know if he's got a knife or what, and I catch myself doing that out here sometimes. And just the speech alone. You get a lot of slang words you use and I'll be talking to someone and somewhere in the conversation all of a sudden you slip back and you'll use these slang words and then you catch yourself and you come out and use the right words.

But it's basically just getting used to having your freedom again where you don't have to depend on somebody else to tell you what to do. You don't have to ask permission to do certain things. You use your own judgment. You know what's right and what's wrong. If you know what's right, you go ahead and do it. If you know what's wrong, you're not supposed to do it. It's part of being in society again, adjusting to society and doing what's expected of you.

Q: What do you think of the parole board?

A: In this state? The parole board is very lenient. Now, that's outside supervision. Inside, I would say the parole board is not quite fair because you may have one guy that's up there for burglary, see the parole board, they might deny him, first offense: "You haven't done enough time. Come back another year." He has a good record but not enough time. Here comes another guy with the same offense. He's been there five times in the penitentiary and they turn him loose. So the scale of justice is not quite even.

Q: Do the guys that are denied even know why?

A: They're told, "We feel that you haven't quite adjusted to where you should go out to society."

Q: What's the effect on them?

A: The majority of them get hard-nosed for a couple of days, then they go right back into the same routine and wait the next year. Some of them rebel against it and end up getting into a lot of trouble. I feel there's a lot of guys up there now that, if they turn them loose after a year or two, they will straighten up and make something out of themselves. Where they keep them five, six, seven years, the longer they stay, the more rebellious they get. A good chance they may never straighten up. I don't believe a man should do more than four or five years, unless he's a habitual criminal, you know, in and out of trouble. Others should be turned loose after a certain period of time.

Q: What would you think of a halfway house program before you go in?

A: What kind of a halfway program?

Q: Say to place guys under close supervision rather than send them up?

A: That would probably be all right because he'd be under strict supervision, but I'd say that would be good for first offenders and then it would be up to the individual whether he wants to straighten out. If he gets in trouble, he gets sent up. A lot of guys, if they have a chance for something like that in the first arrest, they realize, a lot of them will realize, what they're getting themselves into.

Q: How about the sixty-day thing?

A: I don't think that really helps. You go up there for sixty days or six years and you come out and you still have a prison record. You still have a number. You can't be committed to an institution for any length of time without a number.

Q: Well, what I'm getting at is does sixty days give this guy enough of a taste of prison where he doesn't want to go back?

A: I'd say sometimes yes, sometimes no. I wouldn't put a guy in there for sixty days and then turn him loose. Because a lot of times you put a kid in there for sixty days and in sixty days he can get himself into a lot of trouble. It'll scare the hell out of 'em. But as I say, there's a lot of homosexual activity in there and you put a kid in for sixty days and some guys have been in there for six, seven years, they'll pound on that sixty-day kid and give him a hard way to go and I'd say it probably would scare the hell out of him. But I think they ought to have something like a farm, a separate institution where they can send them, or somewhere else for sixty days where they're working, and they can give them counseling and therapy instead of putting them right in there where there are guys that have been there ten years, no counsel, no therapy. But in the penitentiary, so you assign them to the kitchen for sixty days—throw them right out in the middle of the rat pack, nobody to look over them and supervise them, that's what it is. During those sixty days they should have somebody right over them to talk to and answer questions and help out. Then turn them out. Keep them under strict supervision for six months or a year.

Q: I think they're using short sentences in some places.

A: I've seen them come in with thirty days, sixty days, ninety days, and the only answer I ever heard of a guy coming for sixty days was, "I sure got away lucky. I could have got fifty years. I got sentenced to ten to fifty years, all suspended except for sixty days," and they say, "Well, I sure got away clean, didn't I?" And they'll get out and I'd say the majority of them are right back on their old track.

Q: Aren't there a lot of addicts?

A: Up there? No, not really. There are a few but they catch them and they lock them up.

Q: No, I mean aren't there a lot of guys sent up that have been addicts?

A: Yeah, there is. Most of them kick the habit up there. I've heard a lot of guys that say they are junkies.

Q: Don't they get right back at it?

A: Most of them do. I've heard a lot of them say, "I can hardly wait till I get out so I can get a good fix." They don't have a good medical staff up there. The dentist comes in once a week on Wednesday. A guy will have a real bad toothache on Thursday and he'll have to suffer till the following Wednesday. You have a broken arm, break it at two in the morning, you've got to wait until two the next afternoon until the doctor comes in to fix it.

Q: They don't take you out?

A: Unless you're stabbed or really seriously hurt they'll keep you right in the institution. The guy breaks his arm tonight, he doesn't want to wait till the next afternoon to get it fixed. That's basically what it amounts to. If you have a mental problem they'll tell you, "Well, you're faking." And I've seen guys I know they need help and they say, "Well, either you straighten up or we'll lock you up." How can you tell a disturbed person to straighten up? You can't do it.

Q: Did you ever . . . were there a lot of suicide attempts?

A: No, well they probably have maybe two a year up there, or three.

Q: Successful?

A: Yeah. They had two this past year that I knew of.

Q: How did they kill themselves?

A: Well, one of them hung himself. The other one took an overdose of pills. And one got killed, supposed to have hung himself but I think they killed him.

Q: Who?

A: The guards, because of a fight in the population. When the guards came to break it up, he pulled a knife on one of the guards. The guard had a night stick and broke the guy's collarbone and broke his arm at the elbow joint. They took him to the hospital and bandaged him up. So one side is out of commission and the other arm was broke and that night they found him hung up in his cell. I don't see how he could have hung himself up with his limbs broken. They had an investigation and the guard that he originally had the fight with was dismissed. But all that was said was that it was suicide. I think he probably kind of worked him over and he had a heart attack and died or he hit him over the head and killed him, and he strung him up.

Q: When did that happen?

A: In 1968. The kid that supposedly hung himself was Bennie Griego, from this state. You know, it's a funny thing. You've got a lot that goes on that the guards or the wardens are not aware of. You know, you get two or three guards that are doing something and unless it's reported to the warden by another official, there's not going to be too much said about it. Like Mr. Johnson, he was there all the time I was there, deputy warden. He was deputy warden when I went there and warden when I left. He's always been a pretty fair man, as far as the warden goes, you know. He never went out of his way to give you a hard time. If you had a problem, he'd call you and sit down and talk with you and if you had trouble with a guard, he wouldn't take the guard's side. He'd call the guard in and he'd tell him, "You know, this guy says you've done something to him and I don't think it was right." He'd hash it out and if the guard was wrong, the guard was in trouble, which is a pretty good way, you know. But it's kind of hard for one man to oversee several hundred inmates.

Q: What were Davis and Baca?

A: Davis was captain when I went up there. He was associate warden when I left and he never went out of his way to harass you.

He was strict. He went strictly by the rules—guards or inmate. He never took sides. I've seen him call a guard down, call him right down and tell him what he thought of him in front of the inmates, but then he did that to inmates too if they were in the wrong. No matter who you were, if you broke a rule and he knew it, he was on your case. There's no sides about it. Baca was deputy warden and I didn't see too much of him. Mr. Davis, he took care of most of the activities in the population. He was immediate superior over the guards and captains. I've never seen him go out of his way to pick on a guy. If he seen you doing something wrong, he'd make sure you knew about it. He wouldn't wait till tomorrow to tell you about it, he'd tell you right then. And a lot of guys up there were rebellious and some of them even told Davis, "If you wasn't associate warden I'd whip your ass." He'd tell them, "Don't let that bother you— get with it."

He was a pretty good-size man, about six five. If you did something really out of the way he'd get you up in a corner and say, "Well, you think you're a tough guy, fight me." If you was a bully and were bothering one of the other kids and it'd work up to him through the grapevine, he'd come snatch you up and drag you to his office and really get down on your case. And everybody up there, all the inmates, they didn't like him but they respected him because he was fair. He didn't take no crap. Something came up, he'd tell you quick, "You think you're a tough guy, you want to jump on a little guy, I'm your size, jump on me." He'd tell you, "Don't let the title bother you."

Q: Did anybody ever do it?

A: Oh, yeah, he'd get down and fight 'em. I don't know if he ever got whipped or not but he was always fighting in the room or in the gym or somewhere. When trouble broke out he just went in there and broke it up. When the riot started, he was the first one in, came in with a gas mask and tear gas. He told everybody, "Get in your cell or you're gonna get a little tear gas." The ones that didn't get in their cell, he put the tear gas on 'em.

I never liked the guy myself, personally, but I always had respect for him. I've had problems from time to time and he always treated me like a man, you know. He'd tell me, he'd say, "As an individual I don't like you but as a man I respect you." I wouldn't lie to him, if I had a problem I'd tell him. If he caught me doing something wrong, I'd tell him, "Yeah, I did it." Say they catch you drinking beer. They got you and they got the beer. Some guys would tell them, "I wasn't drunk and it's not my beer." They might give 'em sixty days in confinement whereas I'd tell him, "Yeah, you got me, what can I say?," you know. He'd put me on restriction for three days or a week. But they would try to snow him or give him a big lie. He'd treat you accordingly.

Q: What's confinement, solitary?

A: No, confinement is being locked up in segregation. Solitary is the hole. They did away with it for about a year but when the riot started they opened it back up. The hole is an empty cell with a cement floor and a toilet and they strip you down to your shorts. While you're there, they give you a sandwich once a day and a meal every three days.

Q: How long do you spend?

A: Up to six months.

Q: Were you ever there?

A: Yeah, I've been there quite a bit. Out of a period of nine years I was there probably twenty times. You can go to court—the kangaroo court—you've probably heard about it in the papers. He would always hold the court. You figure the minimum was five days in the hole and usually it would be five days or ten days or if you're really doing something it would be fifteen days. And then they'll take you out and keep you in segregation and if you kept on messing up while you're in segregation, they put you back in the hole. And some guys go in the hole ten days, come out and be sentenced to segregation for a year. We used to have a couple of guys up there that were really bad troublemakers, spend most of their time there. One guy, a colored guy, he's in there right now. He's been there for about a year and a half, I guess. Every time he'll come out to the population and he's there for a month, two months, and constantly agitates among the inmates and winds up going off his rocker and beating somebody in the head with a pipe.

Q: Sounds like he's kind of crazy?

A: Oh, yeah, he's one of the guys that needs special help. He belongs in a special institution for that type of guys. Instead of giving him help they put him in segregation. He stays there a year, a year and a half, two years. He must be there now about twelve years in the penitentiary and he's only twenty-nine. He went up when he was seventeen.

Q: What's his name?

A: Bennie Blackbone.

Q: Is he from here?

A: No, I don't think so. He might be, his parents come up and visit him. This guy's been there so long that his mind is just gone. He told me, he says, "These people owe me something. They've kept me here twelve years and I should have been out in five. Now I'm gonna make it hard on them." Well, he's not going to make it hard on them, he's making it hard on himself. But his way of thinking is that he's making it hard on them and he'll probably be in there another twelve years. He's got ninety-nine years. He'll probably be there twenty years.

Q: What was the longest stretch you spent in solitary?
A: In solitary? Fifteen days. That was in 1965.
Q: Down in the basement?
A: Yeah, the basement is the hole.
Q: How many solitaries are there?
A: There's ten actual solitary holes downstairs and they have one padded cell but when I first went there, they'd have probably thirty people a week going to the hole and Cell Block Three was segregation. So they put ten downstairs and maybe double them up two guys to a cell. There would be twenty.
Q: Then that wasn't so bad, when you had somebody down there?
A: Really, I think it was worse, because you had to go ten days on a concrete floor and you don't feel like having company when you're in solitary. You're trying to sleep and this other guy's walking the floor and you're trying to concentrate and he's trying to talk to you. It gets on your nerves. You don't have no cigarettes down there and you get to take a shower once a week and it's just kind of nerve-racking. When Warden Peters came in there, he did away with it and then when Peters left and Johnson took over he kept it like it was till the riot started and then he opened the hole back up.
Q: Let's see. You were under three wardens then?
A: I was there under, I forget his name, but he died, had a heart attack and Johnson took over temporarily. Then Peters came in and then they got him out and Johnson came back in.
Q: In your opinion, who's been the best warden?
A: Johnson, I'd say. He was what you might say experienced. He knew what was going on. He has experience, and he knew how to handle the guys. If you had a problem he'd take time out to talk to you. The other warden, if you had a problem, well, he'd tell you to go see a captain or a deputy warden. He'd never stop and take time out and talk to you about your problems. Well, Johnson, say you had a

major problem and you told him, "I got a real bad problem and only you can handle it." He'd stop and say, "All right, come on in my office," and he might talk to you for two, three hours. He wouldn't say, "I've got an appointment in ten minutes, make it quick." He'd sit there and talk to you for two, three hours and then, whatever your problem was, if he could help you out, he'd try to help you out, which I thought was pretty decent.

You know most of your inmates rebel against officials because officials are officials. Most of them will tell you, "He's a rotten dog." But I'd always tell them, "Guys, this is a penitentiary. It isn't a country club." And actually the rules were relaxed. Where else do you have a TV at night? When you work you don't work hard. There's no real hard work there. You can take up training, be able to go to school. On the weekends, Saturday, Sunday, you're free to do whatever you want, go to the yard, lay in your bed all day if you want, watch TV, play cards, go to the commissary. The institution wasn't too bad, you know. A guy, well, he rebels against that, he wants more. What more can you have? You're not sentenced to have a good time. You're supposed to be getting punished and when you have a set of rules, you have to go by them. Most of the inmates there were always rebelling against the administration because the administration were the keepers, the inmates were the caged animals. Some of them didn't, of course, but the majority were always rebelling, especially your young ones. Young ones in their twenties, you know, try to play the tough guy role, always talking the administration down.

Q: What about attorneys? What has been your experience with attorneys?

A: I haven't had much experience. Some of them will tell you, "We'll try to beat them," you know, get down and try to beat it. Some of them will tell you, "Well, you don't have a chance. Forget it." They're getting paid by the state and they're not getting paid much so they're not gonna give a hundred-percent try. If you're paying an attorney out of your own pocket, they're gonna try harder. But the average guy doesn't have the money to pay for an attorney. As I say, I don't have much experience with them but I imagine it's like anything else—to them it's like a business, their living. They're gonna make a buck if they can and if they're not gonna make that much, they're not gonna go out of their way to help you.

Q: When you got sent up to Santa Fe did you have an attorney appointed?

A: Yeah, and like I say, he didn't go out of his way to really help me. He said, "Well, they've got you on this and they've got you on that and I think what's best is to plead guilty to one of the charges and get the rest of them dropped," and that sounded like a pretty good idea cause I was all uptight about the other charges. If they'd have wanted to really get down with it, they probably could have gotten me for four or five charges which could run into a lot of time.

Q: How do you feel about things now?

A: I have no feeling about it one way or another. You have to have law enforcement. Without it, the country would fall apart. You have to have judges. The sentence he gave me was what the law called for. My record wasn't very clean but I can't really say that they were holding anything against me. If I bumped into him on the street I wouldn't have cussed him out or anything like that. I'd just give him respect and keep on going. I don't have anything against him.

Q: What would you say caused you to select a criminal career over a legitimate one?

A: Well, probably because when I was younger I had no trade. I had no one to lead me in a direction of a trade. I had no one to sit down and talk to me about getting involved in different activities and all that, and when I first started stealing, I had more than when I wasn't stealing and, as time went by, I made more and more. So it was a pretty good deal, just routine.

Q: Do you have any kids with your present wife?

A: She has three and two are teenagers, thirteen and fourteen. I constantly talk with them about staying out of trouble. To my knowledge, they haven't been in trouble yet. The boy is fourteen and I don't see him running around in gangs. He has a minibike that he rides out on the mesa. He's constantly tearing it down. I teach him how to weld, I teach him how to drive. I think he's doing pretty good for a fourteen-year-old.

Q: You met your wife when you got out?

A: Yeah, through some people from here, from Albuquerque.

Q: You knew some people from here when you got out?

A: Well, I was acquainted with Mr. Ortiz. When I left the penitentiary he was a member of the parole board and I was corresponding with him and then, when I got out, I joined an AA group.

Q: Were you an alcoholic?

A: No, but I thought . . . I was drinking a little heavy before I got sent up and I thought maybe just coming out it might help me. When you've been locked up for nine years it won't hurt just to go down and sit in on a few meetings, anyway, and it would give me a chance to meet somebody, which I did. The group used to be at the penitentiary once a week to visit. So it's like anyplace else, you get to meet people and pretty soon you get to meet more and more.

Q: Are you involved in Esperanza?

A: In the Esperanza program I attended a meeting but I didn't like it. I told them I didn't like it because from what I've seen of it, they weren't accomplishing nothing. All I seen was a five- or six-man clique trying to dominate everybody else. A minority clique that was trying to get nothing but ex-convicts into their little crowd and that four or five weren't doing anything good. They weren't helping anybody but themselves and I told them. That was about a month ago. They said, "Come back next week. We're gonna have a meeting at the Mental Health Department next Tuesday." I told them, "I don't think I'll be back" and they asked me why and I told them, "I don't think you're doing any good. I've come to two or three meetings and all I've heard was what you're going to do when you get some money through some grant and what you can do for yourselves. There's no mention about helping other people or getting out and really getting involved in the community. It's just one small circle." There was two or three officers there and some volunteer parole officers attending the meeting and I voiced my opinion. It might not be right but it's my opinion so I'll voice it. I told them, "I appreciate your taking your time but I won't be back," and I never went back. Unless I can see something that's gonna benefit, an overall benefit, everybody instead of a small group, I can't go along with it.

Q: Do you associate with any group now?

A: Yeah, well like I say, I associate with the juveniles and the juvenile court here, the public schools, the parole and probation officers. I figure I can go out and maybe voice my opinion and talk to kids, tell them my experiences and what might happen to them if they continue goofing off, what their options are if they straighten up and go right and just sit down and rap with them. I figure if I could help, out of fifty kids I'm talking to, just two of them, then it's worth my time. Just like I told my parole officer, I'll come and talk to them any time he calls for me as long as the counseling doesn't interfere with my work. I'll come down any afternoon or on a weekend sometime because I've been through it and I don't want to see somebody else follow in the footsteps I followed. It's not a very nice future to go into.

It's a pretty bumpy road and when you get there, when you finally get to the end, it's a dead end. A life of crime—there's strictly no future in it.

Q: Yeah, but people don't see it that way. So many people—

A: Well, most of them just don't want to. Don't want to see it or they don't stop to think what might happen. They always think that if they get away with it once, they're so smart they'll never get caught. No matter if they're smart, they're gonna get caught. Every day in the paper somebody is getting indicted for something, you know, even your politicians.

Q: On fences, do you feel that people who are fences have an acceptable position in their communities besides this illegal activity?

A: To me he's just another thief.

Q: Yes, but how are they generally seen by the rest of the people in the community?

A: Yeah, most of them are businessmen, like Stewart of Arrowhead Auto Sales, he's the biggest fence in town.

Q: Why don't they get busted?

A: They have, over the years, been under suspicion for different things, but I imagine he probably has enough friends in the city government to where if something comes up he can call on them for help. He does them a favor, they do him a favor. To the average citizen the fence runs a car lot or a hock shop. He's a respectable businessman. To the underworld he's a fence and something that's not really major, like buy a hot TV set off you or he might sell you a gun where you were supposed to register it and put down a false name. He's just a thief that hasn't been caught.

Q: But he is seen as a man in a legitimate business.

A: Yeah, but over the years that's how he made his money. True it's probably somebody else doing the stealing. He buys a hot TV set off you for fifty dollars and sells it for two hundred, makes a pretty good profit. And over the years he's got his business built sufficiently that he'll give you credit on a car, three hundred dollars. You get it off the parking lot, you'll be lucky if it runs. I bought a Rambler off Arrowhead and I got to the curb of the parking lot and the battery's dead on it. Just enough charge to get it out into the street, stopped at a stop sign and it died on me. Backed it back to the parking lot and told him, "That damn thing don't run," and he said, "Well, you signed the agreement, buying it as is, but for fifteen more dollars we'll sell you the battery."

Q: And what can you do, huh?

A: Well, I didn't buy a battery there. I pushed it off to the curb and went somewhere else and bought a battery. But to the other person he's a businessman, but to me he's just another thief that hasn't got caught. He's not gonna put himself in a predicament where he's gonna get caught. A guy comes in with a hot TV set, in the hock shop a person doesn't have papers or a bill of sale when he's gonna hock a TV set. The hock shop says, "Well, I didn't know it was stolen." He's a businessman and you're a thief.

Q: Yes, and the worst thing they can do to him is take the TV away.

A: So they confiscate it and he puts down a small loss but he's made a profit off somebody else. At one time, Stewart was involved in other things in this town: gambling, card games, dice games, and if you wanted to borrow ten dollars you'd go see him and he'd charge you fifteen back. Who was going to prove it? The man is not a millionaire but he's well off. He's never worried about where his next meal's coming from.

These guys steal until they accumulate enough money and they go into business for themselves and they see a thief knocking at the door, they'll call the police on you. They got what they wanted. They don't want to jeopardize what they got so they don't want anybody that's crooked around them. They tell you, "I'm a respectable businessman. You've got to get away from me now. I was a thief last week but I'm not a thief no more so you better get away before I have you arrested."

Q: That's the way to make it if you want, I suppose.

A: You steal from a thief and he'll cry the loudest. He'll go for a year and steal a whole bunch of stuff, you know, steal a whole bunch of stuff and accumulate it and get it all piled up but then along comes someone else and robs him. Well, then, he'll have the State Police on them and crying and you can hear him all over town crying about the crime in town and something ought to be done about it. I've seen it time and again.

Q: How about policemen or people like that? Talking about guards in prison being crooked or legitimate businessmen being crooked, have you had any association—

A: In Farmington I heard there was, not in this town. I imagine on any police force you're gonna find some bad, there's gonna be somebody on the take. I'd say overall, you've probably got a pretty good police force here but you're gonna find one that's on the take. In

Farmington I know for a fact that one of them on the police force got
fired. He was a captain of the detectives and he busted several people
down there that are in the penitentiary and he knew 'em as being
local residents. He got caught taking a thousand dollars. Half of it was
given to him by someone that stole it. He let him go and they had an
investigation. This was about six years ago and they even come to the
penitentiary and asked me about it. The sheriff come up and I signed
a statement. I knew some of his activities. I imagine through the
investigation and after they got through talking to thirty, forty people
about it, telling them the same thing, they dismissed him from the
police force. And you always hear of someone on a police force
getting shook up somewhere in the country. You can't control them
all a hundred percent.

Probably the overall average—they're probably pretty straight,
you know. But you've always got somebody someplace that's too far in
debt. He's not making ends meet. He can make an extra dollar, he's
gonna do it. That's not only in the police department. That's
anywhere, you know—any business. A man can really be honest all his
life and get really in a bind with his business in jeopardy or
something. The first thing he thinks is, "How can I get out of debt?"
Burn his establishment down and collect the insurance? And then
they'll do something crooked and get themselves out of a jam and get
themselves back on their feet and all of a sudden they're a good guy
again. Everybody else is doing something wrong except them. They
can't do no wrong. It's human nature. It breaks down to self-
preservation. A guy gets in a bind, he has a nice business going but he
gets a little bit in debt. He has a chance of losing his business and he
has another chance of doing something that's not quite according to
the law, get himself out of debt. He'll go ahead and do it. Then once
he's on his feet again he goes to church every Sunday and becomes a
respectable citizen. He's in there leading the council against crime. It
happens all over the world, I imagine. It's just human nature to look
out for your own welfare.

Q: Were you ever bitter, you know, about the things that
happened to you?
A: Oh, yeah, I used to feel real rebellious against the police and
everybody around me. Always thought, they're doing it and not
getting caught so why should they bother me? That was always my
outlook. I'd read in the paper "Denver Police Department—Fifteen
Police Officers Indicted for Burglary." They had a burglary ring in the

police department and I'd get thinking, "Wow, if they can do it, why can't I do it?" Seven years ago. You probably remember it. And I was always rebellious against . . . they'd get a guy in the police department off duty on a red light and a cop pulls him over and the guy shows him his badge. "All right, Joe. Be careful. See you tomorrow." You go right behind him through the same red light and you get stuck with a twenty-dollar ticket.

A district attorney in the state, what was it, three years ago? He ran over a family in a car accident and killed two of the people in the family and they give him a six-month suspended sentence. Another guy don't stop for a stop sign and hits a car. Somebody gets killed and they give him ten years for manslaughter. The justice of law is not quite fair all the time. That's what it breaks down to, you know. It's not who you are, it's who you know. If you've got a friend that's in a position to help you out then you've got a pretty good stand. You can't do too much wrong, and that was my old way of thinking. I felt real rebellious against it. If they can do it and get away with it, why can't I do it? And when I got caught and found out I couldn't get away with it, then I snapped.

Well, what they do is no concern of mine and I just better not get caught doing something wrong or I better stop doing it altogether, because I'm not gonna get the same deal they are. Like I say, you could have friends or political pull in the state and all of a sudden the DA says, "Charges are dismissed for lack of evidence." You might have twenty witnesses, all of a sudden, "dismissed." Doesn't mean it's gonna happen to you, so you can't look at what's happening to the other guy. You've got to look out for yourself. Everybody knows that the scale of justice is not even, but then you can't live that way. You can't say, well, he got a six-months suspended sentence, I do it, I'll get the same. You're not gonna get the same.

Q: Have you had any harassment since you've been out?
A: No, none at all.
Q: You haven't been picked up on any—
A: They haven't come around at all. Haven't bothered me. They caught me, oh, the first month I was out, I was coming down Central and I didn't have no taillights. It was after dark. A city police officer pulled me over and he wanted to check the car out, so I got in his car and he asked me for my ID and I showed my ID and I had a parole card. "You on parole?" I told him, "Yeah." He kept me in his car for about thirty minutes checking me out and he said, "Well, you better be careful. There's a lot of armed robberies going on in this

town, you know," but he never gave me no real harassment. And after that, nobody's ever bothered me or gone to my house or on the job, nothing.

I used to go down to the parole office probably once or twice a week and now I just go once a month because I get a lot of jobs for them guys that are out of the penitentiary. Like I got a job for four of them yesterday where I work at, and I want to check in there and see if there's guys that need a job, or maybe there's a school down here that maybe they want somebody to come in and talk, you know, to the kids. But I don't have to go in but once a month to file my report.

Q: Do you have a pretty good relationship with your parole officer?

A: Yeah, I talk to him and you might say I don't . . . if I have a problem I just go in and tell him what's on my mind. I don't keep nothing back and he'll sit there and listen to you. He's a pretty understanding old man. If he can give you some advice, he will. If he can't, he'll tell you. But usually there's not much of a problem, never a matter of life and death. You're not gonna get yourself in that situation no way. But whenever I'm down there, you know, whatever he's doing he'll stop and talk to me and ask me, "How are things going? What have you been doing?" So I can't really complain about him because as parole officers go, he's fair, he's pretty strict but fair.

Modesto

When he was younger Modesto was shy and withdrawn. He was uncertain of himself but pretended that he did not care what other people did and thought. He appeared to be suppressing hostility and feelings of rejection. He was of slender build and average height, with black hair and brown eyes, and seemed very conscious of his severe case of acne. He did not spend much time at the Juvenile Detention Home.

Modesto appeared at the interview neatly dressed. He is still slender and has facial scars as a result of the earlier acne. He attempted to analyze himself and talked of his life with an air of detachment, almost as if we were discussing someone else. He tried to convey an air of self-confidence and relaxation, but his manner and posture belied this. He sat with arms and legs crossed, pushing himself back and forth in his chair, almost as if to ward off an attack. Modesto was very aware of the interviewers and the reason for the interview throughout most of the sessions, and seemed to forget himself and become involved only after much of the interview had elapsed.

A: Well, I think it would be best to start when I was around six years old, you know, more or less, relate to you vaguely what I remember. The people that brought me up were my godmother and godfather, *mis padrinos*. My mother got married when I was . . . well, I don't really remember. I think I was very young. I don't remember when she got married to my stepfather. But I never lived with her till now after I got out of Santa Fe. That's the first time I've lived with my mother in my whole life.

Q: Were your parents divorced when you were pretty young?

A: That's what I don't remember—when they were divorced. I never asked and they never told me.

Q: Do you have any recollection of your father?

A: Yes. Oh, yes. He . . . as a matter of fact, the first time I—how do you call it? Intuition or what you call it, but I was working in the sawmill. I used to work for a lumber company, Zuni Lumber Company, and he went to pick up some lumber and something told me that I had seen this man before, that I had knew him from somewhere, because I was real small but I remember going down to his place where he worked. And later on I asked . . . there were some people there that knew him also. They asked me, "Well, did you know who that man was?" And I told them, "Well, I think I've seen him before or something tells me that I know him." They said, "Well, he's your father." And I wasn't too much surprised by this. I mean, I was indifferent toward it. He doesn't mean nothing to me. To be honest, my real father doesn't mean nothing to me.

Q: He never had much influence one way or the other on you? You don't remember any good or bad relationship with him?

A: Sure don't. None whatsoever. If I was to meet him out in the street, he would be like a stranger to me. Because see, as far as I can remember, he never did help us out in any way. That's where it counts.

Q: How many in your family?

A: I have one brother and one sister that are real brother and sister and I have two half-sisters and two half-brothers.

Q: Are you the oldest?

A: No.

Q: There's seven altogether and you and your full brother and sister are the first kids and then your mom remarried?

A: Yeah. And she had two boys and two girls.

Q: When did you start living with your godparents?

A: They took me when I was about a year old or something like that. And I stayed with them until I was . . . I'd say about fourteen or fifteen, then I went to live with my grandmother.

Q: Did you have much contact with your mother when you were growing up?

A: Yes, well, my godmother is sister to my mother so I saw my mother constantly, talked to her.

Q: I think it's kind of a custom with Spanish people here that the godparents are usually selected very carefully, and they're supposed to be parents if for some reason the real parents can't take care of their children. I suppose that's why you ended up living with your godparents.

A: And all the time I was with my *padrinos*—

Q: Did you call them *padrinos?*

A: *Sí.* Well, in the early years I did, and then after I thought that I was grown up, you know, about twelve, thirteen, I called them by their first names. And up to now, today, I would call them by their first names. I wouldn't call them *padrinos.*

Q: Did they have any children of their own?

A: They had two boys and a girl. And one that died. The time that I was with them when I first started school, from the first to the sixth grade, I attended Catholic schools in San Juan and I was involved in the church and I was an altar boy and got good grades in school and everything.

Q: Did you live in the same area you're living in now?

A: Yeah. As a matter of fact, it's only four houses down. And I never did get into no kind of hassles or anything.

Q: Did you go to San Juan for what—the first six years?

A: From the first to the sixth grade. As far as I can remember, I was average in school, I guess. I was poor, you might say, and I used to make some money. I used to caddy at the country club and I involved myself with sports which I like them a lot. There was one thing that bothered me. There were times when we were supposed to have baseball games in the summer. Well, I told my *padrino* that I was going to caddy for some extra money and I didn't do that. I went to go play baseball, then I went to caddy. So actually, there were times that I didn't really enjoy playing baseball because I had guilt feelings about lying to my *padrino.* Then when I went to live with my grandmother, through all this time . . . well, I guess there's nothing I could say that was real bad or—

Q: How did you feel about living with your *padrinos?* Were your brother and sister living with your mom?

A: No. As a matter of fact, none of them lived with my mom. My big brother lived with my grandmother and so did my sister.

Q: Why did your mom not take care of you guys?

A: I don't know. I imagine . . . I don't know. My stepfather must not have wanted us in the house. Did you ask me if—did I feel comfortable or what was it?

Q: Yeah. How did you feel living with your aunt and uncle? Did you feel like you were one of them or or did you feel like—

A: Yeah, I felt like one of them at the time. There was no conflict. Nothing I can remember of there being any conflict. I was treated the same as they were. But as you grow older, you do begin to notice things. I mean, like they're not the same, you know. And I started to have conflict with my *padrino* which ended in the reason I went to live with my grandmother. He was constantly hassling over me for something I did or something I didn't do. That's when I started to feel the difference, you know, that having a real father . . . they started fighting with one another over me. I was around in the sixth grade. I imagine my last year in grade school.

Q: Do you remember real good teachers or bad teachers?

A: Oh, yes. Well, not lousy teachers. I was fortunate enough to have good ones. Cause there was two sisters, Sister Michael and Sister—what was her name? She had an Irish name . . . Murchison or something like that, and Beto Lopez, he was my sixth grade teacher and he's at TVI now. I saw him a while back. I thought they were real good teachers. As a matter of fact, Beto, I've seen him off and on through the years and he's a great teacher. And he's the one that had greater influence on me in the way of awareness toward an education, in better training and things of that nature.

Q: How about your friends at the time? Were they doing some of the same things you were?

A: Yes. Well, I had friends in my grade school years and then when I went to live with my grandmother I picked up a different kind of friend. I mean, I didn't go around with the same guys.

Q: Did your grandmother live in the same area?

A: Yes. She was living on Eighth Street in the same *barrio* and my grandmother and grandfather—well, my grandfather was blind. He was blinded, as a matter of fact, the year I was born.

Q: Were they pretty old when you went to live with them?

A: Yes.

Q: Are they still living?

A: No. I was gonna say, my grandmother—she's been dead for a number of years already. And in that house we had my grandmother and my grandfather, myself, my brother, my aunt, everybody lived in the same house.

Q: Was your brother younger or older?

A: He was older, three years. He had a much rougher time than I did in growing up. And my grandmother and my grandfather, they just got along with a small paycheck and I recall that I was better dressed than he was whenever we got together. I was going to a Catholic school and he was going to a public school. So, in our earliest years, I would say that I had it made compared to him.

Q: So he and your sister lived with your grandparents—were those your mother's parents?

A: Yes.

Q: Did you have much contact with your father's parents?

A: No. I didn't even know him.

Q: So when you went to live with your grandparents you were in junior high?

A: That's when I started at Hamilton Junior High, and I went there for two and a half years. I didn't complete the ninth grade.

Q: You dropped out of school?

A: Yeah.

Q: You were about fourteen, fifteen?

A: Fourteen.

Q: What do you remember about junior high?

A: About junior high, all I remember is that's when I started getting into trouble. Right after I was in junior high.

Q: Was your grandmother not able to give you the supervision or what?

A: That depends on what you mean by supervision.

Q: Well, like when you started coming in late at night . . . and what kinds of trouble you were getting into.

A: Like getting picked up by the police, staying out late at night, or getting into fights at school, and things of that nature. But as far as supervision, well, my grandmother, she always wanted for me to straighten out, you know, but there was hardly anything she could do, really. Just talk to me, and she did, but it went in one ear and out the other.

Q: Were your friends also getting into trouble?

A: Yes. I guess—that's like I said in grade school I had a different kind of friends, and from junior high on they were on the negative side.

Q: How was your brother? Was he also getting into trouble at the time?

A: No. That's one thing that makes him different from me, because he was brought up in poorer conditions, you know, than I was up to that age and our way of life was totally different. I mean, I considered him a square.

Q: Is that right? Were you one of the *pachucos?*

A: Something like that.

Q: Let's see, that must have been in the early fifties.

A: Early fifties, yeah.

Q: So you were a ducktailed stereotype. Were you getting involved with marijuana or anything?

A: That's when I started with marijuana, when I started in junior high.

Q: Where were you getting marijuana? At school?

A: No, well, hardly at school. It was just the friends or the friends of friends, or people that your friends knew or you knew. We started smoking marijuana.

Q: Well, in the fifties, marijuana was really around and heroin also. Don't you think it was about as bad as it is right now? It was readily available and then they had a series of raids when they really cut down on the pushers, and they sent up a lot of the pushers in the late fifties and that put it down for a while, until about the middle sixties, and it's been increasing since then.

A: Well, in my opinion, I think that there's much more illegal drugs available than when I was going to school.

Q: I suppose now it's worse than it's ever been. But I think there for a while in the late fifties and early sixties there wasn't that much around.

A: And it was strictly restricted to the Spanish people.

Q: Right, and especially heroin. I think all of those were really restricted to the lower economic groups, to the slums, people that lived in the poorer sections of town. That's where most of the drug activity was happening then.

A: But today it's different. It's reached all economic levels.

Q: How did you get the money to buy your supplies?

A: Well, sometimes, like I said, I started caddying when I was in grade school and I caddied up to the seventh grade, I think it was. Then I worked once in a while and I went over to the country club district and cleaned yards, raked leaves on Saturdays, in the afternoons, after school, and when that didn't agree with me, I started stealing small things, like shoplifting in the downtown stores.

Q: When was the first time you were busted?

A: I can't remember. I was young, say thirteen.

Q: Do you remember what you were busted for?

A: More than likely it must have been shoplifting, and at that time the roads detour. My outlook changed, my attitudes changed, you might say.

Q: What do you think caused this?

A: I did. Now I realize—

Q: Yes, you did, but what happened to you that you saw two alternatives and you chose to go the crooked way?

A: You can't blame no one but yourself. I mean, of course, like having friends that are in the same boat that you are has something to do with it to a certain extent, but—

Q: You still have a free choice, but up to now you apparently had mostly just the one choice of buddies and everybody you associated with was straight. But now you're faced with a situation where you can have straight friends or friends that are not.

A: But I found that smoking marijuana and taking pills . . . I guess I was not happy with myself or the conditions that were there at the time, having to scrape for a nickel, that gets to you at times. I don't know. I cannot really say. It has something to do with it, the type of crowd you run around with. If they're smoking pot, well naturally, you're gonna smoke pot or drink or whatever they're doing.

Q: Did your grandmother react against those friends? What did she have to say about it? Was she aware of what was going on?

A: To an extent she was aware but that's one thing we never discussed at this house—me smoking marijuana or going with the wrong crowd or whatever. Like even today . . . at that time it was never me that was at fault; it was always my friends that came over and took me out. So that's—*cómo se dice?* What do you call it?

Q: *Te sonsacaron?* They influenced you?

A: She always used to say for me not to go around with such and such and that they were bad company and so forth. But she never told me that I was to blame for it. That it was outside pressure or whatever you want to call it, that made me do the things I did.

Q: And your grandpa? He didn't say too much?

A: Yes, he talked to me a lot, but like I said, my attitude was bad I guess because I didn't pay any attention to him.

Q: How about your sister? Was she living there?

A: Yes.

Q: She's six years older than you?

A: Yeah. Then she got married. I wasn't even there a year, I think, when she got married.

Q: And your brother? What was his reaction to your friends and to . . . I'm sure he was probably more aware than your grandparents of what you were doing.

A: Yeah, but he never did try to influence me or try to interfere. He went his own way and I went my own way. I mean, of course, we had a good relationship. We never fought with each other, or, you know, called names at each other but . . . he was a square to me. And he never did get into no kind of trouble. We lived under the same conditions and it was just me that was all messed up.

Q: And the group of friends he associated with were different than yours?

A: Oh, yeah. *Yo te digo que ellos eran los escuadros en el modo que los viamos nosotros*—I tell you they were the squares from the way we saw them. Like we thought it was a big deal to get a joint, to smoke it, to get high. You forget things just for a moment or just run around, you know.

Q: What did he say when you first were busted?

A: Like I said, he didn't do much to interfere. As a matter of fact, it was in later years when I really started paying attention or looking with my own eyes, the results if I was gonna keep on the same way where I was heading to, and that's when he used to talk to me, you know, concerning this.

Q: So the first time you were busted was probably sometime around when you were thirteen, fourteen?

A: Yes, and I believe it was for shoplifting.

Q: Do you remember what your reaction was at the time? Were you afraid or did this elevate you in your friends' eyes?

A: No, I don't think that it made any difference because at one time or another we all got caught doing something. My reaction to it must have not been so bad or harsh because I kept on getting into trouble.

Q: Do you remember the first time you were locked up in the juvenile home?

A: Yeah, I remember.

Q: About how old were you then?

A: I was going to junior high.

Q: Did they bust you several times before they finally put you in there?

A: Yes, but I was fortunate in one respect because my *padrino*—you know how politics work in this state—my *padrino* was brought up with a probation officer and every time I got into trouble, well, he's the one that took me out, my *padrino*. Because he knew Mr. Ramallo. It finally got to the stage where he had to lock me up because it wouldn't look right for him, I guess. And the first time I remember going to the D home, it did have sort of an impact on me.

It was the first time I experienced knowing that I was locked up, you know. I can't actually tell you how I felt. It's been a long time ago but I didn't like it.

Q: How long were you in the detention home?

A: The most I spent in there was close to thirty days.

Q: You were there several times then?

A: Yeah, but the most the judge sentenced you to was like thirty days, something like that. It wasn't exactly a whole month. It was around thirteen, twenty days.

Q: What did you do when you were in juvenile home?

A: Nothing. Just spent the day bullshitting with the rest of the guys.

Q: In your room? Did you make a lot of friends there?

A: Not really. Mostly, as I can remember, I haven't been able to make friends easy. Acquaintances yes, but what you consider friends . . . I'm not that outgoing, you might say. But as for making friends there, no, just acquaintances.

Q: What were some of the things that were happening in juvenile home, do you remember, then? At the time I guess it was a pretty small place. They had maybe thirty beds for boys and two large dorms.

A: Yeah. One on each side of the hall.

Q: And then the small one behind with four beds and then another one with a couple of beds.

A: And then they had some for the girls.

Q: A few beds for the girls . . . about twelve for the girls, right? It was a pretty small place.

A: There was nothing to do. I mean, you would just—the only time you went out of the room was, say, when you volunteered to mop or sweep or when you went to eat. The rest of the time you just stayed in your room.

Q: No classes?

A: No, there wasn't nothing, I don't think. No recreation, no going outside, nothing like that.

Q: How about the staff?

A: What about them?

Q: What kind of staff, how did they treat you?

A: Oh, Mrs. Helen treated us all very well.

Q: There were only about three or four staff members?

A: Yes, just about three but they all treated me the same as the rest. If I messed up, well, they would punish me in some way, but I never did get punished for going out of my way to do something that I wasn't supposed to do.

Q: Have you always been pretty good when you're locked up?

A: Pretty good. Well, I can't help but be pretty good.

Q: Oh, a lot of people get locked up and continue getting into trouble in lockup, you know. They continue getting busted for having things they're not supposed to or making trouble with other inmates or what have you.

A: I guess I used to get in fights if one of my friends got jumped or something like that. But what is it that you can really do in there that would really be called messing up except fighting?

Q: With drugs around so much, it is very hard to keep drugs out of an institution, and at that time when marijuana was so popular, was there a problem with that, or do you know?

A: Well, at that time, it wasn't exactly considered a problem. I don't think it was. Not in the way we see it now but there used to be some.

Q: Why do you think it wouldn't have been considered a problem?

A: Because it was not known to the majority of the people, and because it was restricted to the poor people. It was something to keep locked away in the back room and not let it out.

Q: And as long as it was down with the poor people in the slums and *barrios* . . .

A: It was just a nuisance. It wasn't considered a problem.

Q: How about your contacts with the police? How were you treated by them?

A: Badly. Up to this day I try to—as you remember your childhood and things . . . I imagine the police, that their age at that time would have been twenty-one and up and the ones that I remember were older than that, in their thirties, and I cannot see two or three of them beating up a fourteen-year-old.

Q: Were you beaten?

A: Yeah, several times.

Q: For what?

A: For trying to stand up for my rights, you might say. Trying to let them know that what they say wasn't all . . . like if I got caught doing something or accused of doing something, that it wasn't the way they viewed it. I tried to tell them my side of the story, but you do get bitter and I mean there's no way. You grow up with this guilt feeling that whenever you see a police car, up to this day man, I mean . . .

Q: You start shaking?

A: No, I don't start shaking because I know it's different now than it was then but still, I'm not comfortable. But that's one of the things I'll never understand. How can one grown man or two or three grown men beat up on a fourteen, fifteen-year-old? I don't know. I couldn't do it.

Q: You were placed on probation?

A: Yeah. Just a few times I remember that I was put on probation. A couple of times I think it was.

Q: Was Mr. Ramallo your probation officer?

A: Yes.

Q: What did your probation reporting consist of?

A: Just go up and report to him and say you were going to school, what you were doing, "Okay, that's all." There was no close times, I guess, as long as you didn't get into trouble. I guess that was their main concern.

Q: How many times as a teenager, before you turned eighteen, would you suspect you were busted?

A: Me? Man, it's hard to say. It was close to twenty times.

Q: And how many times were you in detention? Almost every time?

A: Well, just for a few days. As a matter of fact, once after I had been here for thirty days or something like that, afterwards, I don't remember how long afterwards, I got busted again and they didn't send me to the detention home. They kept me at the county jail for close to thirty days.

Q: You were still under eighteen?

A: Yes.

Q: Why did they keep you there?

A: I guess they figured that I was a troublemaker or something. That I would . . . that the juvenile home didn't do nothing to me in the way of straightening me out or it was too easy for me compared to the county jail. I don't know. I could never understand why they did that.

Q: What was your experience at the county jail then?

A: Same as at the D home, I imagine, only they were older people there but they were still people that I knew.

Q: Were you close to eighteen?

A: No. I was only sixteen.

Q: But you had friends that were older?

A: That's one thing, most of my friends were quite older than I, say three years older, something like that. When I started going to junior high, that's when I used to go around with guys that were about three years older than I. But when I started messing around with marijuana, that's when the trouble started.

Q: Do you think that's the first thing you did, mess around with marijuana, or did you start shoplifting and all this before?

A: No, because when I was going to grade school I never did shoplift or get into any kind of hassle.

Q: So you started doing it all around the same time?

A: Yeah. That's when I became more aware of what money could do for you. I mean, like I said earlier, a person gets tired of being poor. One thing, I worked since I was young. Like I say, I used to caddy and then afterwards I worked at the Ramada. I mean, I earned most of my money. I worked.

Q: But you didn't make enough money?

A: Evidently I didn't.

Q: Did you ever go to the Boys' School at Springer?

A: No.

Q: How come? Politics again?

A: Yeah. It was mostly because of my *padrinos*. All the other friends that I used to hang around with, they went to Springer once or twice. But I did go to Colorado to a reformatory, to Gordon.

Q: Oh, to the federal institution. When you were a juvenile?

A: Yes. I got busted for marijuana.

Q: Were you pushing?

A: No. What do you consider pushing?

Q: Well, I guess selling.

A: No.

Q: Well, what do you consider pushing?

A: A person who does it for profit, who doesn't use it himself. I used to sell some but . . . I used to buy a can and sell five dollars' worth, six dollars' worth, to have money in my pocket.

Q: You got sent up from here?

A: Yes. I was fifteen and I spent eighteen months . . . I guess fifteen and a half, closer to sixteen.

Q: So the strings couldn't be pulled then, huh?

A: No. It was federal.

Q: What were your experiences at the reformatory?

A: The only difference was that there were—the population there was mostly Anglos and blacks. There were very few Spanish people—Chicanos. There was very few. And I imagine you can say that's the time when I started getting along with other nationalities.

Q: You hadn't had much association with blacks or whites before?

A: No. At that time it was just strictly Chicanos. That's one thing that I remember is that's when I got to know other nationalities. We got busted with a can, you know, of Prince Albert. Four of us.

Q: How much in a can of Prince Albert? That's not even an ounce, is it?

A: No.

Q: All four of you had one can each?

A: No, it was one can.

Q: And all four of you got sent up? For eighteen months?

A: Yeah. Maybe it was not eighteen months. It was close to eighteen months. It was a two-year sentence and I know I stayed more than a year because I remember going the first time, I guess it was a parole board. I don't know what it was then. I went before them twice. That time I got busted I was working. I had my own car and everything. As a matter of fact, I lost the first car that I owned because I got busted in my car. They took it away.

Q: You were out of school then?

A: Yeah. I had been working at the Ramada Inn for quite a while already as a busboy.

Q: When you were at reformatory did you go to school or anything?

A: No. I worked in the plumbing shop and in construction. That was outside the fence. That was toward the end of my sentence. I was in trustee status.

Q: Were the other inmates—they go up to age twenty-one there, don't they?

A: Yeah.

Q: So you were one of the youngest kids there?

A: Yes.

Q: Did you have much trouble there?

A: At first I did, when I first got there, you know. Like I said earlier, my attitude was like I knew it all. That I was a big shit in other words and at first I did get into—

Q: And of course you probably felt more comfortable because your friends went with you.

A: Comfortable in what way?

Q: You didn't feel like you were going alone into an unknown situation.

A: Well, none of my friends got sent up to where I did. Because they were older. I think they got sent to Oklahoma. I was the only one that was sent to Gordon.

Q: But you were going to prove that you were a tough guy?

A: Like I said, I had this kind of attitude that I was it.

Q: Did they straighten you out with that attitude there?

A: Well, I never got locked up in solitary confinement or nothing like that. I don't even think they had it because I never did get there. But that's when I started to get along with other people other than the type I used to hang around with.

Q: Were you treated pretty well at Gordon?

A: Yes. Of course, there's always the good and bad in everything, you know. And there was like, I don't know, maybe they had something against marijuana or guys that used it—I don't know what . . . there was a doctor and he used to give me a hard time. Actually, he stereotyped me in a way which I knew was totally wrong. *Era*—he was—some type of psychologist or psychiatrist, something like that. I used to have a lot of interviews with him and he put down a lot of shit that wasn't true, you know. That's the way he saw it. He said I started smoking marijuana to impress people, and that I was antisocial, and I had no motivation or anything like that which, within myself, I knew it wasn't true because I've always had motivation and I didn't smoke pot to impress people. I smoked pot because I liked it. I liked the high. And I don't consider myself antisocial because I . . . that's when I really started getting to know other people, and things of that nature. That's the way he saw me. In other words, he used to give me a hard time. But other than that, that's the only bad experience I had while I was there.

Q: So then you got out from there and you were seventeen. Did you come right back to the same thing?

A: The very first day I got out. I guess it was in the evening, I smoked my first joint.

Q: You got in contact with your friends?

A: No. They went down to the house. That very first night I started smoking pot again.

Q: So what happened?

A: Well, I worked at jobs off and on about for a year. Then I started working for a lumber company, Zuni Lumber Company, in fifty-five and a year later I got married. In fifty-six, fifty-seven I got married.

Q: You got married at about eighteen?

A: I was gonna be nineteen. I got married in December and I turned nineteen in January. Right before I got married, I started using heroin and that's when my troubles really began.

Q: Why did you start using heroin?

A: That's a hard question for me to answer. I don't know why.

Q: Were your friends involved with it?

A: It had something to do with my friends. Some of them were using it, others weren't. I started using heroin when I was around seventeen. I remember when I took my first shot. It was before I started working at Zuni.

Q: How did you feel when you took your first shot of heroin? Do you remember?

A: Yeah. It made me sick and I threw up a lot and I felt weak.

Q: Did you get a high?

A: Not the first time. Maybe because I took too much. I did get sick the first time, but not too sick. I kept on it off and on up till around sixty-seven.

Q: You didn't become addicted?

A: Well, you can say I was addicted because for all that time I use it off and on, not on a day-to-day basis—like once a week, twice a week, maybe I left it for two or three months at a time, but I always went back to it. And I really did get strung out around sixty-seven.

Q: You were married during this time?

A: Yes. I got divorced while I was in Santa Fe.

Q: Did you have any kids?

A: Four. Four boys.

Q: Was your wife aware of what was happening?

A: She was. At first she wasn't aware that I was using heroin because once I started using heroin I put marijuana, pills, everything aside and just used strictly heroin. I could say that for the first year she wasn't aware. She heard from other people, you know, "Don't get married with him. He's . . ."—you know how people are reacting to this type of thing.

Q: Did your wife come from a family that was pretty straight?

A: Yeah. She heard things of the kind of a guy I was, using this, using that. And I guess it was about a year or close to a year that she became aware that I was using heroin on a part-time basis. And how she stayed with me I can never say.

Q: How long were you married?

A: From fifty-six to sixty-nine.

Q: When you finally got sent up, were you badly addicted?

A: Yeah.

Q: How bad?

A: All I could get—I mean there's no—

Q: Ten, twenty?

A: Ten, if I could get ten. The minimum was five.

Q: What were you doing to earn your money?

A: I was working still and another thing I used to do, like payday I used to buy two or three grams at fifty dollars apiece and from there I would sell just enough to get more. I'd just get fifty dollars back so I could buy some more.

Q: Were you using a lot of the money you were earning?

A: Yes.

Q: What was happening to your family at that point?

A: It was going to pieces without me really realizing it. My wife, she worked. As a matter of fact, she's worked since about three or four years after we were married. She didn't feel secure with me, I imagine. She figured that she might as well start earning a living because I wasn't. When I was just using it off and on I didn't spend too much. It was just five dollars a week, ten dollars a week at the most, which wasn't bad because you can spend it on liquor or anything else. So it wasn't bad up till sixty-seven when I got really strung out. But all this time she was working.

Q: Specifically, what were you doing to help support your habit?

A: Let's say I was going down the street and I saw a car unattended with clothes in it or something of value. I'd take it. I'd go steal or shoplift or things of that nature.

Q: How do you shoplift an appliance?

A: It's easy. I mean there's nothing to it. I mean if you're gonna go steal something, you set your mind on it that you're gonna get it without being observed, if you're lucky, without being observed. You put it under your jacket or just walk out with it. I'm not talking about TVs or something like that. A toaster or a blender or something like that.

Q: That's kind of small stuff, isn't it?

A: Well, they'll bring you ten dollars. Also burglaries, but I didn't do too much of that.

Q: Burglarizing what?

A: Homes.

Q: Alone, usually?

A: No. I usually went with somebody else that was in the same boat that I was.

Q: What was your main source of income, then?

A: My job, because I was getting good money. It was close to a hundred and thirty, forty a week. The only thing that I did out of my paycheck usually was to make the house payment and buy a few groceries. And then toward the end I didn't even do that because all my paycheck was going for heroin, till I finally got caught.

Q: How long did you keep your job after you were addicted?

A: Not very long. Just about a year, about a year and a few months.

Q: Did you get fired?

A: Yes.

Q: Because you were addicted? Did they find out or what?

A: Yeah. Well, I imagine they did. Yeah, they did. As a matter of fact, my supervisor more or less could tell that I was addicted because I wasn't responsible on the job no more. I used to go and take off and go back or not go to work in the morning or in the afternoon. When I really, really got addicted, when I really felt dependent on it was when I started working at night. They promoted me to foreman at night at the company there and that meant more money in my pocket for heroin. That's when I really started to use more. I had a responsible job but I wasn't keeping up with it, you know. I would take off and leave the guy alone for half an hour, an hour.

Q: To go get your fix?

A: Yes. That's when I'd get it during the day, you know. I didn't get enough and eventually, well, the supervisor heard that I used to take off and he could tell what was going on. But I don't blame the people because they gave me a lot of breaks and they tolerated a lot of shit that I done.

Q: Where were your kids at this time? Did they know what was going on?

A: No. They really didn't know what was going on. They knew that my wife and I were constantly fighting over this. That's one thing I can't understand. How she stayed with me through all of the years.

Like that was one thing that really bugged her, you know, yet she stayed with me.

Q: How about the rest of your relatives during that time—were they aware of what was going on?

A: Well, no, it was never discussed really. I even went to the County Indian Hospital for eight days to—that's when they first brought the methadone here. Must have been in sixty-eight. I went for eight days to see if I could rid myself of the habit, you know, because I was living in hell, you know—*era un infierno.* Physically, I did get rid of it, but mentally I didn't.

Q: Did you get on methadone?

A: No. I just took methadone for those eight days I was in the hospital and other than that I haven't taken it.

Q: You got out of the hospital and you went right back to it?

A: Three days later. That time that I was addicted I tried other ways, like my wife and I and a friend of ours went for the weekend because I really wanted to quit, you know, and—but I couldn't last. I stayed there—what was it? A day and a half and I got so damn sick.

Q: You were trying to cold turkey?

A: Yeah.

Q: Couldn't make it, huh?

A: No. The only time a person can really cold turkey is when he is knocked out. But out here in the streets I don't see how a person can do it. And I've tried it. I've tried it. I've tried by going to the hospital for eight days. I tried getting out of the city but I mean I couldn't last.

Q: You left the city?

A: Twice. We went to Carlsbad one time.

Q: You and your wife?

A: Yeah.

Q: How long did you stay in Carlsbad?

A: Two days.

Q: You just had to come back, huh?

A: Yes. And the other time, it was during the summer months. We went to a lake and—what's that lake over there?

Q: Fenton?

A: Fenton Lake. We went about twice. Twice I tried but I couldn't make it.

Q: Were you ever busted for a burglary?

A: No, for burglary I wasn't. I got busted for grand larceny.

Q: What did you do?

A: I was stealing a hi-fi from a freighter company. A record player and radio combination.

Q: Were you alone?

A: No, I was with another guy.

Q: And he got busted too?

A: No, just myself.

Q: Was that at night?

A: No, it was in the evening around six—six or six-thirty.

Q: You broke into the place?

A: No, it was open, but the man was in the back part of the store and we were real quiet. We didn't make any noise. That's the thing of it—he saw us when we were going out. In the process I wrecked my car. He went after us and I ran into another car when we were riding away.

Q: And your buddy took off?

A: Yeah. I stayed there. He had my license plates. I mean there was no use of running.

Q: Is that when you got sent up?

A: To Santa Fe? No. I got a suspended sentence for that.

Q: Did they know you were addicted then?

A: I wasn't addicted then. Only on a part-time basis.

Q: Is that the only time you got busted other than when you got sent up?

A: On the felony? That one and yeah . . . on felony, that grand larceny and in sixty-eight I got busted for heroin.

Q: You got sent up then for heroin?

A: Yes.

Q: For using?

A: For selling it.

Q: Is that when you said you were blowing fifty dollars' worth and selling part of it?

A: Yeah.

Q: So you weren't selling it on a big scale?

A: No. Just to survive. And the guy that . . . well, he was an informer. He was an addict himself also. I think he got busted for writing checks, forgery. He must have made a deal with officials or something because he turned informer and he's the one that turned me in, said that I had sold to him.

Q: How easy was it to get hold of the stuff?

A: Heroin? Well, it was fairly easy. I mean it was no big hassle.

Q: You just had your contacts and knew where to go, huh?

A: Uh-huh. As long as you had the money. I mean it was no big hassle.

Q: How about now, if you wanted to get hold of some?

A: Well, what I've heard is there's more drugs around so I imagine that it's easier now. I mean like in the past three years it's been really around, the past three or four years. When I was involved in it, well, it was more a problem.

Q: How about selling the appliances and things you stole? How about the fencing?

A: I sold to different people.

Q: You were selling to individuals or were you selling to a fence?

A: Individuals mostly.

Q: You were fencing your own stuff?

A: Yeah. You never did get a good price. It was like—say you got a fifty-dollar record player or radio. You were lucky if you got twenty, twenty-five dollars, very lucky if you got that.

Q: Why didn't you go to fences?

A: Well, I used a few of them, but you get more money out of selling to individuals than going to a regular fence because they give you one-fourth or something like that. And if you can sell to an individual, you can get more money out of it. The only time I did go to a fence was a last resort, you know. There was no one around that wanted it.

Q: Do you have any idea, if you were to guess, how many times you did things that you could have gotten busted for?

A: Every day. Every day that I was out in the street trying to score or had heroin in my possession . . . well, that's against the law.

Q: What I mean is like burglary and stealing or—

A: That I could have been caught doing these things? How many times? I couldn't answer that.

Q: Just guess.

A: It's hard even to guess because—

Q: Were you at it daily?

A: Daily? Oh, no. I was out stealing day in and day out? No. Twice, three times a week. Three times a week at the most.

Q: And then you'd go out and get what? Something like twenty-five dollars, fifty dollars?

A: Whatever I could.

Q: What was the largest thing you ever stole?

A: You mean merchandise stolen? Coffee.

Q: Coffee? Where did you steal coffee?

A: From a truck. About ten boxes. It was ten dollars a case—about fourteen boxes. A hundred and forty dollars, I think it was.

Q: So you never got involved in anything really big, huh?

A: Well, just imagine how much is a case of coffee.

Q: I have no idea. But that's all you sold it for?

A: Ten dollars a case, that's all. And I think it's worth three times as much as that. It's worth around thirty dollars a box.

Q: What were the best hours? Let's say the best hours to get appliances or some commercial store? In the evening?

A: In the morning.

Q: In the morning? Before the store opens or when the store is open?

A: We used to go to the different warehouses and in the morning, that's when they bring all their stuff out to put in the trucks to deliver. In the early hours of the morning around seven-thirty, eight.

Q: What would you say you specialized in most?

A: I, myself, didn't specialize in nothing in particular. Whatever was available. I used to borrow a lot—never paid back, or paid part of it. I say, "Lend me ten dollars. I'll pay you payday." And I never paid back.

Q: How many times were you ever in city or county jail here?

A: Well, since I got married, I would say just about four times altogether.

Q: In city or county?

A: In city and county. Like when I lost my job—this cop picked me up on suspicion of burglary and took me in. I stayed there a day and a half and when I came out, that's when I lost my job. Boss said, "We can't depend on you. You're not responsible." That was it.

Q: What was your impression of city and county jails?

A: Well, if you were a *tecato*—addict—you know . . .

Q: You had it pretty rough, huh?

A: Yeah.

Q: They don't like *tecatos?*

A: They don't. Not by the way they act. The way they treated us. If they could make it rough on you, they'd make it rough.

Q: When you were in jail did you withdraw?

A: I've withdrawn . . . at the time I was addicted, twice.

Q: In jail?

A: Uh-huh.

Q: What kind of help did you get?

A: None.

Q: Just cold turkey?

A: As a matter of fact, this last time I got busted for heroin, I got to the point where I was thinking of taking my life away but I didn't have something to use to take my life away. I got to that point. Which, now that I think about it, man it's—I don't know. Your frame of mind, once you're addicted to that stuff, your frame of mind, your outlook, everything—there's no describing it. Like now that I'm, *tu sabes*—you know—clear of mind *y todo*, and everything, there's no way I can describe it. Really. Well, it's a living hell, *tu sabes*. I mean, that's all that's on your mind constantly, twenty-four hours a day, every waking moment. I mean you go to bed thinking of that heroin and when you wake up you're thinking of that. Nothing else matters.

Q: But how are you feeling? Are you feeling high? Are you feeling afraid? Are you feeling mad?

A: If you would at least feel high, that would compensate for something else. But once you're addicted, you just take it to feel normal, to function normal. You don't get high—I didn't get no high. The consequence I just gave up asking. Like if I was gonna do something I'd ask, "Well, what will happen if I get caught?" But I didn't give a damn. All I was interested in was my next shot. And that was it . . . from one to the other.

Q: I suppose you didn't care about friends or family or anything?

A: No. I said I cared about my family but in reality I didn't. Not by the way that I was going about it.

Q: Most addicts, after they have been addicted for a while, they don't eat much or anything else. Most addicts that I have known have been very skinny, very undernourished.

A: I didn't have much of an appetite.

Q: Did you steal from your family?

A: I borrowed quite a bit from my family.

Q: I suppose after a while they quit lending?

A: Uh-huh. I stole from my wife.

Q: You don't like to think about that now?

A: Shit, no.

Q: It's kind of hard to imagine, you know. If you haven't been through it, it's a hard thing to imagine—the desire that would completely take over you.

A: It's even hard for me to try to describe to you how a person feels. I mean, after about a year it's sort of a rut—same thing day in and day out. Then like in my case, I got busted, got sent over there. There was times that I didn't sleep at night just thinking *de las cosas que hacía*—about the things I had done. I began to think, *"Como frega'o pudia hacer estas cosas?"*—How the heck could I have done these things? What was it or, well, I know what it was, but how in the hell could I have done a thing like that in my right mind?

Q: But there are people that get addicted, they get locked up and yet they want to go back to it or they think they'll go back to it when they get out.

A: That's what I've seen that . . . I mean it's just . . . they get locked up and they go back in and they start all over again. It's just up to the individual. To my knowledge, I have never talked with a person that has not said, whether he meant it or not I don't know, but has not said that he wished he could quit. There hasn't been one that has said, "Well, I'm always gonna be on it," or . . .

Q: Would you say that a large number of the people that are locked up in jail or a sanitarium are addicts?

A: A large part? In Santa Fe there was a large number that was drug related. They didn't have to be busted for—

Q: Heroin?

A: Or pot or LSD or the other drugs that are in now.

Q: But they got busted in whatever activity they were doing that was drug related?

A: Yeah. A large proportion of your offenses are drug related. I'd say close to half.

Q: Okay, so you were busted for heroin and you stayed in jail until you got sent up?

A: No. I got out on bond.

Q: Who was going your bond?

A: My brother and my stepfather. They took me out on bond. I was out on bond for about a month and a half.

Q: Did you go right back to heroin during that month and a half?

A: Yeah.

Q: Why did they get you out?

A: They didn't want to see me locked up, I imagine. Would you like to see your brother locked up?

Q: Well, it seems to me that if I knew my brother was addicted, that he's probably better off in that jail where he can't get the stuff than out of it. If I knew that when he got out I could control his actions so he couldn't get back on it—

A: I don't know what the reasons were. I imagine they just didn't want to see me in there.

Q: So you were out for six weeks before you went to court?

A: Yeah.

Q: Did you hire your own attorney?

A: No, they appointed one.

Q: Have you ever had to hire your own attorney?

A: Yes. When I got busted for marijuana when I was in junior high I got an attorney.

Q: Do you think there's a difference in the services that you get from an attorney that's appointed and—

A: Well, the experience that I've had, there is a difference. When they see that money's coming in they make quite a lot more effort. Of course, I'm not saying that all the court appointed are bad, you know, but the experience I've had—your court attorney just went through the motions and that was it.

Q: How long were you in Santa Fe?

A: Two and a half years.

Q: What did they sentence you to?

A: Two to ten.

Q: And you were eligible for parole after—

A: Two years.

Q: You didn't make it in two years?

A: I got out on what they call a setup—two years minimum, you go to the parole board. When I went after two years they put it off for six months instead of a year. The standard procedure is you go up to the board every year, but in my case it was for six more months. And that's when I got out.

Q: Before you got sent up, I guess you went to court two or three or four times when you had been charged with other things?

A: Oh, yeah.

Q: What were your experiences in court, your impressions, how do you feel about the court system?

A: It's not fair.

Q: How isn't it fair?

A: I could be caught with a TV in my hands and I couldn't get myself a lawyer or anything like that. I'd probably get sent up to Santa Fe. The next guy could be caught with the same TV in his hands but with money in his pocket or his family with money in their pockets. He wouldn't go to Santa Fe. So it just depends on who you are, who your family is.

Q: In other words, that applied to you at the beginning because you had somebody that knew somebody and then towards the end you didn't have anybody that could really help.

A: Like when I was a juvenile, I never got sent up to Springer because of this—and yet my friends that I used to hang around with, they went to Springer once or twice or they got sent to thirty days in the detention home, whereas I just spent four or five days at detention. But once it was on an equal basis, I guess, well then that's the way I view it; it just depends on who you are, who you know, and who your family is.

Q: But is that the court's fault? Or is it the fault of people before you go to court?

A: It's the system and the court's part of the system, isn't it? So it's the system.

Q: So there is discrimination more at the level of . . . if you're poor or rich.

A: It's obvious. The discrimination is obvious.

Q: Do you feel there's discrimination at the level of whether you're Chicano or white or black?

A: Yeah. Just by their attitudes, just by their actions. Actions speak louder than words. Look at the penitentiary.

Q: Well, can't you—

A: Look! Look at any institution. Look at any jail.

Q: You can't tie that up with the economy? In other words, the blacks are poor, the Chicanos are poor. There are more blacks than Chicanos in jail.

A: And there's Anglos also but they're also poor. You're not gonna see a rich Anglo in jail.

Q: Or a rich Chicano, huh?

A: You might see some.

Q: So you feel that there is discrimination at both levels? The minority group or the Chicano—

A: To some extent. It's not as bad as being rich or poor. I mean, there's a big discrimination there.

Q: How was it in Santa Fe in discrimination? If you're a Chicano you're treated the same way as an Anglo or a black or how is it?

A: I'll be frank with you. If you were a Chicano or an Anglo or a black . . . if you were an informer, you would have it made. I mean no harassment or getting a good job and you'd have nothing against your system. If you would go and tell The Man, "You know what? I saw some guy bringing in some glue from the factory," or doing something against the rules—if you were that type of person. It didn't matter if you were an Anglo, a Chicano, or a black.

Q: So, in other words, there is—as far as you can see, there's no discrimination in there in terms of minority groups.

A: There is discrimination to the point maybe . . . I am not answering your question, right? I myself felt, and the rest of the guys in there for drugs, that there is a discrimination in that area. Where the officers, the system does show a negative attitude towards the individual that is in there for drugs.

Q: It seems like you felt this all through the system, then? The guy that—

A: A heroin addict is always looked upon, stepped upon, and looked upon as not being worth a damn.

Q: How was the system in Santa Fe? What was your experience there, your judgment, your feelings?

A: My judgment and my feelings are that the people that are there are not qualified to be in there.

Q: Why?

A: Because of the way they go about it. They have no understanding whatsoever. You're not a . . . you're just a number, that's all. I mean they're not fit for it. They're not—I'm talking about the officers that work from the lower up to the top man, because even the officers themselves, you're gonna respect a man if he respects himself. But if he goes around bullshitting and carrying on like a kid and, you know, things of that nature, how in the hell are you gonna respect a man like that?

Q: And you're saying that the officers do that?

A: Not all of them . . . I'm not saying that all of them, part of them do. And then they nag you for things, they say, "Act like a man," and they turn around and try to treat you like an eight-year old, seven-year-old.

Q: How do they treat you that puts you down to that level?

A: Well, you know that you're supposed to get up in the morning, right? When you hear that bell, everybody's supposed to get up and be ready for work. Now, they don't have to go around picking up your bunk and throwing it down or going in the dormitory and hollering like wild Indians and all this shit. I mean, a man knows that he's supposed to get up. He don't need to be reminded in this manner. And, let's say like you're walking down the hallway, man, I don't see no difference of walking four feet off the wall or a foot off the wall. I mean, common sense tells you that there's no difference there. And when the man tells you to walk one foot from the wall or close to the wall or walk single file, you know, little things like that you might not think is important and I might not think it's important but after a while it gets to you.

Q: What's the reason for having a rule like that? Do you know?

A: I don't know. They must have a reason. I don't know what reason they have, but those are just little things. Like I say, you might think there's nothing to them, but after a while it gets to you. Or let's say that, like in our case, man, I used to belong to the NA group, the narcotics group that's down there, ex-addicts. We'd meet once a week. Well, the officer that's there, he knows where you're going. He knows your name and yet when you go, you ask permission for him to open that damn grill. He asks you, "Where are you going? What's your name? What's your number? What business do you have over there?" Or, "You can't go out," or "Wait a minute." Little things like that.

Q: How do you suppose something like that can be changed?

A: By having mature men work there. People that have understanding towards human beings, that have some sort of feeling towards their fellow man. Even though if you committed a crime, you're supposed to pay for it. I can see that. But being locked up is enough. I think that's punishment in itself—being locked up. A man with some type of understanding . . .

Q: Could you remember what were your thoughts when you were in Santa Fe, being locked up there?

A: My main thought was that, as I looked around me, I said to myself, "For what purpose was I put on this earth?" Being locked up behind bars was not it. That was my constant thought. Because I feel that being locked up is not for me and by going back to the same thing that I was doing is going to lead to that. So that's what was constantly on my mind, of not going back to the same thing that brought me there. Or, not putting myself in a position where I could fall back.

Q: But mainly because of the fact that you were locked up? That's why you made up your mind that you would not get involved again in a situation that might put you back up there?

A: My freedom, in other words. Let me tell you one thing, though. Even though I lost my wife and to an extent I'm not a complete father to my kids because I'm not with them day in and day out, and even though I lost a lot by being sent up over there, to myself, I mean for my own benefit, it did me a lot of good because, I don't know . . . my outlook changed from what it was. If my outlook wouldn't have changed, well, eventually I would have lost myself also. I would have kept on in the same damn road I was on before. I can't see that.

Q: When you were in prison did you—how did the inmates see you? Were you, as far as most of the inmates were concerned, okay? Did you get along pretty well with most of them?

A: I got along with most of them fairly well. There was no problem there about getting along with—

Q: Did you get along with the staff?

A: No, just very few.

Q: Was that because of this attitude that you think they have about treating you like a kid?

A: Just by the way they present themselves.

Q: What kinds of things happened in prison?

A: Like what?

Q: Among the inmates, are there like leaders and, you know, is there like a system of—

A: I didn't see nothing of that. There's people you respect but you don't consider them as leaders. I mean if they were gonna go jump in the river that don't mean that I was gonna go jump in the river or if they were gonna get into some hassle that I was gonna get into a hassle.

Q: How long have you been out?

A: Since July.

Q: So you weren't up there during the riots?

A: No.

Q: Were you aware that there might be a riot?

A: Oh, yeah. It was about to happen.

Q: Why do you feel that it was about to happen?

A: Because of the tension, lack of communication, the overall picture, the lack of understanding, you might say. It was bound to happen and it's bound to happen again. As long as they keep that staff there, there's no chance. They will have another riot.

Q: Do you see any problems among the inmates? Are there any problems in behavior or—

A: There's a lot of people that shouldn't be there, that's what you mean? They are emotionally disturbed?

Q: What happens to those people that are emotionally disturbed?

A: What do you mean, what happens to them? Well, they just do their time and get out, I guess. What do you mean, what happens to them?

Q: Well, how are they treated by the administration or staff?

A: Just like another number, another inmate, unless your emotional disturbance is real obvious.

Q: Are there any problems with homosexuals in the institution?

A: What?

Q: Homosexuals in the institution?

A: Is there a problem, you say? Oh, yeah.

Q: Where does the problem occur?

A: Inside the penitentiary.

Q: I mean with what group?

A: Mostly Anglos. They are the ones that are homosexuals. I mean, are the ones that are turning to homosexuals or are homosexuals.

Q: Why is that?

A: They must be weaker. They must not have enough character.

Q: Anglos are a minority group in the prison?

A: It's about even. There's not too much of a difference there between the Anglo, the Chicanos, and the Negroes. I mean there's not a big difference. There might be a difference that there is more Chicanos, but it's not like say one hundred to one, or something like that, fifty to one. It's not that much difference.

Q: Are they known, the homosexuals there, to everybody?

A: Well, I imagine, because word gets around. They say, "He's a punk," and that's it. That's all that needs to be said.

Q: How do they practice their homosexuality, like how do they sleep for instance, in big dormitories?

A: Well, all the time that I was there I did my time in the dormitory and as far as actually seeing two men together in a sexual act, I never did see them, but I did see a lot of hand petting and all that shit, you know.

Q: Hand petting?

A: Hand petting, you know, like *acariciandose*—caressing—and everything.

Q: In a homosexual relationship, there has to be like the man and the woman or the guy that's considered the woman. How are the guys that are the men seen by the other inmates? How do the other inmates feel about them?

A: Well, I cannot speak for the inmates but I can speak for myself and how I feel. I, myself, don't have much respect for either one.

Q: You think if wives would be allowed to be there, the thing would change? Conjugal visits?

A: Not only that. Today, the young kid, say eighteen to twenty-two, goes in there. It wouldn't only eliminate that but it would still keep the family together, you know. I mean, it would not only eliminate the homosexual thing in the prison, but your family ties would be much closer and there won't be that lack of contact, even with your kids.

Q: But your kids and wife are allowed to visit, aren't they?

A: Yeah. Twice a week. No, Saturday, Sunday, and Monday. When I was there it was four days a month. I don't know how it is now.

Q: What are some of the things that come into the prison that are illegal?

A: Drugs.

Q: How do they come in?

A: Well, rumors was that some of the guards would bring it in.

Q: But you don't know that?

A: Not for a definite thing. It's just rumors and I cannot say that this happened or that that happened. It's just rumors. Through the guards, through relatives . . .

Q: How through relatives? Aren't the guys searched after they have visitors?

A: Yeah, but that's what they say. The administration says that during visiting hours, that's when the drugs come in or everything illegal. It might be, but you're stripped naked when you go in and out.

Q: So you don't know of any one incident where some drugs came in and you knew definitely how they came in?

A: That I could definitely say, "Well, this is the way it came in"? It was just rumors.

Q: Did you have any occasion to complain, say, write to the judges, to your lawyer, or something about the treatment or the problems you faced?

A: I don't know what you mean.

Q: The treatment—suppose that you wanted to complain. Did you write your judge or write your lawyer or something? Or the judges would go there and visit you or anything of that sort? I think the prison has adopted the Model Act for Rights of Prisoners and in the Model Act there is a vehicle by which they can complain and have their grievances heard. That's after you got out, I'm sure. This was adopted in January or February of this year.

A: Yeah, but is it applied?

Q: I don't know.

A: Yeah, like right now you can go, or anyone can go that's not aware of that place in Santa Fe, and you can go and tour the place and go and actually have dinner there, and you'll say, "Man, you guys have it made. Nice food. Everything's clean. You guys have it made here," you know? But that's just a show. They can show you all types of paper where it says, "We have this program and this program and this program." It looks beautiful in writing, man, but in reality it's not what it says on that piece of paper. They do have a plumbing shop, electrical shop, all the vocational things, but what good if you go over there at eight o'clock in the morning and sit with a magazine? Does that teach you how to be a plumber? Does that teach you how to be a radio repairman?

Q: Is that your choice or theirs?

A: Well, it works both ways, doesn't it? What if your instructor really don't train you? They half-ass train you. Let's put it that way.

Q: Did you get training in anything?

A: Yeah. I worked in the data processing room.

Q: So you learned how to operate a keypunch machine? Was that because you were motivated to do it or because they said you had to do it?

A: I asked for it. I was motivated to do it.

Q: What would have happened if you hadn't done it?

A: I would have probably spent my two and a half years doing nothing.

Q: So you can do—

A: It's up to the individual, yeah. It's up to the individual.

Q: Say you don't ask to go into some program. You just stay in your cell or dormitory or what do you do during the day?

A: You have to have a job, man. You can't just stay without doing nothing.

Q: Do they allow distribution of methadone there?

A: No.

Q: Were you involved in counseling, any type of counseling program?

A: Me? Yeah. I was very fortunate that I had group therapy with Dr. Thomas once a week for an hour and a case . . . well, that was mixed, a caseworker or two, that was mixed, and Dr. Thomas and me.

Q: How large was the group?

A: Oh, it varied from six to eight.

Q: And did you ask for that?

A: Yes.

Q: Did you ask for it because you were motivated to ask for it or because that was a good way to get out?

A: It was a way to get out and also because I wanted to get, you know, who in the hell Modesto was?

Q: Don't a lot of guys just ask for it because they know—Okay, you get involved in this and this and this, and this is how you get out?

A: Yeah, sure. I mean you have to understand that once you're locked up, you're gonna try your damnedest to regain that freedom you lost, man. And if they say, "Get up at six in the morning and walk on your toes," well you're gonna walk on your toes at six in the morning, if that's the way to get out. But at the same time, the way I saw it, my main concern was getting out but yet at the same time getting some help. Like when I tried to get into that Project Newgate I had a big hassle to get into it but I got into it.

Q: Why did you have a hassle?

A: What did I say earlier about that one? Having it in your jacket or your record as being an addict.

Q: Where did you finish school?

A: I got my GED there.

Q: Through Newgate or did you go to school?

A: They had Newgate and they had the regular school there. I got my GED through the regular school there, then afterwards, after I got my GED, I went into Newgate.

Q: Don't they have classes in Santa Fe that some prisoners attend at the college?

A: Well, before I got out, there was talk about it, and I think from what I've heard now that there's some that are going.

Q: But at the time it was just in the prison?

A: Yeah. Well, all the time that I was there, it was just in the prison. Now I heard that some of them are going out in the community, two or three of them. I don't know.

Q: So you took some college courses while you were there?

A: Well, I don't know what type of system they have or nothing like that, but there was no college courses. It was a prep for college. But they do have a college there now.

Q: They have a lot of programs going—but they're not very effective, huh?

A: I don't think they're very effective. It's not that I'm gonna build myself up to anybody but if I was gonna be an instructor in some class, well, I was gonna try to be a spark to the rest of the guys, get 'em off that damned chair and take the magazine away from them and get 'em motivated. That's their job. That's the way I see it.

Q: The instructors don't care?

A: Not the ones that I've seen.

Q: Are all of the men involved in one program or another?

A: Most of them.

Q: Is everybody either in carpentry or plumbing or school, or what have you?

A: Most of them.

Q: How about the hole? Were you ever in the hole?

A: Solitary confinement? Uh-huh.

Q: But you never made the cell block?

A: No.

Q: The cell block is a privilege?

A: Yeah, well, it is, you might say. Because in the dormitory your bed's here and the next bed's right there about two feet away. So a cell is much more private.

And then like, there's another thing, man. I mean when I was going to school, going back to the harassment, you know, well they turned off the lights at ten o'clock. There used to be a lot, like on your own if you wanted to learn something, you could always get a book and read or write something, or do a little bit of something which takes reading and writing. And I used to, when the lights went off, wait about a half an hour till the officer went down, because I lived on the second tier and they went down the stairs. Well, I used to wait for about half an hour till I figured they were downstairs. I'd go into the restroom and read or write or do my homework because I didn't have time to before they turned the lights out or I did have time but maybe I went out to the yard and played baseball, handball, or watched TV, but after ten o'clock anyway. And there was times that they used to run us out of the restroom, and we weren't bothering nobody. We were doing our work, being quiet about it, you know. I mean not making a racket or anything like that. So they used to come turn off the lights for that. Would you call that harassment?

Q: Well, I think it's something that could have been worked out. Those that were interested in studying could have had some time.

A: There was some officers that understood this. There was some officers that left the lights on. I'm not saying that all of them did it, but most of them turned them off or ran you out. And if you didn't go the second time that he told you, he would just write you up.

Q: That's, I suppose, looking at it from their point of view, the problem of security.

A: Security for what? I mean, what do you mean?

Q: Well, the problem of keeping order and trying to keep illegal stuff out and all this.

A: What does that have to do with the light bulbs burning?

Q: I suppose that if a whole bunch of you were talking late at night you might be planning something. I don't know.

A: Yes. But like I say, no disorder or big commotion at that. I mean, when a person is reading or writing, he's quiet, you know. Not making any racket, tending to his own business.

Q: How was the diet? What kind of food did you get? Was it adequate, would you say?

A: Oh, it was adequate—nothing special.

Q: That was one of the complaints during the riot, wasn't it? Food?

A: Yes, but it was adequate. Now it depends on what you call adequate. I feel it was adequate. It was like they gave you a piece of meat, just one piece, cake, just one piece. You were restricted to how much you took.

Q: They gave you three meals a day?

A: Yeah.

Q: Do you have anything else you want to add? Do you have any feelings about anything?

A: You want my personal experiences?

Q: Yes, that would be good.

A: Like what?

Q: Anything. I don't know. What are some of the difficulties? Okay, if you get into trouble, what happens if you break a rule?

A: Well, the time that I was there, there was about four incidents that affected me personally. One of them had to do with medical attention given there. I got the flu or something which really restricted me to the bunk. For three days, I didn't even go to eat at the mess hall, you know. And the third day that I really felt I did need medical attention I went down to the hospital. The hospital there is open from seven to nine, I believe, in the morning and six to eight, eight or nine, in the evening.

Q: Is there always a doctor?

A: No. There's only fellow inmates that serve as interns, you might say, and there's an officer there but he's no doctor at all. He just dispenses medication and there's a doctor which I don't believe he's a doctor either. He's had some kind of training in that area. Well, in this case, I went down there and I asked him for medication. I talked with Ramirez. I remember his name. I'll never forget it. The officer that was dispensing medication. And I asked him for some medication. He said what was the matter with me and I told him, "Well, I feel weak. I can't eat. I imagine it's the flu. I don't know what it is *porque yo no soy doctor*—because I'm not a doctor."

And I didn't speak to him in no harsh words or acted sarcastic with him you know, *con buenas palabras*—with nice words. And he didn't pay any attention to me so then I went when the other shift came in—it was in the evening. I asked again for some help so they set an appointment for me the next morning for the doctor and I didn't make it. I couldn't get up to see the doctor. I was sick. I couldn't get up. I got up around ten and I went down to the hospital and what the guy told me was, "Well, being that you were a narcotics addict, I think that these are delayed symptoms that you get."

Q: How long had you been in?

A: I had been in there about a year and a half, close to two years.

Q: And the doctor told you that?

A: No, it wasn't the doctor. It was the officer that dispenses the medication. He was just being sarcastic. He says, "Well, I guess you was a narcotics addict so I guess these are just like symptoms you know. Go back to your dormitory." So that was one incident that I was denied medical attention because I was hurting.

The other time was during the summer. We had our softball games in the morning, Sunday morning. I was on the softball team in the institution and I sprained my leg sliding out, at the time it didn't hurt me, you know. We got through playing by eleven-thirty but it didn't hurt me at all. But about one-thirty, it really started to hurt, you know the pain, I couldn't stand the pain. So I went about two o'clock to the hospital and they wouldn't open the door for me. They said, "You have to wait till regular hours," or, "If you're hurting or you sprained your leg, well, why didn't you have Adams, the coach, call us and make a note that you had hurt yourself?" When that happened I wasn't swollen. It takes time for a thing like that to swell up, you know, and I told them exactly what happened; that it was about a couple of hours earlier, that it got swollen and started hurting me. And he didn't open the door for me. He said, "Come back at six." So I went back at six but through all this time I even went to the lieutenant that was in the hallway. I explained to him the situation, that the guy didn't want to give me no kind of medication or at least a hot water treatment or something you know for the swelling and the pain, and even the lieutenant didn't do anything. He said, "Well, those are the rules and we have to abide by them. You can come back at six." And then I went and they put me in a whirlpool, sort of a revolving whatever it is, and that's all they did to it. But those two incidences in there when I was really hurting—I wasn't making excuses to be off work or you know . . .

Q: Is that used a lot by the inmates? Making excuses to get out of work?

A: That's the attitude that they had—that you just make an excuse to lay around in bed. To be honest with you, I never did see any of the inmates abusing this, faking it, in other words. Because the persons that I saw, like myself, that actually did go to the doctor—it was that they were hurting. But those two instances in there when I was really hurting, I knew I was sick and in pain but I was denied medical attention, for the rules that they have are from seven to nine or six to nine and I didn't go at the proper time. Now, is a person supposed to get sick at eight o'clock in the morning or from seven to nine? Even by looking at a person, you know he's not well. I mean you can tell right off if he's faking it or not or if he's in pain. You can tell. I mean you're not blind, and that was just one small way of telling you who you were and who they were.

Q: Did you ever have reason to be disciplined for anything?

A: Yes. One occasion that I felt was really totally unnecessary.

It happened during the summer. I was on the softball team and we used to practice about two or three times a day in the afternoons or a couple of hours in the morning, according to the weather. So it happened that the day before, Adams, he's the one that runs the recreation, he said, "Go for your baseball shoes at the yard and bring them in and shine them up for our game Sunday." So that evening I didn't plan to go to the yard because I had some schoolwork to do, get it out of the way, so I went for my shoes and there they close the grill and the yard at a certain hour.

Q: So you can't get into the yard?

A: Yeah, you're supposed to go to the yard within a certain time and you all come back within a certain time.

Q: You all stay at the yard?

A: Yeah, or stay inside either one. Well, it just so happened that when your dormitory eats last, shoot, if you want to make it to the yard, you have to eat fast and make it by six-thirty or whatever time they're gonna close that grill and not let you out. So I ate fast, my supper, and I went for my shoes and when I was coming back, the officer that was in the grill when I was going to my dormitory said, "Well, you can't come in." And I explained to him the situation, that I had gone for my baseball shoes and I don't plan on going out to the yard. He told me, "Well, why did you go out in the first place?" That's when I told him, "Well, the baseball shoes." I even had them with me. I had my glove and he gave me a hassle. He didn't let me in, you know.

Q: So you stayed in the yard?

A: No, I stayed beside the door until he opened it and the other guys went out to the yard. So the minute his back was turned, I sneaked in and went on to my dormitory. So he wrote me up and he used the "big word" in his report.

Q: Insubordination?

A: Yeah, something like that, refusing an officer and he made a big deal out of it and a couple of days later I had to go before the adjustment committee, the committee that takes care of matters of that nature.

Q: What do the inmates call it?

A: They call it the kangaroo court. So anyway, I went before Mr. Baca and there was—I was explaining to him the situation. Well, he had the officer's report in front of him more or less what had happened and then it was my mistake because I mentioned the word "man," you know, I was telling him something and mentioned the

word, "Well, man, I don't know," and he blew his top. He said,
"You're supposed to be a man and by using those words—" and so
forth.

Q: Baca did?

A: Yeah, because I used that word "man" you know. "Man, I
didn't want to go to the yard." I don't recall exactly what I said but I
used that word so he blew his top off, gave me a lecture that if I didn't
know the rules, how long I had been there, that if I didn't know the
rules that once you go out you can't come in until a specific time . . .
in case of emergency I imagine. I explained to him, man, that I didn't
. . . I just went out for my shoes and came right back. And he said,
"Well, we're gonna restrict you for thirty days from any of the yard
privileges." So right there and then that automatically put me off the
team because I couldn't practice, I couldn't play and we played every
Sunday—once a week. And that is—I guess he doesn't understand that
a person looks forward to going out to the yard.

Q: So you got the feeling that there is no relationship between
what you do and the punishment they gave you?

A: No. They had no understanding whatsoever as to the
situation. I mean they just have one outlook and that's it. They don't
try to understand. There was nothing out of the ordinary involved.

Ralph

Ralph, the only black interviewed during this study, first came to the Juvenile Detention Home approximately five years ago. He was in the home on two different occasions, once on a burglary charge (which was dropped) and again on a runaway charge. Both times he spent only a few days there. His family was difficult to contact, and the concern of his family after learning of his arrest was similar to concern for an acquaintance rather than for a son or family member.

Ralph is a good-looking young man who doesn't seem to have been hardened by his life's experiences. He is eager to please and soft spoken. With Ralph, one almost gets the impression that he is a well-adjusted, crime-oriented personality, and it seems likely that the main reason Ralph turned to crime was that he had no access to a legitimate role. Everything in his environment was crime oriented, and there were no models or opportunities for alternate types of behavior. Ralph appears to be of average intelligence. It was obvious, however, that he has not received much education.

Q: Start out as far back as you remember and, you know, give us an idea of who was living at home and what the relationships were and things like that.

A: Well, let's see. As far back as I can remember it's always been me and my mother and my grandmother. I was the only child in the family for fifteen years.

Q: Are you originally from Albuquerque?

A: No, I'm originally from Roswell.

Q: How long did you live in Roswell?

A: My mother, she's married to a serviceman and she traveled quite a bit so off and on for I'd say twelve and a half, thirteen years in

Roswell. And we traveled a lot, coast to coast. She was married quite a few times, all of them were in the service.

Q: Who was your dad?

A: Roger Wilson. He's from Texas. The last time I seen him was in fifty-seven. He left in fifty-seven and the way my grandmother and my mother explained to me, he liked to travel a lot so he stayed away from home quite a lot.

Q: How old are you?

A: Twenty-one.

Q: So in fifty-seven you were just seven?

A: Yeah.

Q: So he was gone anyway, even when they were married?

A: Right, so you know, like I was raised mostly by my great-grandmother. She passed away in sixty-six. Then, from there, my grandmother raised me, so like I was kind of raised in what you might call a highly criminal environment. Like back then there was a lot of gambling going on, a lot of dope, you know, marijuana. I don't think they were too hooked on the pills but marijuana was smoked a lot. You know, I was exposed to a lot of older people whereas, you know, most kids would rather have some place to go instead of staying at home, we got a chance to get wrapped up in illegal activities at home. Actually, to the best of my knowledge, she tried to steer me away from my mother's house, steer me away from a lot of bad habits I picked up.

Q: I guess then when your mother moved out to another campground—army base—you stayed behind with your grandma?

A: No, she always took me with her. Wherever she went I always went with her.

Q: Well, why was your grandma so much in the picture? Did she live with your mother?

A: Yeah. They stayed together until around fifty-nine and then my mother started getting her own place to stay, apartment. All in all, I guess you'd say I had a great childhood as far as being raised and that sort of thing. I never wanted for anything. My family went generally towards criminal activities and I guess it seemed like fun when we were kids. Through the years, you know, kids didn't have any place to go except, you know, in the streets and this is when eventually they come in contact with people who commit crime. They see an older person ripping off something, they figure that's an easy way to get something.

Q: Where did you go to school?

A: I went to Roswell for elementary all the way through to sixth, and my seventh and eighth grade years were spent in Roswell and I went to Lubbock, Texas for the ninth year and then I went back to Roswell for my tenth year and then I quit. I started traveling around when I was about sixteen.

Q: Was this with your mother when she was moving around?

A: No.

Q: You were on your own, then, more or less?

A: Right.

Q: Do you remember back to grade school—were there any teachers or any people that you feel had a special interest or a special impact on you?

A: Yeah. I remember two. My first grade teacher, Mrs. Blackburn, she—I don't know. I guess I was attracted to her. She showed special interest in me so I got the encouragement to go to school; and my sixth grade teacher, Mrs. Shaw, she was great.

Q: They kind of stand out in your mind as being special for some reason. Were both of these teachers black or were they white or what?

A: They were both white.

Q: Roswell has a high percentage of blacks, doesn't it? I mean higher than Albuquerque, for instance.

A: No, not quite. There's more blacks in Albuquerque than Roswell. There's still about somewhere between two and three hundred in Roswell.

Q: Do most of the blacks live in the same area?

A: No, I guess you could say they're partly spread around. It only took—it occurred about six years ago, they started migrating out.

Q: While you were growing up there, then most of the blacks were living—

A: They were living in slum areas while I was there.

Q: Would most of the blacks that were there at that time be living in an area that was a lower part of town, you know, the poor part of town?

A: Right. Like they used to have an old saying, "across the tracks."

Q: And you lived "across the tracks"?

A: Yeah. So like it was a—most of them thought it was a bad thing, you know, to be living "across the tracks," so they started migrating and going to different neighborhoods. At first, you know, a lot of black families were rejected on account of the kids. They had too many kids and they were so destructive. That's why most of the people didn't like them.

Q: In other areas of town?

A: Right.

Q: So they were really kind of stuck in that area? What was the resistance when they started moving out, from the white people?

A: Well, they were—some of the whites moved and some, you know, protested or signed petitions. But, you know, after a couple of years they got used to it—the idea that blacks aren't gonna steal. The blacks just want to better themselves so they might as well forget it and let them stay there.

Q: Do you think there was a lot of prejudice?

A: Oh, yeah, there was a considerable amount but it wasn't to the point that you couldn't handle it, you know, if you knew how. A lot of blacks there, of course, are not educated, so their main means of taking care of situations like this is force themselves on them and a lot of times they start fights and stuff like that but there never was a race riot.

Q: Did you ever, when you were growing up, come up to situations where somebody was outwardly discriminating against you?

A: No, I never ran into that situation but I've seen others that have. Like, it was funny to me, you know. I guess I never was exposed to this race thing. To me, you know, if he doesn't want me in his place, well, that's cool. I don't want to be there, it belongs to him. So I wouldn't go in there.

Q: So that never bothered you too much?

A: I guess I'm—my mother says I'm gifted with a personality that people like. I get along with people pretty well. I've always gotten along with white people there in Roswell to a certain extent. I was one of the first blacks to ever mix, the girlfriend-boyfriend thing.

Q: You went out with some white girls?

A: Yeah, and that was during my grade school.

Q: And you didn't feel that there was pressure from the white parents?

A: No, her parents, they thought I was the coolest dude in town. Like now, if I go back there, if I needed something, she'd be more than glad to give it to me.

Q: Is this with an Anglo family or a Chicano family?

A: Anglo.

Q: What kind of grades did you make in school?

A: I kept a B average. I had a B average in everything except math. I kept an A in it. That's my special subject.

Q: What kind of woman was your grandmother?

A: She's well liked. All the whites there in Roswell like her because she was so kind and she had real strong standards. Because they all remember when she first came to Roswell, she brought about fifty blacks with her.

Q: Did you mean they followed her?

A: Right. She was a gambler.

Q: What kind of gambler?

A: Dice, cards . . .

Q: So in her house she ran this thing? Is that how she made her living?

A: Yes, until her eyes started getting bad.

Q: And then she retired?

A: Yeah. She's working for a store in Roswell now.

Q: Oh, I thought she died?

A: That's my great-grandmother that died.

Q: Then it was your grandmother that you spent most of your time with or your great-grandmother?

A: Well, actually, all four of us stayed in the house together.

Q: All four of you—your mother, your grandmother, your great-grandmother, and you—all lived there most of the time. I see. And your dad was really never around much?

A: No.

Q: Did he . . . what kind of a guy do you remember him as being?

A: Well, he was a gambler, too. As a matter of fact, the whole family is. Some way or another, cards, dice, pool, stuff like that. Like I can remember in 1958 my mother brought home a whole tub of weed, you know, in one of those big tin tubs.

Q: Marijuana?

A: Right. She picked it out of a field.

Q: In Roswell?

A: Yeah. First time I had ever seen any weed.

Q: Did they bring it in to sell or smoke it or—

A: They sold it and smoked it. She was about eighteen, nineteen, something like that.

Q: Your mother?

A: Yeah.

Q: She was pretty young, then, when she had you?

A: Right.

Q: How old was she?

A: I think . . .

Q: How much older than you is she now?

A: Let's see, she's thirty-nine.

Q: She's thirty-nine and you're twenty-one so that would make her eighteen, around there when she had you. Was she married?

A: No, they were going together at the time and after I was born they got married. And like he stayed around till I was about six. But I hardly knew him.

Q: So he really didn't have much of an influence on you, either good or bad, huh?

A: No. Really, as the years went by, I kind of grew a minor hate for him, you know. Because I don't feel it's right that a—you know, if a man loves his wife and she has a child, you know, that he should up and split. I don't dig his philosophy.

Q: You think he should have stuck around and—

A: Yeah and, you know, try to give her a—some kind of help.

Q: Did he ever give her any money to support you or anything like that?

A: No, he never did.

Q: So your mother and your grandmother supported you?

A: Right.

Q: How about your friends? Who were your best friends? Were they kids like you or—

A: Yeah. This one guy, you've probably heard of him, Randy Watson, national Golden Gloves champion. He still has some bad habits. He's frequently doing something to get himself sent up. You know, like I turn to him for the worst. I guess because he was very interested in boxing whereas I really didn't have any interet in it at the time. Actually, I didn't start getting interested in sports until I went to Springer in sixty-six.

Q: When did you . . . your mother and grandparents were not on welfare?

A: No.

Q: Did your mother work?

A: Yes, she had a job. Like she was working for a night club downtown at night. You know, cleaning up from about two to four. Jobs like cleaning house for other people.

Q: Did you help much?

A: No, I stayed around, you know, when they left my great-grandmother a lot.

Q: Your grandmother also went out to work like that?

A: Yes. Actually, she got my mother a lot of her jobs because she was so well known, my grandmother was. Practically everybody that's old-timers there in Roswell knows her.

Q: When she had this gambling thing going on at her house, did the white people as well as the black people come in?

A: Oh, yeah. Well, actually, she had more white friends than she had blacks. I guess it would still be pretty hard for a kid not to gamble once he got out into society because like this was an every-night thing, you know. Drinking, smoking, gambling.

Q: Going on until—

A: Four or five in the morning. We used, like when we were going to school you know, we wouldn't want to go and she'd say "Okay," and we'd stay home. We were all well provided for; two uncles, my aunts, my mother's brothers.

Q: They lived there too?

A: Yeah. We moved around quite a bit, you know, from house to house trying to find one large enough for all of us.

Q: How do you remember starting, when you started getting into trouble?

A: It was back then when movies were a nickel. To go to the movies it only cost you a nickel and a lot of times I'd go home and I couldn't find my mother, my grandmother. My great-grandmother, she might be at church.

Q: Did she go to church quite a bit?

A: Yeah. She was a Jehovah's Witness. Very religious, and so—

Q: Was your grandmother religious?

A: No, she didn't go to church.

Q: What did your great-grandmother think of that?

A: She really didn't like it, but, you know, she didn't say anything. Our family was more or less . . . we acted like brothers or sisters. We'd get into arguments like brothers or sisters. Actually, we functioned as a family.

Q: In other words, there were no real authority lines or anything. More or less everybody's equal and everybody has the right to—

A: Voice their opinions. I'd see a lot of families, like you know, if someone's been gone a long time, when they do see each other they hug and kiss each other, you know. But in my family, like I've stayed gone three and a half years in Santa Fe and I come back and everybody's standing there and saying, "Look," "Wild," like I had never been gone.

Q: Yeah, just like "Hi" or like you've always been around. People might leave for a week or a year and then come back and nobody would question where they were going or when they would be back or anything else.

A: Right. All that was required was to let each other know where they were going in case they got in trouble or got sick.

Q: You were talking about when you started getting in trouble when movies were a nickel.

A: Right. Well, I went downtown and this bank deposit box was wide open and I was curious and I reached in there and pulled out these two big money bags. Like I didn't have a sense of value of money, so there I go, and after then I started picking other things, I started shoplifting—

Q: What did you do with that money?

A: Well, actually it's funny because most of it I threw away, tore up, gave it away. I think my mother told me that there was about a thousand dollars.

Q: That much, huh? That was, as far as you remember, the first time you had ever taken anything?

A: Right.

Q: How old were you then?

A: I was nine. No, I was younger than that. I'd say I was about seven. I guess that was where one of the stores had deposited their money for the night. When it was placed in the box, nobody noticed it was open.

We didn't have any restrictions around the house like most kids, their mother'd say, "You can't go anyplace," you know. If I felt like going, I just went.

Q: Everybody else was probably too busy doing their own thing to know that you were going.

A: By the time they realized I was gone, I was back. So I started going to the stores and the little shops and things like that.

Q: This money you brought back, you gave some to your mother?

A: Right.

Q: Did she ask you where you got it?

A: Yeah. She asked, "Where'd you get all this?" "I got it from downtown." You know, "found it," and then she turned it in. Even though she was breaking the law in some ways, you know, she would have turned it back in if I had taken it from someplace. Especially an amount that large. Like back then, money was pretty easy to get a hold to because it was floating so freely around Roswell.

Q: You started shoplifting after that?

A: Yeah. Then I graduated to cars.

Q: What kinds of things would you shoplift?

A: Well, I'd shoplift knives, guns, maybe a ring, a watch. I kept them. I took clothes and stuff like this. You know, things that I felt like I wanted and I didn't have the money for. I just ripped them off.

I believe the first time I was picked up was for shoplifting. A store detective caught me and called my mother. He kept me there for a while. He got in touch with my mother and she came down. He said it was going to be a warning this time. So like I laughed about it, you know. I didn't pay much attention to it. I just kept progressing till finally they got tired and they locked me up for about three days. They figured this would shake me up.

Q: You were in jail, I guess?

A: Yeah. I was nine then.

Q: Nine years old and you spent three days in jail.

A: Yeah. They figured this would shake me up. Actually, all it did was made me angry, you know. I thought, "Wow, she'd let them lock me up like this."

Q: You got angry at your mom?

A: Right. And ever since then we haven't been able to get along. We talk, we see each other, you know, but as far as staying around, you know, trying to get along with her, there ain't no way.

Q: What was your impression of the police, do you remember then, were you afraid of them?

A: No, I guess that's why I continued to get in trouble because I never feared the police. I've seen a lot of guys that shake just at the mere sight of them. To me it was just . . . it was funny. You know, here's this guy in a uniform telling me what to do. I just crack up. And then I started traveling when I was ten. In sixty I started going to Texas and like I came here to Albuquerque for two or three days. I'd just get on the road and hitchhike.

Q: And you never had trouble getting picked up?

A: No.

Q: They'd give you a ride. What would you tell them? I mean, if I pick up a ten-year-old I might ask him, "What are you doing?" or "Where are you going?"

A: Those are the type of questions they asked me and I always figured something to tell them. Like one time I was picked up and this dude asked me where I was going.

"I'm going to Lubbock, Texas."

He asked me, he said, "You running off?"

I said, "No. My mother's dead, my father's dead and I'm staying with my grandmother," and the like, it was a continuous conversation all the way over. He took me all the way to my aunt's house. I knew where she lived because I had been over with my mother once or twice. Then, after that, whenever they threatened to put me away, I'd take off.

Q: Did your mother ever report you had run away?

A: Oh, no. Well, actually, I think she did. The first two times I ran off I think she did. The first two times because she didn't know where I went. After that, I kept doing it and she forgot about it because she knew I'd probably be at a relative's house somewhere.

Q: Did your relatives ever call her and tell her you were there?

A: Yeah, always. As soon as I'd get there they'd call her and let her know. It would be four or five hours, she'd come after me. She'd always come get me. As far as being a mother, I think she's the best mother a kid could have. We just don't see eye to eye on anything.

Q: What—you didn't mind being in jail?

A: Well, it kind of made me hostile really. More and more, every time I got locked up, I was growing more and more hostile toward my parents, toward the family, stuff like this.

Q: So you started growing away from your grandmother also? She didn't like what you were getting involved in?

A: No. She failed to realize, you know. What else could I grow up to do? I was raised in this type of environment. Like I skipped school. I wouldn't go to school. I'd get picked up by the truant officer and I'd write notes and keep myself out of school, stuff like that.

Q: Your grandmother's still in Roswell—and your mother?

A: She's still there.

Q: She's still there but you moved to Albuquerque?

A: Yeah, I moved.

Q: Who did you live with?

A: The first time I came down—I met a guy while driving down the street, told him I didn't have a place to stay so he offered me a place to stay, and like the first night I was there, that's when I got picked up and sent to the D home. Vagrancy. We were sitting out right in front of his apartment and the cops came up and said "Vagrancy" and locked me up.

Q: How long were you here when that happened?

A: I'd say about three days. They got in touch with my mother and they released me. The Salvation Army sent me back home.

Q: What do you remember about your stay at the D home?

A: I remember at the time I was smoking and we had a couple of older guys and they sneaked me cigarettes and I'd smoke. I didn't have no complaints, no problems. I was treated nice and I realized that this was a detention home and the officer that took me up there, like he brought me a candy bar and he rapped with me, you know. He told me I'd probably be here two or three days till they got in touch with my parents. The second time I came back—

Q: You went back to Roswell and you didn't stay very long?

A: No, about three weeks.

Q: Then you came back to Albuquerque?

A: Came back to Albuquerque and I stayed here for a year. The second time I came to the D home I stayed about six days then and I had an aunt who lived here in Albuquerque and she came after me. Mrs. Helen told me I'd better not come back to the D home. That's the last time I was in Albuquerque.

Q: So you were only in the D home a couple of times?

A: Right. Yeah, I got picked up for a car burglary.

Q: Was that when you came back the second time?

A: Right.

Q: Had you stolen a car or had you stolen something from a car?

A: No, we were trying to break into this car. There were a couple of radios and stuff like that. There was people eating lunch at Denny's coffee shop and they spotted us and someone called in and they picked us up. We gave them a couple of aliases and this guy, he's on the police force and he had just come from Roswell and he knew who I was so I told him my real name.

Q: During the year that you were here in Albuquerque, how were you supporting yourself?

A: I was stealing.

Q Did you sell the stuff you were stealing?

A: Yeah.

Q: Where did you sell it?

A: Older guys like their older brothers. They'd take it and get rid of it.

Q: What kinds of things were you stealing, things from cars?

A: No. Mostly house burglaries, like rifles, TV sets.

Q: You'd break into homes?

A: Right.

Q: Were you doing this pretty often?

A: Something like at least four a night.

Q: Four a night? In the year you were here you must have burglarized quite a few homes. How many?

A: I got all of Paradise Hills and—

Q: How did you break into them?

A: Through the windows, pick the lock. I guess in the year I was here, I ripped off about two or three hundred houses. It was about three hundred.

Q: And you were doing this mostly at night, huh?

A: Yeah.

Q: Empty homes? Homes where the people were gone?

A: They'd be gone to movies and they'd go out to eat, something like that.

Q: And you would steal mostly guns or were you stealing everything?

A: Everything of value that I could sell.

Q: But you would sell mostly to individual people you knew? Like, you weren't fencing to a big outfit or anything?

A: No, just—they were people that knew fences, you know. I'd give it to them and they'd take it to the fence. And they'd come back and we'd split the profit.

Q: But you never did get picked up for any of those burglaries?

A: No.

Q: After you were picked up the second time for the auto burglary you went back to Roswell?

A: Right. I went back to Roswell and then I started burglarizing over there and I got busted quite a few times.

Q: For the same kind of things, residential?

A: Right. Pulled a couple of store burglaries, which was new to me, too. Like I graduated from there and I wrote checks . . .

Q: You wrote checks before you went to Springer?

A: Yeah.

Q: So you were only, when you went to Springer, about what? About fifteen?

A: Well, yeah, fifteen and I went in the first part of sixty-six and got released the latter part of sixty-six. I was there about eight months.

Q: When you went back to Roswell, then, you did have a probation officer?

A: Right.

Q: What was your relationship with him?

A: Well, he tried to get me interested in sports. He gave me odd jobs around his house trying to keep me out of trouble, but I really didn't dig it. He wanted me to get involved in sports but I always ran off to Texas.

Q: Were you also pulling stuff in Texas?

A: It had become an obsession.

Q: You never got busted in Texas?

A: No, I only got busted when I came back here to Roswell.

Q: How did you choose the places you were going to break into?

A: Well, maybe I'd walk past this certain house. Maybe I'd walk past it three times in a couple of hours or sometimes I would pretend like I was looking for someone and, if they didn't answer the door, I'd just go around back and break on in. Unless it was in the earlier part of the day, I didn't have time to case it and nine times out of ten I was successful with it.

Q: Would you say most of the time you had a couple of friends along with you?

A: Yeah, most of the time I did—seventy-five percent of the time. I'd probably steal a car to go where I was going and I'd leave it about six, seven blocks away from the house I was gonna burglarize.

Q: And you'd case the house and go out to your car and what?

A: No, I always picked . . . every time I'd burglarize a house I'd leave walking, down the alley. It would be late at night.

Q: You never burglarized in daylight—morning or early afternoon?

A: Every once in a while I would. Like I'd be walking down the street and, you know, they have those big picture windows that you can see right through and I'd look at it and nobody would be there so I'd go ahead and go in. I'd go out the back and down the alley and take it to the pawn shop most of the time.

Q: You never had trouble pawning your stuff, huh?

A: No, cause I had a false ID. In one of the burglaries I pulled, I had acquired a false moustache, a wig, and even as young as I was, I looked a lot older. I dyed my hair sometimes. After I got through with those house burglaries I started on stores.

Q: At night?

A: Yeah.

Q: How did you get into stores?

A: Through the roof. I used glass cutters to cut a pattern out and go through it. Put tape over it so the glass wouldn't fall and break. If it didn't have a burglar alarm I'd pick the lock, something I picked up when I was younger. This elderly dude, that's all he used to do was fix locks and I used to sit around and watch him. So one day I just tried it and after I got started, I started using it.

Q: Once you know how, it's pretty easy to pick them, huh?

A: Yeah.

Q: Then, actually, homes in Albuquerque are not so safe?

A: Well, the burglar alarm system gives them sort of a secure feeling, but actually it's no good because you can take a . . . you've got anywhere from two hundred to two hundred and fifty burglars in Albuquerque. These are guys that strictly burglarize houses and like, they're getting where they pick up these books on electronics, you know, and they learn how to read them. They spend all day familiarizing themselves with these different types of burglar alarms. So if they run into one tomorrow night, they know how to handle it.

A guy that just really wants to get into some place, it's really not safe, because they go as far as knocking holes through the walls, you know, or cutting a hole through the ceiling or, if it has a basement, they go through it. A home is not safe if a burglar really wants to get into it.

Q: Do they burglarize places where there is somebody there?

A: At night, this is a famous thing in Texas, down around Fort Worth and Houston. Like they go to the bars and sit there four or five hours and they watch maybe ten, twelve people and they'll follow one home. Be about twelve guys so they all get one person. He'll be pretty high and they'll follow him home, wait until he gets in bed and passes out, then they'll clean out the house. And, if he wakes up, they might have a black jack or something to knock him out. That was the favorite game going down in Texas around sixty to sixty-five. They still do it a lot here. I've heard of a couple of cases like that here in Albuquerque.

It's a bad profession. Most of the guys that turn towards it have some reason, maybe they don't have an education. I figure, you know, if a lot of them had the opportunity to go ahead and get their education . . . like, you know, cosmetology or something like this. Your only chance, you know, is to become interested in something that can help yourself. But the main problem today is, a lot of kids, they don't have any place to go.

Q: What was the biggest job you ever pulled?

A: Biggest burglaries? Oh, it was about three thousand dollars' worth of merchandise. In Texas. It was a rancher. He was pretty wealthy. He had rifles, he had several places and never stayed home. He had a color TV. So like we ripped him off for everything he had.

Q: What kind of guy would you say you are? How would you characterize yourself?

A: Now?

Q: Uh-huh.

A: Well, right now I'd say that I was completely stopped.

Q: What made you change?

A: I kind of snapped, you know, when the judge gave my sentence. "These people are really taking my freedom," but by that time it was too late. Actually, I was reformed before I ever went to the penitentiary.

Q: When you went up to Springer, what did you get sent up for?

A: Car theft.

Q: They picked you up in Roswell?

A: Right.

Q: And you had already been busted so many times that they didn't give you another chance?

A: Right. They had overlooked it something like nine times. I'd been to court about three or four times. Most of the time I wouldn't even get to court.

Q: Your probation officer would give you a break?

A: Right. You know, like I say, they would always show special interest in me for some reason and I wouldn't pay any attention.

Q: Were you a pretty good con guy, maybe?

A: Well, I really don't like to talk that much. I'd always say, "Yes, sir," or "No, sir." And there would always be my mother, you know. She'd always be there and they'd always give me a break. So finally they said they couldn't give me any more breaks and sent me to Springer.

Q: How did you feel about the judge that sent you up?

A: I guess you could say I really dislike the dude. Almost to the point of hate. But you know, after I was up there a while I finally realized, "Wow! You know, they gave me every break in the book." But then I still, you know, I still had this feeling that I had to go out and rip off something. Even after I got out, because like I told the guy that was up at Springer, well he asked me how I feel that I was going home. I told him it was something like a vacation to me because after I stayed there a while they started having dances with the girls' welfare home. I'd go to parties and I got visitors pretty regularly from home.

Q: You considered going home a vacation or being at Springer a vacation?

A: Being in Springer a vacation, a resting period. When I got out, you know, I started the same day I got out.

Q: What were your experiences at Springer? Were you afraid when you first went up?

A: No, I wasn't afraid because it was like he told me. He says, "Just watch the guys up there," you know. So I figured if any other guy got to playing around, anything could happen. I'm not gonna take any chances. Then, like I said, I got in a hassle the first day I got there. A Spanish dude thought he was the power there—tried to take me. But after they seen that they couldn't push me around, we all started getting pretty close together—got along with each other.

Q: Were you considered one of the top guys at Springer?

A: Yeah. Well, actually, there was about seven of us there so I was considered, you know, one of the leaders.

Q: Did you have much trouble there, you know, getting placed in solitary, treatment, or whatever?

A: No. I was put on restriction shortly after I was there, plus I was put in segregation. I was put there once because I was in the hospital and I was supposed to have been sick with asthma and so when the guard, the night watchman, came around, we were jumping up and down on the bed shooting rubber bands, shooting at each other, so I was isolated. The next morning the officer in my dormitory, he came down and got me out.

Q: Actually, all in all, you probably got along pretty well at Springer?

A: Yeah. I got along with all of them. I was working in the kitchen and I was learning how to cook. Like the lady that was over in the kitchen, Mrs. Betts. I looked up to her a lot you know, because she showed special interest in me.

Q: Did you learn how to cook from her?

A: A little.

Q: I ate some of her cooking and it was great. She was a good cook.

A: Mrs. Betts is a great cook. She used to bring over recipes and we used to test them, try them out, like pea soup, barbecues, burritos, and so on. She was really nice.

Q: Was she one of the people at Springer that stand out in your mind?

A: Uh-huh, her and Mr. Ford. I believe you know him, don't you?

Q: I don't remember the name.

A: He taught me how to play ping-pong, you know. Every evening he'd come on duty and we'd play ping-pong. We'd always mess around, joke, go on hikes, stuff like this. We'd get out and play football and he'd be right in there with us. Like I remember I dug him a lot. Those were about the only two people that I really liked. I never did try to do anything to mess 'em around, didn't act like we did with the others, you know. I'd always do something, you know, to the others. Like keep'em angry all the time. Really, I didn't like them.

A lot of people thought that would slow me down, you know, going up to Springer, but I built up animosity towards the whole system. Because actually, you know, I realized that a person is not gonna change unless he wants to and this is more or less forcing a change on them and I don't think it's right. Because like now, I finally realized, well, a long time ago, that crime was one thing. But now, you know, get him a job, get him to know people, show a little bit of respect. This is where it's at. I still have a lot of buddies that come around and want to do things. I turn them off because I am not going to mess around.

Q: How did you feel when you were burglarizing these people? Did you ever put yourself in their situation?

A: I realize how they would feel, after they come home and find all their things gone, but most of the people that are burglarized, they almost have everything insured, even down to the ashtrays and they were pretty well off. So I didn't mind too much about them. I figured all they have to do is call up the insurance man to get the money.

Insurance will take care of it. I hardly messed with blacks, only middle-class blacks and middle-class whites, Chicanos—I always felt they were pretty well off.

Q: So you'd go to the best area of the town—because the take was better there or because you felt that they were better able to—

A: They were better able to replace it, you know, and nine times out of ten, they were getting what they got out of life illegally but legally, if you know what I mean. So I didn't have no feelings at all towards them.

Q: Did you feel that if they are getting their stuff illegally, they had it coming to them?

A: Right, and I like . . . I went as far as, after I made some money, you know, I'd see a lot of neighborhood kids, a lot of kids without clothes so I'd just give it to their parents, you know. They never knew where it came from. Either I'd leave it in the mailbox or I'd leave it on the doorstep without no one seeing me.

I guess in a way, you know, I wasn't really doing it for myself because even now I hate to see kids running around ragged. Of course, I guess it's an emotional thing. Most of the guys that burglarize are doing it strictly for themselves, get their clothes, their houses, their cars and stuff. Really that wasn't my main purpose for doing the things I did.

Like for instance, there was a Spanish lady. I didn't even know her, you know. I had just met her, knew her name was Lucy. She had two little girls and two little boys. So one day I just went and cashed a check. I bought about seventy, eighty dollars in groceries and I just carried them to her and I left Albuquerque. Like helping people has always been my bag.

I've always been against the rich, you know. I feel like they got theirs illegally but legally. I never dug that. The whole thing is, it would be something really . . . I'd have to be really depressed and really in need of something before I'd take something from just anybody.

Q: When you got out of Springer, did you go back to Roswell?

A: Yeah, I went back to Roswell.

Q: You say you started the day you got out again?

A: Right. I went into a store and this lady, she was back in the storeroom, so I just ripped off the whole cash register and split. I stayed in Roswell about two months.

Q: You were almost seventeen when you got out of Springer?

A: Right, and I went to Texas and on my seventeenth birthday I got married.

Q: To a girl from Texas?

A: Right. Like me and her parents couldn't get along so we got a divorce.

Q: How long were you married?

A: Oh, about three weeks. We couldn't get along.

Q: Were you working at all?

A: No, just stealing, that's all. Stealing and gambling, that's about it.

Q: Are you a pretty good gambler?

A: I used to be. I used to shoot dice and play cards and shoot pool. I've just about quit. After I got a divorce from her, I remarried and we stayed together for about a year. As a matter of fact, when I went to the penitentiary, we were still married.

Q: Was this also a girl from Texas you married a second time?

A: Yeah.

Q: Did you come back to New Mexico?

A: I came back in the last part of sixty-eight.

Q: Both of you?

A: Yes. I rented a house that was pretty close to my mother's house in Roswell and we stayed there about two or three months before I got busted.

Q: You were still making a living by—

A: Stealing.

Q: Did your wife know about it?

A: Oh yeah, she knew. And in a way, she didn't approve of it. She was the one who worked whereas I wasn't.

Q: Do you have any kids?

A: I've got two twins and I have a little boy. My second wife had the twins and my first wife had the little boy. We had been going together so after she had the kid, we got married.

Q: Your first wife?

A: Yeah.

Q: You were going together before you went to Springer?

A: Yes, we'd been going together for pretty close to two and a half years.

Q: So she had the baby while you were in Springer?

A: Yes.

Q: What did you get busted for in Roswell again?

A: When I went to Santa Fe? I got busted for aggravated burglary and carrying a concealed deadly weapon. I was carrying a .22. I had a .22 and a .25.

Q: Was it during the daytime?

A: No, it was at night.

Q: Was anybody in the store?

A: No, there wasn't anyone in it. It was a pawnshop.

Q: You broke into it and got busted inside?

A: Yes.

Q: What mistake did you make?

A: Curiosity. There was another door inside the store. I had everything I wanted and I was getting ready to split, so my curiosity busted me. I wanted to see what was behind that door so I wouldn't feel like I left something. So, I opened the door, you know. There was a silent burglar alarm that went off and in a matter of seconds, about two or three carloads of cops came.

Q: Did you give yourself up?

A: Yes.

Q: And you went to jail?

A: Yeah.

Q: You weren't quite eighteen, were you?

A: Yes, I was already eighteen.

Q: During the time you got out of Springer to that time, had you gotten picked up for anything at all?

A: Yes, I did. I was busted in Texas on my eighteenth birthday. I gave a birthday party and me and a couple of friends, we got pretty high off this weed. We decided to burglarize this place. We just ripped off all this stuff, everything, you know. We just—it was a practical joke to us, you know, because we were high. When they found us, here we all stood in the middle of all this stuff. We was at one of my friend's brother's restaurants. We had picked up a lot of stuff and had it all laid out. Officers came and caught us.

Q: But they let you go on that, huh?

A: Right. Everything was recovered and we made restitution for the damage.

Q: And you moved back to Roswell?

A: Roswell. That's when I was with my second wife.

Q: Were you . . . did you mention barbiturates and marijuana? Were you really involved with that stuff?

A: Yeah, like I was smoking something like thirty, thirty-five joints a day. And I was popping pills, you know. I was keeping high taking as many as two thousand milligrams.

Q: What kinds of pills were you taking?

A: Reds, whites.

Q: Were most of your friends involved in that too?

A: Oh, yeah. Actually, when I went to this little town called Littlefield, Texas, the pills were pretty well new to those people at the time, until I started to bring them in.

Q: Did you ever sell the stuff?

A: No, never. I always used it for my personal use. I got turned on with reds. As for selling it—never.

Q: You were using them daily?

A: Right. It almost got to the point you know, where every morning when I got up I'd light up a joint. After a while I got to where I kind of needed it. It was a psychological thing, really. I really didn't have to have them but it kept me happy all the time, and I didn't have to worry about anything and actually I kind of started getting worried when I was going to go out. I'd always get high before I went out and it showed up on my burglaries too.

Q: Were you making a pretty good living?

A: I was making, at least, anywhere from five hundred to five fifty a week, and that was pretty good, considering.

Q: When you burglarized something, what value did you get out of it? I mean, like if you stole something worth three hundred, what would you get out of it?

A: I'd easily get two seventy-five.

Q: You'd get almost full value?

A: Right. Almost full value because I knew after I got rid of it he was gonna jack the price up—so actually he's gonna make his money back. So I'd get as much as, I'd say, seventy-five percent most of the time. After I had been doing it, through the years I started finding out what a good fence was, so as I was going down through Texas, I picked up more of them and started taking 'em stuff.

Q: How do you spot a fence? How do you know them?

A: Well, most fences, you know, they'll come to you. They'll look through the records and say, like they'll go around town and check your record. They'll go down to the police department and ask them to check this guy's record, let them have the information. And if he feels like you're a pretty safe dude, he'll stop you one day and he might tell you, "Well, I need a typewriter, an adding machine, stereo console," or something like that.

You can spot one. Like in most of your bars you can spot them easy, most of the time. You know, he's the businessman type dude. Every time you see him he has the expression of a . . . he's taking care of business, you know, and he's easy to spot. He's always, or most of the time, dressed in suits and stuff like that. He has a certain air about him, you know. You can detect it right away, after you've been burglarizing, stealing for a long time. You can tell him from the regular burglar or person.

Q: Most of the guys that are fences are legitimate businessmen, are running a front where they are actually in legitimate business?

A: Right. A lot of them are pretty wealthy. One man runs a barbershop, that's to give him a legitimate front. And one guy, he may run a bar, grocery store, shoeshine parlor. Just something to put up a front so he won't get busted. There's all types of different businesses he could be in.

Q: And he would sell directly to the people?

A: Yeah, and like the people that he would deal with were usually well-to-do. The word would get around town that they wanted stereo consoles, a piece of furniture or something like that.

Q: He would come to you and put in an order for a stereo console and you'd go out and lift one and bring it back to him.

A: That's right, color TVs, motorcycles, every now and then cars. Like they had a pretty good car racket down in eastern Louisiana. They were taking all the Cadillacs, El Dorados, Mach 3s, Mach 4s and they would bring them back this way and sell them to these car dealers. They'd repaint them and change the serial numbers. New Mexico, Arizona, to North Dakota, South Dakota, up north. They finally got busted, though.

Like I've been exposed to dope, prostitutes, junkies. I've been exposed to this all my life, you know. It's a terrible thing but what else is there left to do when you don't see nothing else?

Q: When you went to court in Roswell and got sent up to the pen, what kind of sentence did you get?

A: Ten to fifteen.

Q: And you spent three and a half years there?

A: Yeah.

Q: You were just past eighteen when you went?

A: I'd been eighteen for a couple of months.

Q: And you were on probation in Texas?

A: Right. I was looking for Texas to put a detainer on me but they didn't. They probably, you know, just forgot about it. The crime I committed there really wasn't too serious.

Q: So actually, you say when you were committed you were already reformed?

A: Really, because I finally realized that they were taking away my freedom, you know, which was what meant so much to me and I finally knew what freedom meant. So really they didn't have to send me up because I was already reformed just by fear alone.

After I got up there it wasn't as bad as it seemed. There was a lot of people that I already knew that were already up there. It took a little while for me to get adjusted. Like I got into quite a few fights, arguments. I couldn't get along with a lot of the guards that worked up there. Because, in my opinion, they're not qualified to be a guard, over me anyway. Over children, I could see it if they were watching kids. But over me, they're not qualified to hold their job. I found out that most of them don't even have a high school education and when a guy comes to them with a problem, instead of sitting down and trying to help the guy out, keep him from getting hostile, you know, they would get quite indignant. Like there was about two or three that really had intelligence and would really try to help a guy out.

A lot of the restrictions they put on the guys up there is really unnecessary, totally unnecessary. Like sending a guy to bed at ten-thirty. If a guy, if he's not gonna work, he's not gonna work anyway, so why restrict him from watching TV? If he wants to stay up until two and watch TV, well that's cool as long as he gets up in the morning and goes to work like he's supposed to. If he doesn't, you know, then he's supposed to be locked up.

Q: In other words, you feel you're treated like children?

A: Right. They treat you as though . . . they try to use reverse psychology on you up there and actually, all the guys up there, what they're doing is turning around and they're using reverse psychology on them. Take for instance, like every week they shake down the dorm. They're looking for knives, dope, and cash money, you know, contraband that you're not supposed to have. So instead of the guys finding the hardest place to hide the stuff, they just simply put it under the bunk and they leave it there and when you come back, everything else is torn up except the bunk. It's the simplest thing in the world to hold a conversation with one of them, you really have to fall down around a sixth-grade level where they could understand what you're talking about. Like the guy I was working with, he's educated, he's had a pretty good education.

Q: What were you doing?

A: Electronics, TV and radio repairs and like me and him got along pretty well. We communicated with each other. We talked without going into a stage of anger.

The guards, they harassed the dudes a lot up there. For instance, "Get up against the wall," you know. This is ridiculous. Why get so close to the wall? The wall is not gonna fall. But I can see their point again on that, because if everybody walked down the corridor like they wanted to, there would be a fight every day because a lot of guys up there don't like each other. But they should figure out something a little better than that.

You know, little bitty things that guards pick on you about, like your shirt. You're supposed to have it buttoned all the way up. If you don't, you know, he writes out a little report on you. They don't allow you to have a needle and thread in your possession and a button falls off your shirt and they expect you to sew it on. With what, if they don't give you a needle and thread? So they give you a report knowing all the time that this report can hinder your getting out of there.

Q: The reports, they go on your record?

A: Yeah. This guy's been there as long as seven years, you know, just on account of one report. And if a guard doesn't like you, you can have a rough time. Like they have a hospital there. You got three hours to go to the hospital—eight, twelve, and six. If you get sick any time after six, you're gonna have to wait until eight in the morning, which is really ridiculous because that's just like telling you, "You get sick when I tell you to get sick."

Their education system is poor as far as school is concerned. They have dudes from the penitentiary that's doing time there teaching school. There's a fifty-fifty chance that they know what they're doing.

Q: Some of them haven't been to high school?

A: Right and those guys aren't qualified to teach anywhere. So it's almost impossible to learn and plus they turn the lights off, you know, about ten o'clock so you leave school about four and if you don't do your homework then you're just out of luck. And then they restrict how much you spend in canteen. Like you can't spend but ten dollars a week, which is insufficient for some guys.

Q: Where do you get your money?

A: Your money is sent up from your folks. They won't allow you to have cash money with you but some guys get it anyway through visits. They sneak in cash money.

Q: They get searched after the visits, don't they?

A: Yeah, but they manage to bring it in anyway.

Q: How about other stuff like drugs—do you get much drugs in there?

A: Oh, yeah. Well, when I first went in there, getting drugs was just like getting drugs out here in the street. All kinds. That was sixty-eight, sixty-nine, about half of seventy. That's when they really started getting strict. It's like, you know, the guards get pretty tight with some of the criminals up there and like they would bring it in.

Q: The guards would?

A: Yeah, and you get most of the barbiturates from the hospital, guys that work in there.

Q: Does any stuff come in during visiting?

A: From the street? Yeah, quite a bit of it. They've got that under control now. They just busted a guy in there not too long ago. He was a guard, and a resident and he passed off some barbiturates.

Q: A resident?

A: An inmate. An inmate and a guard got busted.

Q: Oh, the guard was bringing stuff to the inmate?

A: Right.

Q: Was this inmate using it or selling it?

A: He was using it. They've tightened down quite a bit.

Q: Did you ever get hold of stuff like that?

A: No. I never had anyone bring it in but I know dudes that did. Mostly pills.

Q: Not too much marijuana?

A: No, not that much. In fact, maybe at one time there might be a hundred pills, over a hundred pills, floating around, you know.

Their church situation is something else. It's a poor way of having church. Like guys would go over there and they'd take these guys and the gays there, you know.

Q: The what?

A: They take gays into the church. That's where they have sex acts, in church. During church, because you know he never comes towards the back. He stays in the front. Like maybe a whole group will go in just to go for these two guys.

Q: Is that a big problem there?

A: Yes, it really is. A young guy, going in there, you know, if he's not too tough, he's in trouble. Like most of the young guys that come in there, they seek protection right off. They have themselves locked up, you know. They'll do their time locked up.

Q: So they don't get out into general population?

A: Right.

Q: Did you have any problems?

A: No, I didn't have any problems. It's like I say, most of the guys up there I already knew from the streets and I really wasn't worried. But like the first two or three days there, I had a weapon. I had a spoon from chow hall and ground it down and sharpened it.

Q: Did you get approached?

A: No, I never did get approached. As a matter of fact, I kept it for three years in one spot. I never did move it. They never found it. It was right under my bed. I had some green tape. Well, my bed was green so I had it camouflaged.

Q: Was everybody aware of the queers, the homosexuals? Did everybody know who they were?

A: Just about. You know every queer there, plus they have ten, fifteen locked up.

Q: Did they lock them up because the administration knew they were queer or because they requested it?

A: They knew they were queer. They come from the outside like that, you know.

Q: So they locked them up?

A: Yeah. Perhaps the change of administrations with the new warden and the place was wide open then. Didn't make it any better or worse, just about the same, I guess you would say. Like I had a . . . I didn't pull hard time. I kept myself occupied, doing something all the time. Like I didn't give nobody no hassles, you know, and nobody gave me a hassle.

Q: How about among the prisoners, do the Chicanos and Anglos and the blacks kind of stick together? Or do they mix in pretty well?

A: No, well there's sort of all feelings against each other because, you know, out here the whites are in the majority and we follow right behind them. All the whites there, if they can't more or less . . . if they can't hold their own, they're seeking protection from the blacks or the Chicanos, which causes some conflict. They have quite a few stabbings up there.

Q: The Chicanos and the blacks are really the ones that are always—

A: Clashing.

Q: And the whites have to choose one side or the other?

A: Right, because you know, they come in and they realize they're not in the majority anymore so they have to choose sides.

Q: You were up there during the riots?

A: Right.

Q: Were you involved in it?

A: No. There was . . . I tried to discourage as many blacks as possible, you know, for the simple reason that what was supposed to take place was we were just to sit there, you know, until they granted our grievances. But the Chicanos and the whites, they didn't see it that way. They wanted to destroy the place. They had a couple of blacks in there. I didn't see any sense in it really, because some of the things that they were asking for, sure it wouldn't have hurt to have, but why go through all that to try to get it? Seeing that the administration had already refused, you know that they won't get anything that they were asking for. So they couldn't come to any other conclusion on how to go back on their demands, so they started rioting.

Q: There weren't a lot of blacks involved in it?

A: No, they refused, but after it all happened they blamed it on the blacks. They said the blacks were the main cause of it, which was an injustice really. All in all, even though I had to do my time like I did, I was glad to get out of there.

Q: Did you spend all your time at the walls or were you in Los Lunas?

A: No, I never did get a chance to make it to Los Lunas. I stayed in the walls all the time.

Q: When did you get out?

A: In February.

Q: How did you feel about getting out?

A: I was really happy. I couldn't hardly believe it because I . . . I went in and I had placed my mind at a state where time just didn't mean anything, just from day to day. Like the first few years I was there, you know, I hadn't really snapped, till I had been there two years. I think that's when I started snapping a little bit because time was slowing up. It seemed like time was getting slower and was getting closer, getting ready to go up before the board.

Q: You had to do a third of your time?

A: Right. Well, actually, you know, I did three years and five months. I got out a month earlier than I was supposed to. Plus, you know, I had pretty good counselors backing me up.

Q: What kinds of things did you think about when you were in there?

A: Oh, I thought about getting married.

Q: Your wife divorced you while you were in there?

A: Right. Get married, settle down, get a job. You know, play it straight when you're out. Because the guy in there truly realizes the value of his freedom, stay out of the place. Like I've seen quite a few losers that won't ever come out and I've seen a lot of them return and I've tried to figure out why. I guess they say they get institutionalized, you know. Like they stay there so long that's all they know. When they're free, they can't face reality out here. It's supposed to be a cold dark world.

Q: You didn't feel like that?

A: No, I've always felt that anywhere I go, you know, I could get along with people no matter who they were or how they were. Given half a chance, you know, I can get along with a person. I feel like all you have to do is to speak to know people. And some of the dudes up there, they're afraid of people actually and they just haven't realized that every type of criminal in the world is up there and those are the most hardest people in the world to get along with. People out here are much easier to get along with because if a person likes you, he likes you. If he doesn't, he doesn't. Like they say, "If you don't like it, lump it," you know.

But up there, up there is a different kind of mental thing, you know. It works on your mind because the physical labor is not that hard, and it works on you mentally because every day there's something different, you know. It mounts up and you try to relieve it the best way you know how and so most of the guys stay in the gym and play basketball. They get in a couple of fights but it don't amount to anything.

Q: Do you have pressures both from the prisoners and the staff?

A: Right. If you can—if you can learn to maintain through both pressures, you've pretty well got it made.

Q: Pressures from the prisoners are to not conform and pressures from the staff are to conform?

A: Right. A lot of dudes, you know, like mostly around convicts they act like a convict, you know, but when he gets around an officer, he straightens up. Two roles. It's a role which doesn't necessarily have to be played because just like I said, just go ahead and be yourself wherever you are.

Q: But can you, really?

A: Yeah, it can be that way. Really, it depends on the kind of person you are. That's the main factor. If you're not used to being exposed to different types of pressures that's around you, then it's pretty hard to get along with everybody. That's why you have a lot of guys that end up in the mental hospital in Las Vegas.

Q: They can't take the pressure.

A: Right.

Q: Do you think that the pressures there are worse than the pressures out here?

A: I'd say yeah. Pressures up there are really tough on a guy because out here, you can, you know, like if the pressure gets to you, you can always go to the mountains. Try to come up with some kind of solution to the problem. Up there, you know, there's no place to go. Like I was saying, the intelligence level up there is so low, you know, you can't go to just anyone to converse.

Q: Did you have some pretty good friends among the prisoners there?

A: No, not really. I didn't make any friends, you know, because I didn't want to become familiar with other dudes up there. You know, like maybe he gets in a fight and if me and him are friends, I have to get into it. There's a couple of guys up there, you know, I used to run around with but mostly I stayed away from them as much as possible, you know, because they were up there for something different and what I was going for was to get out of that place.

Q: How did you feel about the place?

A: As a whole?

Q: Yes.

A: Pretty rotten. It's really pretty rotten because, like I say, the intelligence level there. Like one of the guys who wears the suits, one of the administrators, he can't talk to you normally, you know. It's always got to be an order and if you try to talk to some of them, they look at you and give you a go-to-hell look. It's really a rotten place. What it really needs is a whole new administration.

Q: When you came out did you go back to living alone or did you go back with your mother?

A: No, I came to Albuquerque.

Q: Directly to Albuquerque? On your own?

A: Yeah.

Q: So what are some of the problems that you see now for yourself?

A: Really, the biggest one is trying to settle down in a permanent residence. Once I accomplish this, everything else will be pretty easy.

Q: Are you working?

A: Yes, I've had a part-time job. I haven't been able to get full time yet. I'm going to try to get into TVI and follow my electronics training. This way I would be more qualified to work at maybe G.E.

Q: Did you get your GED?

A: Yes, I acquired it at the penitentiary.

Q: You're not married right now?

A: No. I don't plan to get married till I get fully situated. That way I won't have any problems in the future. Like you know, I'm trying to get into different groups, you know, organizations and things like that.

Q: Like what?

A: Like Omega Psi Phi. That's a fraternity of brothers and they have an association which is run by blacks. It's to help people, you know. Not necessarily blacks, like they take kids that don't have any place to go and they try to appropriate lots to build, you know, a small park to give the kids somewhere to go. They have one in the Heights. It's a ball field. They just appropriated money from the government and everybody gets together and they're building. They built this park. All the little kids have a place to go. Those in that area. And like this TVI, it's a pretty nice way to get involved, get a chance to meet different people. That's a familiar problem today—a lot of kids and teenagers, they don't have any place to go. They don't have anything to occupy their minds besides school. After three and a half years I've changed my whole outlook on life.

Q: You don't appear to be bitter.

A: To tell the truth, I am, but I don't like to show it.

Q: What are you bitter about?

A: The way they treat you. The treatment that I received when I was up there, the harassment that I experienced . . . I can't blame anyone for why I was up there. Actually, it's nobody's fault but my own.

Q: So maybe you're not bitter about getting caught and getting sent up there, but you're bitter about how you were treated while you were up there?

A: Right.

Q: Are you bitter against the state pen or are you bitter against the system?

A: No, it's just individuals. I couldn't be bitter against the institution as a whole because like they got a saying up there, "Nobody invited you," or "Nobody asked you to come up here." No, I couldn't be bitter at the thing as a whole but I still feel badly. It's pretty easy to do parole here in Albuquerque. You don't have your parole officer riding your back, you know, and actually, if you get sent back from here, you send yourself back, because they don't bother you as long as you report and stay out of trouble, get yourself a job.

Q: Do you see him often, the parole officer?

A: Yes, I see him every fourth.

Q: Once a month?

A: Right, and I go in sometimes just to rap. I have a counselor that I rap to. He was helping me while I was up there. As a matter of fact, he helped me get out.

Q: Who is the counselor with?

A: DVR.

Q: So you still see him now that you're out?

A: I see him often. He's trying to find me a job working with the public schools or somewhere where I can put my knowledge of electronics to use. As soon as I find a job in electronics, you know, some place like a TV shop, something like that, that's all I ask for me.

Soledad

Soledad came to the juvenile home for the first time approximately seven years ago. She had been taken into custody for running away from home and incorrigibility. First and subsequent impressions were of a young woman who was innocent, hurt, and striking back at those things that were completely altering her life. It was obvious that she was hostile and angry. Counseling revealed a person suffering from feelings of rejection and bitterness.

Soledad was a nice-looking small girl, dark haired and clear skinned. She dressed well and was of at least average intelligence.

When interviewed she was still attractive but somewhat harsher and coarser. There was still a very obvious track down the veins of one arm as a result of her earlier severe heroin addiction.

Soledad attempted to appear very certain of herself, her goals, and her means of achieving them. However, she still seemed to be looking for the security and love that had always escaped her.

Soledad was nervous at the beginning of the interview but relaxed as the interview progressed, until she became completely engrossed in the conversation. Emotions and feelings were very apparent as she related various stressful or emotional moments of her life.

Q: How we've done it with the other people—we've tried to go as far back as they can remember, when they were kids and the situation at home, who was there and maybe some of the relationships.

A: You mean just as far back as I can remember where I started having trouble?

Q: Well, no. Really, just as far back when you were growing up.

A: Okay, I'd say like I was about ten years old. At that time, I was living here in Albuquerque in the south side and there was

144

myself, my two sisters, and my brother were living with my mother. My mother was alive then. My father wasn't—well, my father would come and he'd stay a couple of months and then he'd go again.

Q: Were you the oldest?

A: I'm the oldest of the girls. I have a brother that's older than me but he's a half-brother. My mother was married before. She had my brother and then she married my dad. She had three girls and I'm the oldest of the girls.

Q: She got divorced from the first husband?

A: Uh-huh. Well, she dated my father before he went into the service and when he went into the service I don't know what happened but he got married when he was out there, so she got married too and that's when she had my brother.

Q: So she married her first husband on the rebound?

A: Yeah, because he married, you know, first. But then when my dad did come out they started seeing each other again, and she divorced her first husband and married my dad. She cared for my dad an awful lot.

Q: Was your mother pretty young when she got married?

A: Oh, let's see . . .

Q: How much older than you is she?

A: She died when she was thirty-eight. I was twelve then.

Q: So she's twenty-six years older than you, if you were twelve then.

A: That must be about how old she was because, see, my father did want to marry her before he went into the service but she had a thing about wanting to finish school before she got married. She was going to high school and she wanted to finish this before she got married. So he went into the service. I guess he thought maybe she never wanted to marry him and she was just using that as an excuse. He got married and when she found that out, she married Joe.

Q: Was she married to Joe for long?

A: Oh, just two or three years, I think. I don't know how long but around that length of time. Then my dad came back and they got together. I was born and my next sister to me was born, there was five years difference between us. There's only eleven months difference between my two sisters, and during that time was when my dad started stepping out and this and that. At this time I was about ten or eleven.

Q: Were you aware that this was going on?

A: Oh, yeah. I was old enough to know what was going on. My

mother used to cry a lot and talk to me about it and my brother too. We were the closest to her, mainly because I guess she felt she had to talk to somebody and we were the oldest of her children so she talked to us about it a lot.

Q: What was your feeling about your dad? Were you angry at him?

A: I don't know. I just guess I had pity for my mother. It hurt me so much to see what she was going through that I had a little bitterness towards my father. All this caused her to start drinking. My mom became an alcoholic and she took it very hard. She cared for my father an awful lot and by the time I was twelve . . . well, see, one thing that always bothered my mom—because I remember talking about it, you know off and on—was that she had a son but it was Joe's, you know, but she had given my dad only us three girls and she wanted very much to give him a son and she never did. So he's stepping out quite a bit with just this one woman who's my stepmother now, and when I was twelve, Dora got pregnant.

Q: Who's Dora?

A: My stepmother. She got pregnant from dad and she gave him a son.

Q: Was he already married to her or was he still married to your mother?

A: No, he divorced my mom but the divorce was final just a few months before she had my little brother. Anyway, during this time that my dad was stepping out on my mother, you know, he was worried. Well, she had started drinking pretty heavily and he wanted us to be taken care of and everything else so he decided to—he sent her to the state institution in Las Vegas for alcoholics, the hospital there because she had a whole lot on her mind. She was going through the change of life and all this had an effect on her. She was really in bad shape.

And it hurt me—it hurt me to see her going through what she was going, you know. Especially when they took her, when they took her away from us, they put all of us in a children's home. They took her up there and from then on we've been scattered all over. I've never been with my brothers and sisters since I was about eleven. All right, they put me in with my dad, one of my sisters with my aunt and the other one with my grandma, and my brother went to live with his father. From then on we've been separated.

My mom stayed up there a year and after that year she came out.

She was doing pretty good. She was healthy again, happy, you know. They cured her from her drinking, so she said. But still she was going through the change of life and I think that had a mental effect on her because when she came out, I was twelve then, and my stepmother did have my dad's first son. She read about it in the paper . . .

Q: Did your dad divorce your mom, then, while she was at the state hospital?

A: Yes. Okay, and when she came out we were still in school. It was April, March when she came out. The end of March and we decided, or my dad decided, to keep us where we were until the summer came and then we'd go back with my mom, you know. So we'd go with her on weekends and things like that. Anyway, this one weekend we went with her, it was a Friday. Let's see, it was a Friday when Dora had her son, you know, and being that my mom had been up there and everything, I don't know if her mind was all together or what, but it hit her so hard she cried and cried and cried all weekend that we were with her, she cried about that, you know. It really had an effect on her.

It was Friday when she read about it in the paper and then Monday she committed suicide. She took rat poison. She took rat poison and committed suicide.

Q: Did you blame your dad for it?

A: Yes, and my stepmother. I was very bitter towards them. I couldn't stand her. Now we get along because I've grown up and I can understand better that what happened, happened, and it can't be changed, you know. Two people fall in love and it's just human nature. There's nothing that can be done about it. You can't force yourself to live with somebody just to keep them happy because they have your kids. My dad, she's made my dad a good woman.

But at that time I blamed her for my mom's death, and I couldn't get along with her and then they . . . when my mom died, well, I had to go live with them, so my dad and my grandma especially, saw that I wasn't getting along with her. I was very bitter towards her, very bitter towards my dad. I was very rebellious.

Q: Did you tell them that you were bitter?

A: Not in so many words, but they could see it because I was rebelling against them, doing everything possible that they didn't like that I wasn't supposed to be doing and I mean, I can realize that now. At the time I didn't know why I was doing it. I just knew I hated her, but now I know why. I did blame her for that, you know, and now I

can see I was wrong. But at that time, I did rebel against them. I did
everything. They'd tell me to do certain things and I'd do just the
opposite.

So finally they had to get rid of me. They sent me to a boarding
school in California. Before I went to the boarding school they sent
me up there for the summer to spend it with an aunt that I had living
up there. She's here now.

Q: How old were you at the time?

A: Twelve, thirteen. It was April when she died and as soon as
school finished that summer they sent me out there. I spent the
summer out there with my aunt and when the school semester came
back, instead of letting me come back home, they told me that they
were gonna keep me out there and I didn't have any say-so
whatsoever about it. I just had to do what they said.

Q: How did you feel about it?

A: I felt unwanted.

Q: You didn't really want to live with your dad, but—

A: But he was my dad and I felt that, all right, my mom was
dead and I felt like I was, being that my mom died, like he cut me off
too and I wasn't a part of him or something, you know.

Q: How about your brothers and sisters, how were they getting
along?

A: They were very small. Rosa was six and Maria was . . . five,
and you know, like they were still babies. They didn't know what was
going on, you know.

Q: And you say that your half-brother went to live with his dad?

A: Yeah. One of my sisters was living with an aunt. I was living
with my dad, one of them was staying with my grandmother, and the
other one was with an aunt. So I stayed out there. They put me in this
boarding school and it wasn't that bad. I got interested in school and
made good grades. The year passed pretty fast.

Q: Did you like the school?

A: Well, I can't say if I really did or didn't, you know. I didn't
like it because I felt neglected but I liked it because I was away from
my stepmother. So I did and I didn't but I just made up my mind to
make the best of things and I got interested in school and did my best.
I only stayed a year. It got pretty expensive for my dad. I think he
spent three thousand dollars, something like that, for tuition a year.
That was tuition, not counting my laundry bill and things like that. So
I only stayed up there one year.

When I came back to live with my father and my stepmother again, I made up my mind that I was gonna try my best to get along with her for my dad's sake, you know, to make him happy. So I tried but I'd just keep getting this feeling that I really hated her deep inside, you know. Like it was very hard to do, you know. Then I felt that she was like, when she'd tell me, "Clean the house," or do something, I felt that she was telling me to punish me because she didn't like me.

She knew. She could tell. She knew I didn't like her and I felt like she was telling me to do things because she didn't like me also, you know, because she hated me too. She hated me being there or something, you know. And now that I'm older I look back and it wasn't really that way. It was just a feeling I had, you know. I was very young. When I came back I was only thirteen, fourteen—fourteen, I was when I came back.

I came back and they put me in Saint Paul's Catholic School and I stayed there a year after that. I stayed there a year when I was fifteen and then I finally ran away from home. I don't know where I thought I was going but I ran away, and that's when they brought me to the D home.

Q: Did you have a fight?

A: No, it was just everything, every day, and I thought, I've got to get away from this. You know, I couldn't stand it anymore and I don't know where I thought I was going. I was only fifteen but I thought, "I'll take off," and on top of that I had a boyfriend that I thought would take care of me. He was only fifteen, a little kid, but I thought that we were old enough and that he was old enough to take care of me. I'll live with him and everything will be all right, you know.

So I ran away from home. One day instead of going to school in the morning, I took off and I met this guy, and I stayed with him a couple of days. I was fifteen then and my dad sent some detectives after me and they picked me up and that's when I went to the detention home. He kept me there for two weeks. Besides, the time that I ran away I was so hurt. I don't know. I had a feeling like I didn't even feel I belonged anywhere. I didn't care if I was dead or alive really at that time. It was a silly attitude, you know, but that's the way I felt at the time.

And this guy that I was with, well, he was a pusher. He dealt a lot in drugs, you know, and I was feeling so bad this one night. I had been gone, it was about the second day that I had been gone and I had all these things going through my mind. I really wanted to be home but I wanted to be happy at home. That's what I really had in my mind. But I couldn't be, you know, so I just didn't know what to do. I was lost. Anyway, this is when I first started getting involved with drugs—fifteen, fifteen and a half, around there. This guy was dealing a lot of drugs and I didn't know that he was . . . you know, I thought he was dealing with pills and marijuana and all this, but when I was with him those few days, during that time, about the second day I was with him, I caught him fixing—

Q: He was addicted?

A: Yeah. He was an addict. When I saw this, I became curious, you know. I was very curious. That's what got me started using drugs. Not only was I curious but I was looking for a way out, and so I asked him, I told him I wanted to try it out too, and he didn't want me to but I argued so much that he gave it to me. Like, "Go ahead and see what you get yourself into," you know. "You want it that badly?"

He didn't want me to at first but I argued so much. I started fighting with him and he said . . . well, he didn't care about me, you know. If he cared about me I know he would have never let me start. Anyway, that's the first time I ever fixed with heroin. And I just fixed one time and it made me sicker than hell, it made me sick yet after the sick wore off, throwing up and all that, I just felt so content. It made me forget about all the problems that I had at home, you know, and my body just felt so relaxed. I felt like I didn't have no problems in the world. It was an escape.

I didn't get addicted then. I started when I was . . . yeah, I was almost sixteen, but I didn't become addicted till I was nineteen. So all through these years, whenever I'd feel that way, whenever I'd feel left out and, you know, get in these moods and feel like nobody cared about me at home and I wanted a way out, I'd go out and I'd fix.

My dad used to give me a pretty good allowance. He used to give me twenty, thirty dollars a week and that was my money to use however I wanted, on clothes, for lunch at school, and things like that. So I had plenty of money. My dad was pretty well off then. And I guess he was trying to give me money to show me that he cared about me or I don't know why, but that's not what I wanted. I wanted him to love me, you know. I didn't want material things but that's the way he was doing. He was giving me money because he couldn't be with me. He was working. I'd see him in the morning. I mean, when I'd get up in the morning, I'd go to school and he was asleep. When I'd come back, he was already gone to the bar and he'd come back about six-thirty in the evening and sleep until about eight and then he'd go to the bar. He had the Rio Grande Lounge and then he wouldn't come back until two in the morning. By that time I was already in bed so all this time I wasn't seeing him. So he was giving me money, giving me money, you know. That was his way, I guess, of showing me that he was my father and he did care about me.

Anyway, every once in a while, when I had these problems with Dora, and I got really down and felt like they didn't care, I'd go out and I'd spend my money and get my drugs and I'd fix, you know, because they made me feel like I didn't care. Once I'd fix, I just didn't care. I didn't have to. The problems, they weren't a reality anymore. It was like if they weren't there. I escaped from it for a while. After it'd wear off, I'd go fix again but I never did become addicted in all that time.

Q: Going back a little, during the time you were living with your own mother, apparently you had a pretty good relationship with her.

A: Oh, yeah, very close.

Q: Was there anybody else that you were really close with?

A: My brother.

Q: Your older brother? Did you have a grandmother or aunt, uncle or anybody like that that you were—

A: The rest of the family, I mean, the way I'm related to the rest of the family, I consider myself—I still do and even now that I'm older and I realize everything that was going on, I have a clear mind about everything and this isn't a fantasy that I have in my head—I still believe that I'm the black sheep of the family. I've always been, because see, I don't know if this is the reason for it, but my grandma's mentioned it before and so this is why I believe that she feels this way and treats me like she does. Because my mom . . . I was born before my mom and dad were married. They got married a couple months later.

I was illegitimate, you know, and so that's why I feel my grandma doesn't really consider me a grandchild like she does the rest, you know. Just like she treats my daughter now. My daughter, Lisa, she's illegitimate. I had her while I was still single and she doesn't treat her—they don't treat her like she's part of the family, you know. She's just nothing, and that hurts me. It doesn't hurt me that they treat me that way but that they treat her like that, it really hurts me. But I have to be real about it.

Q: Your grandmother that you mention, was that your mother's—

A: No, my father's mother. My grandmother, my mother's mother, died when I was eight. She was an alcoholic too but she got killed in an accident.

Q: You never really had any family?

A: No, no family on my mother's side, just my mother. Because my mother didn't have any sisters. She was the only one.

Q: So these relatives that your sisters went to live with were all—

A: My dad's. My dad's mother and my dad's sister.

Q: How about schools during that time that you were in grade school? Were there any teachers that you felt . . .

A: Close to?

Q: Yeah.

A: Not really. The closest person I had was my mother. That's why when she killed herself and all that happened, that's why I was so rebellious towards my stepmother because they took away . . . I felt she caused to take away the most important thing I had in the world, you know.

Q: Looking back on it, was your attitude all that time you were growing up kind of rebellious and angry?

A: What do you mean?

Q: Do you feel now that you were angry toward other people or that other people perceived you as being angry and rebellious?

A: Oh, I guess, not really. It just depended on how people treated me, you know. That's the way I've always been. It just depends on how people treat me. Nobody else was at fault but my stepmother, I thought. I just couldn't ever get along with her until I moved out. I moved out, you know, the day I became eighteen.

All this money that my dad was giving me, when I'd feel like it, I'd fix and this and that, you know. I'd buy my own clothes. I had money saved. I'd save money in the bank and when I was seventeen I decided to quit school. What I wanted more, what was more important to me, was I wanted to go to beauty school. So I started going. My dad paid my tuition and I started going here to the Albuquerque Beauty School. I told him, you know, "You only need a tenth grade education to go to beauty school. What do I need my diploma for if that's going to be my trade?"

So I dropped out after I finished eleventh and I started in beauty school. I was seventeen then and I went for ten months. That was about the summer of 1967. I was seventeen and when January came I turned eighteen. I bought my car to go to beauty school. My dad went with me. I took money out of the bank. I gave the down payment and then I paid my payments after that. I only had thirty-dollar payments. I had a real nice, it was a Buick Special so I could go to school, you know.

Then I was eighteen, I turned eighteen. I only needed a few more months to finish beauty school but I decided . . . I moved out, you know, because like when I was fifteen I ran away and they put me in the D home and I stayed two weeks. After that I went home and I said to myself, "Well, if I run away I'm gonna go to the same place so what I'm gonna have to do; I'm gonna have to stick it out here till I'm eighteen and if I leave they can't bring me back." I turned eighteen, and it was just a couple of days later that I left. I got all my things together and I told my daddy, "Well, Daddy, I'm leaving." I rented a little house that was right in back of my grandmother's. She rented it to me for forty-five dollars and I still was going to beauty school. The day that I tried to leave, I started to leave and pack my clothes. My dad and I had talked before about it but I guess he didn't really believe it.

I just got my things together and he came into the bedroom and he asked me why, you know, "Why are you leaving?"

I could see in his eyes that I was hurting him. He wanted me to stay but I just explained to him, "I just can't make it with Dora." It's like if she was jealous of me, you know, and I told him, "Two women can't live in the same house loving the same man. It's just not possible. It can't work, you know. So that's why I've got to leave," I told him. "I've got to leave."

And what he tried to do, he tried to bribe me. He pulled out a twenty-dollar bill and he said, "Here, go buy yourself something. Go settle yourself down. Go cool down, here's twenty dollars. Go buy yourself a dress. Go to a store and look around and it'll settle you down and think about it, you know."

He thought that giving me the money and sending me out to buy a dress would cool me down and I wouldn't leave, you know. But that's not what I wanted. I had to get out of there and I did. When I did, I got pretty wild. I started going to night clubs and going out with different guys and this guy that I went around with . . . I was sixteen in school, sixteen, seventeen. He came back from the service. He came back and I became pregnant. I was going to beauty school all this time and I started getting morning sickness and I couldn't finish beauty school. I'd be combing somebody and all of a sudden I'd get this morning sickness and I just couldn't hack it. I had to quit.

Q: How were you supporting yourself?

A: Well, I wasn't on welfare yet so when I first got out, I moved out in January and got pregnant in April. So during these months I used to make money by ironing clothes for people and—

Q: Your dad wasn't giving you any money then?

A: No. As soon as I moved out, my dad cut me off and the most money I made . . . I was working for this one lady, cleaning her house and all this and she'd get appointments for me during the evening. I'd comb her hair. All her friends and all. I was making pretty good money. They gave me two dollars each, you know, or if I gave 'em a haircut, three dollars. I was making pretty good money.

Q: You were making enough money to live on?

A: He was still paying my tuition. Let's see—I was also working at the Rialto Theater. Then after that, you know, I wasn't making enough at the Rialto to pay my grandmother rent and all this, you know, so that's why I started working for this lady and cleaning house and ironing for her and I'd get all these other ladies, combing hair, and make better money that way, you know. I was just waiting to finish school and take my state board examination and get my license and then I'd start working as a beautician but it never worked out that way.

So after I quit beauty school and I found out for sure that I was pregnant, I went to the welfare office and I told them the situation and they started me on welfare.

Q: You didn't want to get married?

A: I didn't want to marry this boy. I didn't want him to marry me because I was gonna have his baby, you know. I want a man to marry me because he loves me so I never told him. My brother told him when he came back on leave and then he came to see me and he said he wanted to marry me. By that time I didn't have any feelings for him whatever, I didn't love him, so I didn't marry him.

Q: Were you scared?

A: No, I was happy. I was happy . . . I figured that finally I'm gonna have somebody that nobody can take away from me, you know. I needed her. I needed somebody that I could call my own and nobody could take her from me, you know. She's gonna be mine. And it didn't really hurt me that much that she didn't have a father, that I wasn't married.

Q: It didn't scare you to think that you were going to have to support her or anything like that?

A: No. Well, I was on welfare. I wasn't married. They were sending me my checks and I was doing all right. That was enough to pay my rent and buy my groceries. I was pretty settled down then when I got pregnant and even after I had the baby I was real settled down. I stayed home all the time, watching TV, just taking care of my baby, you know. I was very settled down at that time.

By this time I had moved. I was still renting from my grandmother but I had moved from in back of her over right next door to my aunt, the one who took care of one of my sisters. And, let me see, my two sisters were with my dad. They were together with my dad.

Okay, and until Lisa was, let's see, Lisa was five months, all this time I was alone. And when she was five months I met the man that I'm married to now, Tony del Valle, I started going out with him and right away he moved in with me and started living with me. We lived together ten months and then we got married. I've been married two years now. When he first came out, it was June. He came out here from the narcotic hospital in Fort Worth and when he first came out here we were real happy. We were doing real good and he was working and he'd come home, just like a regular family routine. I was really happy.

All during the time I was pregnant and taking care of my baby . . . I told you I was real happy and all that time I never shot any stuff. I stayed away from it for a long time. Then my husband started messing around. He worked about two months, that's all, after he came out of Fort Worth. And about two months after that, this guy he was working with, he started getting pretty messed up. He started using stuff every Friday when he'd come home from work and after Friday he'd use twice a week and then three times a week and pretty soon, before you knew it, he was hooked, you know. So I got the attitude, "Well, if the man really cares for me, I'll start using it too and if he really cares for me, he'll stop," you know. But he wouldn't stop and I got hooked too and I stayed hooked for a year and a half. And this is where we started stealing, shoplifting and burglarizing and doing things like this, and this is when they caught me for the burglaries and sent me to the penitentiary.

Q: Both you and your husband, then, were going out and stealing. That's how you were supporting your habit?

A: Uh-huh.

Q: Specifically, what kinds of things were you doing?

A: Mostly shoplifting. Every day we would have to steal. We'd have to steal at least three hundred dollars' worth of merchandise a day to support the habit we had. At first it started out to be about five dollars, you know. After you've fixed a week, it takes two or three caps, but by the time we were at the end of the line, when they caught us for the burglaries and sentenced us, we had already been hooked for a year and a half.

Q: You were shooting up how much?

A: About a gram each, a little over a gram. A little over fifty dollars a day, each.

Q: So you had to steal actually two, three hundred dollars' worth of merchandise to support your habit?

A: Oh, by the end we had to steal four or five hundred dollars' worth of merchandise a day to support our habit. And like days that we would do pretty good, we'd go into a store and we just had good luck. Like this one time we went to a jewelry store and we went in for ten minutes and we came out with nine thousand dollars' worth of diamonds. When we'd do something like that, we really let it go for nothing. We got a hundred dollars for each thousand. So we got nine hundred dollars cash plus a car that they had just rebuilt—engine, transmission, and everything. It was a good car. That nine hundred dollars lasted only three days.

But that's what I mean. Days that we would have good luck like that and get a whole lot of money, you know, like people would think it would last us for week but an addict isn't that way. The more money he has, the more he shoots, you know. It was gone in three days.

Q: The jewelry store—how did you do it?

A: We walked into the store. We acted like we weren't together and I went over and stood by the counter. The people were working over there. I went and stood right in front to block him. I stood between him and the people, blocking him, like as if I was looking, and he opened the case and took out the diamonds and then we walked out after that.

But there were other times. The days weren't that easy, you know. It would take us . . . we'd have to go into four or five stores to get two or three hundred dollars' worth of merchandise. We couldn't just come in, take it, and walk out. We had to . . . we were still hooked, you know, and we didn't want to get caught and have to be put in jail to break cold turkey. That's the worst thing an addict can go through. That's the worst kind of sickness. It's the worst pain there is in the world, I think, and I had more pain when I was breaking the habit than I had when I was having my daughter. It's a terrible pain, really bad.

Q: During the year and a half that you both were hooked, what would you say was the number of burglaries, shoplifting, and so forth that you pulled?

A: Mostly shoplifting, but burglaries about five. The rest was shoplifting and that was every day. Every day we'd go to about eight stores. We'd get orders for people, you know. We'd have a bunch of fences and we'd get orders. "Clothes for our daughter and clothes for us." They'd give us the size and more or less how many they wanted, what price range, and we'd go out and we'd get these things for them and we'd bring them back and sell it to them half-price.

Q: Were these people in the community or—

A: Yeah, all over Albuquerque there's people like that, that would buy stolen goods.

Q: So you weren't actually selling to one individual. You were selling to a lot of people?

A: We had about four or five fences that we could sell anything to and then he knew all the people in San Felipe where he lived. So he knew all the people there and if we couldn't sell whatever we had, he'd go literally door-to-door selling, asking them, you know, if they wanted to buy and we sold it. Because I mean, like let's say an impact wrench is worth a hundred and fifty, two hundred dollars, and we sold them for thirty.

Q: So you really didn't have much trouble getting rid of your stuff?

A: No, except that we gave it away. Any addict will give things away. I mean, something worth a hundred dollars and an addict would let it go for twenty-five, you know, because it's hot or stolen. There's been times that we were so sick, then we'd have something that was worth maybe fifty, sixty dollars and we'd say, "Here, just give me five dollars," enough for a cap, you know. I mean it was really bad because you go through all the trouble to steal and you take a big risk of getting caught, spending months out of your life for stealing and then you give it away. It's really bad.

Q: How about your daughter during that time?

A: I was leaving her with different babysitters. A lot of the times I had her with me, but most of the time I wanted to leave her with the babysitter because I didn't want her to get caught with us. But as far as her being neglected, she was neglected to an extent where I wasn't taking care of her myself but I did take care of her where she had nice clothes, she was healthy and she was eating good. But she just wasn't with me all the time, you know.

Q: Before that, the only time that you had been busted was the time when you were picked up for running away and you had been brought out to the detention home?

A: Uh-huh, and a couple of other times. One time this girl asked me to steal something for her in Woolworth's and I went and stole it and they caught me. A pair of tennis shoes, I believe it was. But they took me, I don't know where I was, but they took me and they called my parents and they came and picked me up, you know. Then when I ran away and after that I didn't get in trouble anymore until I got hooked.

After that I got in a whole lot of messes; shoplifting and I even had one child abandonment where I left the baby alone for about an hour and somebody reported me. They took her away and put her in the children's home and I had to go talk to the welfare people to get her back. Oh, besides stealing, I was still getting my welfare check. But see, my welfare check, when I'd get that I always paid my rent, you know. I always had my rent paid, my bills paid and that was for that, you know.

Q: You weren't married yet then?

A: Well, let's see. I met him in June, June of 1968 and we got married April 11 of 1969.

Q: And you went up when?

A: March of 1970. That's why I'm giving my husband a divorce, because I've heard many people say that he's told them that if he ever goes back he'll take me with him again.

Q: Is he out now?

A: No, he'll be out in about fifteen more days and I don't want to mess around anymore. I've come out. I realize where I'm at now.

I've met a man that I care for very much and that can give me a good life. He's also an ex-convict. He's able to give me the life that I want to lead. He's interested in going to these groups with me, Esperanza and things like that and we're happy just doing simple things in life, taking a walk, going out in the park, things like that, you know. And I'm happy with him.

So I mean, I was with my husband for three years and I don't have anything to show for those three years. The little things that I did have before, like the bedroom set that my mother left me, he sold when I was in jail for shoplifting last year.

Q: What were your experiences with the police? What was your attitude toward the police?

A: You mean all during this time that I was shoplifting and they'd catch me, what was my attitude? I hated them. Well, you know, they picked me up and they'd throw me in jail, you know, and I'm not a criminal. What I was doing was because I was sick, you know. Just like an alcoholic. But they were doing their job.

I hated them, you know, but when they sent me up to the penitentiary I was weighing eighty-two pounds after being hooked for a year and a half. I felt rescued, I really did.

Q: You had to cold turkey?

A: Oh, yeah . . . I feel that the penitentiary did me a whole lot of good. It gave me a whole lot of time to open my mind and think and stand up and say, "Well, where am I? Where am I going?" you know. And I found myself. I found Soledad and I know what I want now and I'm out to get it.

Q: Did the penitentiary do you good because it gave you time to think or because it has people there that could help you?

A: No, I think I helped myself because it gave me time to think. Because they didn't really help me. They talk about rehabilitating and all this but really what it is, is just the time. The time for you to find yourself and where you're going, what you want.

It won't work on everybody that way. With some other convicts, it'll just make 'em bitter and they'll come out and do the same things all over again, you know. But it did help me. I think it did. Because I was lost. Let's say, what if I had kept going on the same way I was? I would have ended up killing myself with an overdose or during a burglary some cop would have shot me and where would my daughter be? I don't want her to be an orphan like I was.

So I'm glad of what happened. I don't want it to happen again. That's not what I'm saying, you know, but it did do me a whole lot of good. I finally found myself and found direction. It took me a long time. I went about it the hard way, but I did, you know.

Q: What do you think could have been done earlier to help you?

A: I don't think nothing could have been done. It was the circumstances. I think it had to be done the way it was. I don't think anything else could have been done with me at all before because my mind was all corrupted, you know. I had these false notions about my stepmother. All this stuff in my head and nothing was going to change me. I was just set on . . . I was stubborn. Just set on . . . I don't know what. I was just out to escape the kind of life I had, you know, the circumstances that I was in and I didn't know how to do it. I went about it all this long hard way but in the end I figure it did me some good because now I know it'll never happen again. I've found it out and I know what I want. I'm out to get it and I think I'm gonna get it, you know.

Q: Do you want to talk about your experiences at the pen?

A: Okay. See, I was hooked for a year and a half. It was a Sunday when they picked us up. We were gonna go out and steal meat. On Sundays we used to steal meat because the butchers aren't in the store. We'd just walk in and shoplift food. I carried this great big purse. Anyway, that's what we were gonna do that Sunday and we were renting a motel.

Q: Were you living there?

A: Yeah, we were living in a motel and all of a sudden, you know, the cops knock on our door and I thought it was the maid to let her come in and clean, so I said, "We'll be out in a minute," and he says, "Soledad, open up," you know. So that's when I realized it wasn't the maid, that it was a cop.

I jumped out of bed and I panicked because I knew I was gonna go to jail and I was gonna have to break, you know, so I did panic and I told Tony, "It's the cops." The reason they picked us up is because of failure—the warrant that they had was failure to comply with our lawyer. It was time for us to go to court for the burglary that they had caught us for. The burglary that they sent us up for. It took a whole year before we went to court to trial.

Q: So actually you were picked up for a burglary pretty early when you started getting involved in—

A: We were picked up for this burglary in May of 1969. We had only been married a month. When they picked us up, you know, they give you all your rights and all this and I was so bitter towards them I didn't even give them my name, you know. I wouldn't talk to a cop at that time. I hated them.

I told them, "You're a cop, if you want my name you find it out for yourself. I've been here before. Look at the records. Find out my name yourself."

I was that kind of person, you know, and they found it out. They took out my records. That's why I went up as Parale, because they got my record and they put me down with my maiden name, Parale. I was already del Valle but they wrote me down as Parale. Okay, this was April the nineteenth, I think, when they picked us up. It was a Sunday.

Q: What did you do at the burglary?

A: Oh, the burglary, right. Okay, it was May 1969. This was the burglary that we did over here on . . . I can't remember the street, but right off Lomas a couple of blocks that way. We went up to the house and Tony went and knocked at the door. At first, when he drove to the house, I didn't know he was gonna do a burglary, you know, because he had just picked up his methadone.

Q: He was on methadone—

A: Yeah, he was on methadone too. He had just picked up his methadone but he had a hassle with them. They didn't give him the right dose or I don't know what and he said he was gonna be sick, so he went up and parked in front of this house. I thought it was somebody he knew and that he was going to ask them for some, you know.

But he knocked at the door and when he came back, he came out the side and went in the window. When I saw him do that, then I knew what was going on and he came out. He put a TV in the car. He went back in the house and took something else. I don't know.

Anyway, while he was back in the house, the cops drove up and I started the ignition but they came up to the car and they took the keys from me. The baby was with me.

He asks, "What are you doing?"

I panicked. I didn't know what to say, you know. I said I was out of gas or something like that and then he asked me about the TV, what was I doing with the TV, and I said it was mine, that I was taking it to be fixed. That's why they convicted me, because I said the TV was mine, you know. What was I supposed to say? That's what I told them, "What was I supposed to say? My husband stole it?" That's the grounds that they convicted me on, as an accessory because I covered up for him.

Q: Did they pick him up that day too?

A: Yeah. They held me there and then a couple of cops went after him and they picked him up and the guy that was with him, Carlos Loretto and that guy, he testified against me when we went to court. So they convicted me and he pleaded guilty because he had other charges. I only had that one burglary plus shoplifting. But Tony, he had that burglary and another burglary. He stole a seat from a car and an aggravated burglary, which was really a purse snatching, and then also the jewelry. Remember I told you about the jewelry?

Q: You did get busted for the jewelry?

A: He did. He did but he never went to trial for it because they made a deal with him that if he would plead guilty to that burglary, the burglary that he went up for, they'd drop all those other charges. So he did and all the charges were dropped. So, that was May of 1969 we went to arraignment and they set our court date. They told us, you know, that we were out on bond.

Q: Who made your bond?

A: His sister and a neighbor of his mother's made our bond. And we got out on bond and they told us that we'd go to court when our name came out in the dockets, you know. So this was May of 1969 and our name didn't come out on the dockets until April 1970. So it was a whole year and during that whole year we were hooked and doing more things but they never caught us.

Q: Did they realize you were hooked when they picked you up for that burglary?

A: No.

Q: Were you on methadone?

A: No, I was using stuff. I had just barely started then to get hooked.

Q: But Tony was on methadone. He was also using stuff?

A: Uh-huh. What he would do, he would sell his methadone and get stuff. So I hadn't been hooked too long, but I broke there. We stayed in there about six days and I broke. When we got out I started all over again, you know, and this time we stayed hooked for a whole year, except for times that they'd throw me in jail.

Like, I think after that I got caught once or twice for shoplifting. They gave me thirty days for one shoplifting. See, I had one shoplifting and they told me that I had ninety days advisement and if I didn't get in any more trouble, they'd drop it. But it wasn't ninety days. It was only about forty days when they caught me for a second one so they gave me thirty days for the first one and thirty days for the second shoplifting. I did thirty days and they appealed the second thirty. My husband got me out. It was November of 1969. I got out a day before Thanksgiving.

Then, in January, we decided to go to Sacramento. These people we knew wanted to go out there and also we thought maybe we could get a job out there. We knew that our court was gonna come up and we kind of wanted to run away because we were so hooked. We knew that our court was gonna come up sooner or later and that we would have to break so we thought that we would run away and not come back.

Q: Each of these times that you went to jail you had to cold turkey?

A: Yeah. But like in November when I did the shoplifting, I did break, but it wasn't too hard because my husband came up to the jail and gave me some methadone pills through the screen and that helped me break.

When we went to Sacramento, they caught us for two shopliftings up there too. They caught me once. I was so used to stealing that I'd go in a store and if I'd see something I wanted or needed, I'd just take it, you know. And this time we had . . . I had just gotten there, you know. I didn't know how things were there. I thought I could go into a store like I did here, because I knew the stores here in Albuquerque but I didn't when I walked in there. I took a can of hair spray and they caught me. They booked me and the next day I went to court. They couldn't bond me out because I wasn't a resident there so I had to go to court the next day and I went to court and I guess the judge saw that I was new there and I didn't have a record or nothing.

Well, I was really sick, you know. I was already starting to break and I was sick but I put on a pretty good act. I told the judge that I wasn't from there and I had a daughter to take care of, like if that was the first time I had ever taken anything, just a can of hair spray and he let me go. But it was the same thing like here; the ninety days advisement thing. Anyway, a couple of weeks later they caught both of us, me and him, taking meat from a store and they took us again and I thought, "Oh wow. They're gonna pull that advisory on me and give me thirty days." So when I went to court I had to give 'em a real good story, you know, because I was hooked. Each time that I went to court I was sick but I gave 'em a good story. And it's like when you're that way, you learn to talk yourself out of things. So I went to court and I told 'em if he'd let me go home, let me go home and make arrangements, first. I'm gonna take care of my baby because I wasn't from there, you know, and I'd come back for sentencing in a week, you know. So he did. He let me go and I never went back to court.

So they put out word for my arrest and by this time it was already April and our names had come out on the dockets over here.

One night Tony called his mother and she told him that our name was gonna come out on the dockets and we'd better come home or else his sister was gonna lose her house because she had made our bond.

So he told her, "Well, we'd like to leave but we can't get home," you know. "The money that we made, we were using it to fix and we just can't make the money to get home on the bus."

Q: His mother knew all the time that you were both addicted?

A: Yeah. She went for us and brought us back. While she was bringing us back, we were breaking, you know. We wanted to break for her, but we just couldn't make it. We had been hooked for so long. It was a year that we had been hooked and we were really sick. I have never been that sick in all my life. We were really sick and she saw how sick we were.

We tried to stick it out but we had been about sixteen hours without using anything and we just couldn't stand it anymore. We were in Long Beach at that time. She went to go visit her brother and we were going to let her down. We were gonna leave and take off to L.A. and see what we could do, shoplift something. We had to fix. So rather than have us go do that, she gave us twenty dollars and took us to L.A. and we fixed and with the stuff that we had connected we used just a little bit at a time till we got home, you know. We used half and saved the rest because we knew we'd be sick coming and we didn't want to be sick coming through Arizona or some place like that.

Q: Did you ever have any trouble making connections?

A: No. In L.A., no, you go into L.A. and they're all over the streets. You can tell. I can, anyway. All you have to do is to walk down the street and you can tell, the way they dress or you can walk down the street and you see people that are hooked, there's something, you can tell. And we went and connected and came back and as soon as we came back she lent us another five dollars for another fix because we figured that as soon as we got back we'd go to Dr. Strett and get our methadone and break, you know.

But we didn't and so we didn't get back in time for the dockets. So we had to go to court and they reinstated our bonds. We told them we were in Sacramento, that that's where we had come from so they reinstated our bond and set our day for trial. We were supposed to talk to our lawyers during that time. It was a couple of weeks and we didn't. We were so busy stealing and all that, that we didn't talk to our lawyers, and so on April nineteenth they picked us up, like I told you, at the motel. The put us in jail.

Q: They didn't really bust you, then, for a burglary?

A: No, just failing to comply with our lawyer. They thought we weren't gonna show up in court so they put us in jail. It was April nineteenth and about May first we went to court.

Q: Did you have to cold turkey then?

A: Yeah. It was really bad. About May first we went to court. He pleaded guilty. They found me guilty and a couple of days later we went for sentencing and they sentenced us both to one to five years in prison. And so on May fifth they took me up and on May thirteenth they took him up.

Q: Did you ever think it would come to that?

A: I thought that they'd take him. I didn't think that they'd take me because I didn't have any other burglaries. I thought they'd give me a break but they didn't. They sent us both. But I really think they sentenced us as an example to the other people, as man and wife, you know.

Q: What about . . . you did time in county jail, you were in there several times, or was it the city?

A: The thirty days I was in the city. I was in the county when they picked me up for the burglaries and when they picked us up to send us up there and one other time for the aggravated burglary, purse snatching. They put me in a lineup and all that but when they couldn't prove anything they let me go.

Q: What were your impressions of city and county jail? What did you do when you were there?

A: Nothing. They would send me into those jails and I really wouldn't think that much of it. I'd break and after I'd break I knew I was getting out in a matter of days so it didn't affect me that much. It didn't really bother me. I'd joke about it and things like that. But I never thought it would come to be spending eight months in jail or in prison, you know.

Q: What happened to your daughter when you were in jail?

A: Those times? Which times?

Q: A couple of days, thirty days.

A: She would be with a babysitter. The time I was in for thirty days, I had a friend take care of her and when we got out we paid her. We paid her two hundred dollars' worth of stolen merchandise for taking care of her. But when they were sending me on the one to five, when they were sending me up there, a lady from the welfare came out and had me sign a paper about putting her in a foster home. I signed the paper but I signed a certain name that I wanted her to be put in with, the people that she was with there, the lady that she's with now.

Yesterday I tried to go get my daughter and the lady won't let me have her. She's gotten attached to her and I think the main reason she won't let me have her is because she's been getting the check all the time that Lisa's been there and she knows that when I take her, that check is gonna stop, you know. So we had a hassle about that yesterday. I wanted to be with her for Mother's Day and she wouldn't let me take her. She said the welfare said if I came for the baby to call the police and all this and I don't think she's right.

The main thing is that my parole people have to say that it's all right for me to get her and they already did, so after I leave here today I'm going over to the parole office and ask them to go with me to pick up my daughter. Anyway, that's how I ended up there.

Q: Did you and your husband see each other when you were up there?

A: On Saturdays.

Q: They'd let you visit?

A: Yes, for an hour. We couldn't see each other or write to each other until we proved our marriage. We had to send for our marriage license. But it was completely different from the time I spent in the city, in the county, just a matter of days compared to eight months. There's a whole lot of difference because over there, they really mess with your mind, you know. One matron will tell you to do something and another will tell you to do something else and you have to do what they want or they can snap your parole up and take it away and you don't know what to do first.

Or like these little windows . . . there's lots and lots of windows over there and like they'd have us washing them with Bon Ami, then wiping them off. Let's say they'd been washed just the day before or in the morning, and they decide they want you to wash them again just to have you doing something. They'll tell you to do 'em again and you have to or they can take away your parole, you know. Crazy things like that.

Q: What's your impression of what happens to people in institutions?

A: Well, like I told you, if you're in an institution, they take away your right of making decisions for yourself, deciding what time you're going to bed, what movies you're gonna watch. They have a TV and things like that but if there's more colored people than

Chicanos, they have control over these things, the TV, the radio, you know. I mean, you can't decide to do nothing. They decide it for you. What time you're going to bed, what time you get up. They even have hours for taking showers and baths and what time you eat, what time you get up, your job has to be done by eight o'clock, things like this.

And then when they let you out, they release you and out here you have to make all these decisions for yourself and it's kind of hard. It really is. You have to get adjusted to a whole new routine. But I was only there eight months. What if I had been there five years or something and everything changed out here, you know?

Then you come out and you try to get a job and they don't want you because you're an ex-convict. It's hard for an ex-convict to get a job when you get out. Nobody trusts you. How can they trust you? How can you do anything, accomplish anything, if nobody will give you a chance? You have to be given a chance to show you're rehabilitated, you know. So I got a job at the Holiday Inn through the parole office and I did pretty good there but then I was offered this other job combing wigs and I like that better.

Q: So you quit at the Holiday?

A: Yeah. I quit the job at the Holiday. What kind of career can you get making beds and cleaning bathrooms? And I enjoy combing wigs.

But what I really want for a lifetime career—all I want is to live a normal family life and, you know, be happily married, take care of my husband and children. That's what I want and that's what I'm going to get and I think I've found the right man to give it to me. I'm filing for divorce now.

Q: How many women are there in the prison in Santa Fe?

A: When I was up there, there was about twenty-four, twenty-two, and when I left there was eleven. Way different from the men's side. We fix our own meals. We don't have as much privileges as the men. The men have more recreation. They have their gym, if they want. After their jobs are done during the day they can go to their gym or they can go to arts and crafts and make things out of leather or paint, you know. They have DVR where they make furniture or carving or making things like that.

Women don't have anything like that at all. The only thing you have to do is, if you have the money, like you can send to town for yarn and things like that, or crochet, you know. Other than that, there's nothing. That's why I got involved in IBM. They have two

IBM machines, one on each side. I got in there and started keypunch because it helped the time go a little faster. It gave me something to do during the day and it was a paying job. I mean like you start out at five cents an hour and then ten cents, fifteen . . . no, five, ten, twelve, and then fifteen. It wouldn't go higher than that. But at least you could earn a little bit of money for cigarettes and things like that.

Q: Did you have somebody sending you money when you were up there?

A: No, not on my side. The money that my mother-in-law would take my husband, he'd send me half. But I made cigarettes and that by combing people's hair all the time.

Q: Your dad didn't send you anything while you were up there?

A: He didn't even write to me. But now that I got out I went to see him, you know, and I told him how I felt. I told him I found myself, I'm going to straighten up, you know, and he was happy to hear it but that's not enough for him. I have to show it to him and it's gonna take a couple of years for my dad to see that I meant what I said, you know. But I think it's gonna work out all right. It'll take a while but I just want him to be happy before he dies, you know.

Q: Were there hassles between the women inmates, you know, like the Chicanos, the blacks—

A: Yes, over things like the TV and radio.

Q: No big things to really hassle about?

A: No, but any women living together are going to hassle about anything, you know. But just little things like that . . . the TV and radio. It's silly but I guess they got to argue about something. But they don't have things for the women to do like they do for the men. Like arts and crafts, you know, and things to keep you busy. They don't have anything like that, just idle time, day after day, you know, just trying to think.

Q: Did they have group counseling or any kind of counseling for the women?

A: No. The man that's in charge of the women's division, Mr. Durbin, he's supposed to be the superintendent of the women's division. You'd see that man maybe once every two months. He'll come in and talk to each girl about five minutes and then he's gone and you don't see him for another couple of months.

That's what I mean. I mean, we're just there in a hole and if you have a problem you can't talk to anybody about it. He only comes over once a month or something like that, you know, once every two months. When he goes, he'll talk to you. What can you get out of talking to somebody for five minutes? You have all these things piled 'up for about a month or a month and a half and all of a sudden he comes and what can you put on the table and solve in five minutes that he gives you to talk to him?

Q: Did he ask you about problems there or—

A: No, he doesn't really ask you anything. We just line up and shoot 'em at him and he writes them down on a piece of paper. He goes back and I think he throws them away because nothing ever gets done about the things you ask him.

They need some good people in there. What I think are the best people that could run an institution like that are doctors because these men aren't qualified. He's just a family man. What kind of qualifications does he have to run an institution for social problems and things like that when he's just a family man himself? I think what they need in there are doctors, psychologists, or something, you know.

Q: They don't have anything like that?

A: No.

Q: You were never involved in a counseling situation while you were there?

A: No, just when I was gonna make parole they talked to me for a couple of hours, asked me what I planned to do when I got out, that's it. And then I was involved in a drug rehabilitation program for a while but I didn't like it because they were making monkeys out of you.

Q: Like how?

A: Like you'd go in and she'd want you to put everything on the table. Say what you thought about yourself, why you started drugs and this and that and she wouldn't feed anything back to you, you know. You'd just tell her all this and she wouldn't give you anything back to take up here [head], you know. You'd just tell her everything about yourself and she'd say "all right," and then she wouldn't give you any ideas.

And then crazy things like . . . I don't know what kind of therapy she thinks she was doing but things like, it felt to me that she was belittling me because I was an addict, you know. She said it was therapy but I don't know what kind of therapy it was, you know, because the other girls are standing outside looking in and she has you lying on the floor covering your head and things like that. I dropped out. It wasn't doing anything for me.

Q: Were most of the women that were up there in for drug-related offenses?

A: No, just a couple, two, three. There was one girl that was in for murder. She was doing life. Another girl was there for life for murder, she's been there one year. She has nine years to go. She killed her husband because she found him with another woman.

Then there was myself and there was this girl I was really close to. She was there for the sale of heroin. She did two years and she got out in September. Then myself, I was there for burglary. There was another girl there for burglary. Let me see, one girl was there for forgery, another one for checks too. Another colored girl was there for manslaughter. She shot a girl.

Q: Did you have a lot of hassles with the colored girls?

A: I didn't get along with them at all. I considered them all rats and I just didn't get along with them. I kept away from them. It was really disgusting to see two girls making out.

Q: Was there a lot of that?

A: Yes, some of the colored girls and a few of the *gabachas*—Anglos. I think the Spanish girls were the straightest ones that were up there. There was only three of us, four, but they're not only on drug-related charges. There's different things; manslaughter, passing checks . . .

Q: Did you get any visits during the year?

A: Yeah. This lady would go and take my baby every two months.

Q: The one who was keeping her?

A: Yeah. She'd go up with my husband's mother. My husband's mother used to go up about every three weeks. But I never got any visits from the family. I just stayed there eight months and finally the eight months were up and I got out. When I went to the board, one thing that they specified was that they wanted me to participate in the Colony drug program when I got out so I am, plus I'm involving myself in things to keep me busy, with Esperanza, things like that and I think I'm doing real good.

Q: Are you on methadone?

A: Uh-huh.

Q: Why did they put you on methadone?

A: I was on the drug-free program for a while and then I started getting the urge to, not really an urge, but I found myself getting weak because I had these problems of my mother-in-law, you know. I don't get along with her at all and all this. How was I gonna leave my husband? Should I leave him now or wait until he gets out or what, you know? I've been wanting to leave him for about a year and a half but I'm afraid of him.

All this is going through my head. I don't have my baby because I'm working, all kinds of problems, that I thought, "All these things are gonna get me weak and I'm gonna start to shoot stuff." So I asked them to put me on methadone for a while. It's helped me. I just want to stay on it a little while until everything is settled and I have my divorce on its way and almost final and until I get my daughter and all this and then I'll get off of methadone. I'm just using it like a crutch.

Q: Are you afraid that you'll have to use something?

A: Especially now that I'm getting my divorce and I've been involved with this other man. But we talked to the parole officer about it. They asked us . . . you know, they said that they're just happy for us, that two people can come out if it and do so much for each other. We're going to marry each other as soon as my divorce comes through. We talked to the parole people about it and everything. They asked us . . . you know, they're happy for us and this is what they want, our happiness, but they want us to go about it in the right way. They want us to be discreet in seeing each other until my divorce is final, you know. And we care enough about each other to go about it in that way. We don't want any trouble. I don't want him to get hurt or Tony or myself.

But I think it'll work out. But Tony is extremely jealous, and he's threatened that if I ever leave him, he'll kill me and things like that, but I think he has a better head on his shoulders than to, you know, go out and do something crazy like that. He can't force me to live with him when I don't care for him anymore. Plus, I'm afraid of him and I'm tired of his way of life. I'm tired of using stuff and crime and all these things. I don't want to ever go back, and other people have told me that he's said that if he ever goes back, he'll drag me along with him again. What kind of a man is that? That doesn't show me that he cares for me at all, like he used to. If he cared for me he'd want me to stay here and take care of my daughter and not want to drag me back with him. But he's just so afriad that I'll leave him that he wants to have me with him everywhere he goes.

I would have made him a beautiful wife. I'm very . . . I have a good heart. I can be a good woman to any man that'll take care of me and show me at least half of the love that I give him in return. But Tony just took my love for granted and treated me terrible, like a dog, you know? He didn't take care of me. He had me using stuff. He had me skinny as hell, I wasn't dressed right or anything and I think he had me that way on purpose because he didn't want me to be desirable to anybody else. He was happy with the way he had the situation, and he took me up there and he said that if he ever goes back he'll take me with him again. Well, I'm not a puppet, you know.

Q: When you got out, I suppose you were very happy to be out?

A: Oh, yeah.

Q: Were you afraid, also, coming out?

A: Yeah, like I said, I was, because I'd been used to them making my decisions for me. I didn't know what I was gonna do. I'd never worked really in my life. I just worked a little while at the Rialto Theater but to support myself I had never worked. And then, plus that, I didn't want to work. I wanted to take care of my daughter but my parole officer won't let me be on welfare or anything like that.

But things are working out pretty well. My divorce will be final pretty soon and then I can marry Ned and do what I want; stay home and take care of my baby and my husband because he does make good money. He makes six dollars an hour as a carpenter. But in the meanwhile, while my divorce is going through, they want me to keep working and, you know, stand on my own two feet till things settle down. They care about the safety of all three of us because there is things that have happened before with a triangle like this. One or two of the people have gotten killed. Well, I don't want anything like that to happen to us. Things are too good. I'm too happy for anything like that to happen.

But like I say, all this that has happened to me, it was the long way to grow up, you know. The long hard way but I've finally come to the end and I've grown up and I feel I'm mature and I know what I want. I've found myself and I'm happy. I'm happy that what happened, happened and they did send me up there before it was too late and I killed myself or something. So I'm happy at what happened. I think it did me a lot of good and like I told you a while ago, I don't think there could have been anything else. I don't think there could have been any other way for me to, you know, change and come to realize where I was.

Q: Was there anybody along the way that you felt was really interested in helping you?

A: My dad, I guess. My dad is cold, real cold, but deep inside he wants the best for me, and that's how come I've got to prove myself to him and make him happy before he dies. He is old, and really no one else, just my daughter, but she's not old enough, you know.

Q: How old is she now?

A: She's three years. And then the people in the Colony. They're trying to help me. And that's about it until now. Until I met Ned, and Ned wants the best for me. He's ready to give me anything I ever wanted. Not material things but the happiness I've always been looking for, you know. So we're happy and I think things are going to work out.

Q: How old is he?

A: He's thirty-eight.

Q: How long has he been out?

A: Three months.

Q: Oh, is that all?

A: But I've known him for a long time.

Q: Did you get together up there or since he got out?

A: Since he got out, but I knew him a long time ago. Him and my husband are cousins and I met him a long time ago. But we never got anything going . . . I was too afraid of leaving Tony, you know. I've never met a man with such a good heart as Ned has. Like I mean, he's interested in other people.

I think we're gonna help a lot of convicts through that group. Of course, we need time and we need more funds. But it's nice. It feels good to get involved in something like that and know that you're helping other people, you know, plus we're helping ourselves. Like Tuesdays, they're to help other people. Anybody can come on Tuesday. On Thursdays it's just ex-cons. On Thursday we help ourselves and Tuesday we try and help other people, you know. It's really a good group. Plus, he's in AA. He used to be an alcoholic. He hasn't gone to any of their groups and I don't think he's gonna need to because he hasn't been drinking since he got out, you know.

And I think we're helping each other. I think that he really needed a woman who really cares for him, a woman that would make him interested in having a good life, because before he'd come out and he didn't have anybody, he had started drinking and that's what would send him back up, you know. He's been there three times but I think he's ready to settle down. He's been ready a long time. He's a hell of a man, you know, but he just didn't have anybody. He didn't have anybody that cared, you know. A man needs somebody that cares.

Q: Everybody does.

A: Yeah, I'm really happy. It was a long road, you know, but I've finally come to the end of it and I know where I'm at now.

You know, I wish for the other people that are even going back to these institutions . . . I wish that they would do something. Like Dr. Romero, he could have really done something that was good because he wants to help, you know. He cares and these other people that are there just . . . I don't know. They're not qualified to be in the positions that they're in. Like Baca—the things that he did, you wouldn't believe, you know. Like you get little reports for—oh, let me see. Let's say you go back and steal a sandwich, you know, or you get an extra roll or something like that. They take you to court for that and take away five days good time for a thing like that. Take away your parole for something like that.

Q: What court?

A: His own court. Him and another officer and like Mr. Zelada, you know, correctional officers. They get together and if he feels like taking away twenty years good time, he takes it. If he feels like taking away your parole, he'd do that, you know.

I think they've changed that now where, if they charge you with something and give you a report, I think you have the right to have a lawyer present at the court. But before, it wasn't that way. You get a report, you go to court with him and if he felt like taking away your parole, he'd do it. For a whole year, you know. That's crazy.

Like when you went to visit, they said you could kiss your husband once when you go in and once when you come out. All right, I kissed him when I went in, I kissed him when I was leaving and we stood up, and when we were walking out, I just got him and gave him another kiss. I didn't think anything of it, you know, but I got a report for giving him a third kiss. Can you believe that? They took us both to court. They took away our visits for a week and they took away five days good time from each of us. That's at the end of our sentence. But five days good time doesn't really mean five days. Five days good time is ninety days.

Q: Oh, right. Because you get a day good time for every month.

A: Ninety days they took off, plus they took away our visits for a week. Just for giving him another kiss. Can you believe that? And then when we had the riots up there, I didn't see my husband for two months. We had to get a lawyer to go up there and get our visiting privileges back. They had him locked up because they said he had inspired the other men to . . . that he had started the conspiracy and all these things. They had him locked up and they wouldn't let us see each other for two months.

Q: On your sentence of one to five you were eligible for parole at—

A: In six months. But he got a report for sniffing glue or something so they took away his parole from November to December. I changed mine to go out together with him because he wanted me to do that. He had my mind so burned. I did everything he asked me to do. He wanted me to change my parole hearing to go together with him because he said it would be a better chance for him to get out if we went together. He said if they let me go, they would keep him there forever, you know. But if I'd do that, they'd let us go together because of the baby or something like that. I don't know. But it didn't work that way because the board let me go immediately. I got straight out and he got a six months' date.

Q: Are you on parole for five years?

A: Yeah. That will be all right. I don't plan to get into any kind of trouble whatsoever.

Q: How are the parole rules, do you think?

A: Pretty strict.

Q: Do you agree with them?

A: Not all of them because I have a direction now towards life and what I want to do. I have no desires, no thoughts whatsoever of committing a crime ever again in my life and some of the things, I think they're really silly, you know. Like you are not to associate with ex-convicts or anyone that your parole officer forbids you to see. I can understand their point of view, conspiring to commit a crime or something like that, but Ned is an ex-convict too, you know, and this is what I explained to them. He's an ex-convict too and they can't forbid me to see him because what we have is something good, you know. What we have involves our whole future and our happiness. We're not conspiring to commit any crime, and so there I don't feel that that should apply.

My parole officer said it does but we talked to the head man, Mr. Klein, and he said that he would permit it but he just wanted us to be discreet in seeing each other until my divorce was final and I agree with him. I think he's right because I don't want anybody to get hurt.

And like you're not to go into a bar. Well, if someday me and Ned were married and we would go night-clubbing, you know, nice clean fun, we'd go to a bar and dance and go home. I don't feel it should apply either. Little things like that you have to ask permission for and it's kind of funny. You're a mature woman and mature man and you have to ask permission to go out night-clubbing and it's silly. But then, they're concerned with your future, your rehabilitation and making a good life for yourself so these are all precautions.

Q: But some of them you feel should be changed?

A: Yeah, or if not changed, I mean they shouldn't apply in every situation.

Q: But I guess you're finding out, actually they don't apply in every situation. This thing with you and Ned, it's okay.

A: Yeah. We talked to them about it. You have to get permission for anything that's contrary to what the rules say. If you have a job and you want to quit that job, you have to ask permission ahead of time. What if something happened at the job where you have to quit right then? You don't have time to go ask them. Have you read those rules?

Q: No.

A: Here, I'll show them to you.

Q: In other words, it's a continuation of the institution, where you're not free to make your own decisions?

A: Yeah, that's exactly what it is. All those rules in the back are what I was supposed to comply with when they let me go on parole. I signed it. My parole officer is new. I'm just about her third client. She's really strict. She's going strictly by the rules, you know. That's why me and Ned went to talk to Klein; because he's the head man. He's been there for a longer period of time and it was easier for us to make him understand the situation, you know. But she was going strictly by the rules and she forbid me to see him. Like she was forbidding me to see him or marry him ever until we were both out of parole. But we got Mr. Klein to approve it.

Q: I see. Okay, let's go through a brief summary of some of the things that you feel really affected what you've done. Maybe the relationship between your parents, the relationship between you and your mother and your bitterness against your stepmother and somewhat your father.

A: That was then, you know. I mean now that I've grown up and I've gone through everything that I have, I think differently about it. Because I know what it is to care for somebody and be in love and I now realize when my dad fell in love with this woman, she cared for him and it's his right to be happy. Even though he had a responsibility towards us, as being his children, he still had a right to be happy, you know. But at the time, I just couldn't see it. It was just hurting me so much about what he was making my mother go through. But what happened, happened. What hurt me so much was that he deprived my mother of her happiness because she cared for him an awful lot and that's what started everything. That's what started my being . . . like I said, I'm not a criminal.

Q: You got involved in crime because you became addicted.

A: Yeah, and I became addicted because of the problems that I had at home in my childhood, you know, and everything. I was trying to escape those problems and I found that every time I would drop some stuff, it would help me to forget about it, at least for a good seven, eight hours.

Q: And your husband supported that kind of thing.

A: That's why I guess I looked up to him. Like he was taking care of me. Not really, because I was going out stealing for it too. Afterwards I realized, well, you know, the man couldn't care for me. Any man that cares for his woman doesn't have her out stealing and things like that. But we were more, my husband and I, more of a partnership. A partnership of taking care of each other's life, than really a husband and wife relationship, because we shoplifted together and we were supporting our habit together. We cared for each other because we were helping each other keep from being sick, you know. And when I got tired of that and I realized what kind of relationship we had, I wanted to escape it. I wanted it to end but I was so afraid of him that I didn't do it until now, and I'm afraid because he's still a kid. He hasn't grown up yet. I don't think all this time of spending in the penitentiary has changed him like it's changed me. I think he still wants to use drugs and I don't think he's ready to settle down and forget about 'em yet.

As far as I can see, Ned is. He's interested in helping himself and helping other people as well to better their life. He's interested in it. And to get a high feeling just out of being yourself and being sober and going out to a park and buying an ice cream cone and running around. That's the kind of high I want, you know. Just a high from being yourself and being happy. That's the perfect high.

Q: You don't need the other kind of high, the artificial high?

A: No. Don't you think so? The perfect kind of high. I mean to . . . if you can go to a park, or the mountains and look at, you know, nature and get a kick out of just eating an ice cream cone, chewing bubble gum, you get where I'm coming from? Just being a happy human being, you know, clean and sober. That's what I want and that's what I'm working for and we're doing it together, me and Ned.

And that's why I'm so sure we have a beautiful life, you know, ahead of us, because that's what I've always wanted.

Q: If nothing else, that's not asking anything unreasonable.

A: And you see we talked to Mr. Klein about this and he conceded we were serious about it, and that's why he said it was all right. We're good for each other, you know, and that's what he's concerned with is that we be happy. And that we're ex-convicts doesn't make any difference.

Everything that happened, I guess it was because of that. I know that my crimes were because I was addicted and I became addicted, started using drugs, because I was looking for something, you know. I was looking for attention and love and I just couldn't find it and when I dropped stuff I forgot about it.

Q: When you shoot up, is it always in the arm or where?

A: In the veins, mainlining.

Q: Is there any other place that you shoot up?

A: No, my veins, all my veins on my arms. I used to have tracks real bad. They used to be black when I first went up, from every day, every day for a year and a half.

Q: Two or three or four times a day?

A: Oh, no, about seven. Yeah, they were pretty bad. They were black. They've gone away a whole lot. You can still kind of tell, but not that much.

Q: Did you ever get hold of any stuff at the pen?

A: No.

Q: You never tried, never wanted to?

A: No. I wanted to straighten up. But it's boring. If I would have gotten some I would have used it because it was so boring, you know.

Q: So you didn't see any or you weren't aware that there was any?

A: Oh, there was some. If I really wanted it I could have gotten it but it was hard. To me it was more important to stay clean and not get caught because they would take away my parole and that would be harder on my chances of getting out, if they ever caught me. So to me it was more important to stay clean and straighten up my head and find myself, you know. I wanted to be with my daughter. She's three now. She deserves more than what I've given her.

Q: How long have you been out?

A: Six months.

Q: That was a nice Christmas, huh?

A: Yeah. I was with her for Christmas. And I'm doing all right.

Q: Did you work at the Holiday Inn all the time till now?

A: No. I started at the Holiday Inn in January. Before that, about a week before, I was working at the Howard Johnson but it didn't work at all. I was in the pantry and the boss wasn't satisfied with my qualifications for working in the kitchen. Like I worked before when I was up there at the penitentiary. I worked in the kitchen but the Howard Johnson is a rather exclusive place. Everything has to be perfect and like one day I was making these ham sandwiches and I was just learning. I was in training, you know, and I had to ask about it, and so he asked me, "Have you ever worked in a pantry before?" And I told him that I hadn't and a couple of days later he asked them to get rid of me. I don't know if he found out I was a convict or what, but they laid me off.

Then I went to the parole officer and I got the job at the Holiday and I stayed there about four months, five months. I just quit last week when I started working at the shop. I like it there because I think it's more opportunity and now I can get my daughter and take care of her in the day. See, I'll take care of my daughter in the daytime and Ned's sister, she owns the beauty shop, and I'll take care of her son during the day while she goes. When she comes, she'll take care of my daughter. I like it that way better because I want to take care of my daughter myself.

So a little at a time I'm getting what I want. I found a man that cares for me and wants to give me a normal, real happy life and I'm getting my daughter and I feel very good. That's why I say, all this, going to the penitentiary and all this, it did do me some good, you know. I'm not saying it's the best thing in the world to do for all these kids. It's not the solution to go all the way up to the penitentiary and that's gonna solve everything. Help 'em to find themselves. I hope these kids nowadays find a better way of finding themselves than to go all the way to the penitentiary before finding where they're at, you know. But I don't know what solution there is. I don't know. I know there couldn't have been any other way for me cause I was just going, going, going, running away, you know.

Q: Perhaps, had you found someone really caring for you—

A: I just had to mature. I wasn't growing up, you know. I just hope the other kids nowadays find a better way of growing up before they find out the hard way. But you can't tell kids and it looks like they want to find out for themselves, you know. Like my dad used to tell me . . . he even used to tell me, "You're gonna end up in the penitentiary," you know, and I just had to find out for myself. And now I know who was right but it's too late. But it's better that it worked out this way than if I would have ended up killing myself with an overdose or something like that.

Francisco

As a teenager, Francisco was a gregarious youngster, easy to get along with and accustomed to the structure of an institution. He was in custody at the juvenile home a number of times for various reasons, ranging from curfew violation to rape.

In the institution, he knew how to get along, always managing to remain on the good side of staff and peer group. From the staff's point of view, he might be considered a "con man," an inmate who always managed to get what he wanted within the institution without alienating anybody.. Always in Francisco's family there has been grave concern for all its members, even though it appears that for most of the time when the children were growing up the family was completely disintegrated.

Francisco was a good-looking teenager, short and stocky. He was always neat and clean, and his mother brought clean clothes to him in the juvenile home several times a week. He always had a ready smile and a joke. He is about five feet six or seven inches and has a medium complexion, dark hair, and brown eyes.

At the interview, Francisco appeared in a pair of jockey pants, black shoes, and a long-sleeved shirt, dressed somewhat like the *pachuco* of the early 1960s. His good looks have been marred somewhat by a broken nose and a scar over one eye. At this time Francisco was more serious. However, he was able to relate very well with the interviewers and seemed to discuss most things openly and with conviction. He is somewhat hostile toward the correctional system and expresses much bitterness toward police officers and the penal institution. He professes strong family ties and deep concern for all members of his family.

Q: I think what we'd like is for you to start back as far as you can remember. Start out with the family and environment and as far back as you can remember—who lived at home?

A: Oh, I'll tell you as far back as I can remember, we were living in Santa Fe and I was attending school—

Q: You can talk Spanish if you want to.

181

A: And, I don't even remember what grade I was in but I can slightly remember . . . and the way it started out with me, I used to hang around with some older fellows than me, you know.

Q: In Santa Fe?

A: Yeah. But anyway, as far as stealing goes, I don't know how that started, you know. I mean, I can't remember how I started stealing but that's what I started doing then . . . oh, yes. I do remember now. It started out with bikes. I wanted a bike and my dad didn't want to buy me a bike.

Q: Was your dad living at home then?

A: Yes. And my mom, well, she was always for us but him, he was always—so anyway I guess I decided to, you know, get a bike for myself so I got me one.

Q: How old were you?

A: I was around . . . couldn't be no more than nine or ten, maybe even younger, I don't know.

Q: You said that you lived in Santa Fe for eight or nine years?

A: Yeah. So I stole the bike and my dad busted me and knocked the shit out of me and all that, you know. So these two guys that I'm telling you that I used to hang around with as I was getting older . . . I was learning a little more, just a little more. I remember every time I used to come from school my dad used to hide my shoes because he was afraid I might cut out again. So I just let him cut out and I just looked for the shoes and I'd find the shoes and I'd just cut out myself.

Q: What kind of a guy was your dad?

A: I guess you could say that he was more or less something like me, I guess, because that's what my mom says, what my other brothers say, that we were a lot alike.

Q: Did he die?

A: Yes, he died last year. You might remember, they found him dead on North Fourth in a parking lot.

Q: Oh, yes, I remember that.

A: He used to drink a lot, you know, *tomaba mucho* wine.

Q: Did he drink when you were living in Santa Fe? When you were that young?

A: Yeah, he used to, not quite as much, but he used to. I think that's where he really started, you know, drinking that wine. So anyway, as the years went by, I . . . . so now I wasn't getting any more bikes. That wasn't my kick anymore. Now I was just a little older and I was already burglarizing. So I got busted in—*cómo se llama?*—Jim's Drive-in, Santa Fe. We did a burglary there and then went down to

Española, did some more over there and came back to Santa Fe, and they were already waiting for us, the cops.

Q: How old were you at that time?

A: I don't know. I was about nine or ten, maybe younger, maybe older. I just don't quite remember.

Q: Who was living at home then?

A: There was me, my mom and dad, Juan and Ernesto, Pancho, Maria, and the Corregidors, Max and Manuel.

Q: Were the Corregidors your half-brothers?

A: Yeah. Oh, maybe I should mention this. I used to argue a lot with my brothers and I was always—

Q: Your half-brothers?

A: Yeah.

Q: Were your half-brothers also getting into trouble?

A: They've never been in trouble except one. He's been to Santa Fe.

Q: So they were pretty straight?

A: Now. They weren't. They just, uh, they just don't like the idea of going around stealing and nothing like that. And I used to get into fights with them cause of my dad, you know. I didn't like the way they treated my dad. Of course it was dad's fault, but—

Q: He was their stepfather?

A: Yeah. He was my father. So anyway, when I was younger I didn't like any of them and I don't think the rest of my brothers . . . they were maybe younger, maybe they were just seeing things different or they were just young, I guess.

Q: That's your real brothers? ·

A: Yeah. So my father and my mother, they were always arguing . . .

Q: Did your father work?

A: Yeah. He was a painter and at one time he was even a schoolteacher. So anyway, let's see—

Q: Your mother didn't work while you were living there?

A: Naw. He was working—my dad. And these burglaries, as the years went by . . . I'm just saying what I can more or less remember, and we got busted for that there in Santa Fe. As a matter of fact my dad was the one that busted me.

Q: For the burglaries?

A: Yeah. So going back a little now . . . I remember when I used to come home late, one time my dad was drunk and he didn't like for me to be out so late, you know. Well, I was young but when I was hanging around with older guys and we used to hang around *allá en la arroya*—there in the arroyo—and we used to drink and all that—

Q: Were you sniffing at that time?

A: No.

Q: Sniffing hadn't come in or you never got involved?

A: Well, yes, but later on. And I came home one night about . . . well, actually I came home around nine o'clock but I stayed out on the porch because I was afraid of my dad. And then he was drunk and my mom, she told me to stay out there for a while so he could more or less, *para que se aliviara un poco y se duerma*—so he would calm down a little and sleep. So I went in and my mom, she didn't want me to sleep in our room because she was afraid that he might get up and see me. So I sneaked in the bathroom through the back door and we just laid a rug *allí* and I just went to sleep there.

So the next thing I knew when I woke up, there was my dad and he was at the faucet, and I think I remember very well he said, *"Para que aprendas"*—"So you'll learn," you know. He just turned on the faucet, so there I was right under the faucet.

So now he and my mom are arguing and my mom is telling him, "What's the matter with you? You crazy?"

Q: Was he holding you down?

A: Yeah. He wasn't really gonna drown me or anything, you know. He was just—he used to drink a lot and he used to have faults, but . . . he was very strict and he never did like anything about all that stealing or nothing like that. As a matter of fact, the reason why my mom and my dad got a divorce was because of the Corregidors, you know. My dad was always saying, "Well, these guys are big enough to go out and work," or "Why don't they go out and work and get their own place or get married or something?"

Q: How much older than you are they?

A: The youngest is Max and he's thirty-four . . .

Q: So they're about . . . you're twenty-six, right?

A: I'm twenty-six, yeah. So they're in their late thirties except Max. Anyway, that's the reason why I think they got a divorce.

Q: Most of the fighting was over the Corregidors?

A: Yeah. And because of my dad's drinking and all that.

Q: Do you think that you were poor or do you think you had enough?

A: Well, I think we were poor because I remember very well I was out selling papers with a shine box, you know, shining shoes and selling papers and things like that. And whatever I could steal on the side—well, that's what I'd steal.

Q: Did your dad have a steady job or was he working?

A: He had a steady job.

Q: He was working for somebody else?

A: Yeah. On the side he used to paint houses. He used to make pretty good money. As a matter of fact, real good. And getting back, you know, to them burglaries, when I got busted there, I was already a little older and I was already through selling papers, giving shines and all that. So they gave me—well, they didn't give me a break, but—

Q: Did you go to probation at that time?

A: No. They thought that it would be better if I was sent to school. So I was sent to Saint Peter's home for boys. Saint Peter's orphanage. So I was sent there and I stayed there about four and a half years.

Q: You came from Santa Fe to Saint Peter's.

A: Yes, and since that time I never gone back to Santa Fe.

Q: While you were there your parents moved here to Albuquerque. Is that when your parents got a divorce?

A: Yeah, about five years later actually, they moved here and they finally got a divorce.

Q: Oh. So they didn't divorce while you were at Saint Peter's?

A: No. *Estaban apartes pero se juntaban y logo se apartaban y logo se juntaban por un rato*—they were apart but they would get together and then separate and then back together for a while.

Q: Whose idea do you think the divorce was?

A: Oh, my mom's.

Q: She would kick him out or something?

A: Yeah. By that time, you know, his problem was drinking. So I went to Saint Peter's. When I had about two years there, they brought—I don't know if it was Nesto, Pancho, or Juan. I think we were all there, but finally she took us out. As a matter of fact, *a mí me quiquiaron de allí de* Saint Peter's—they kicked me out of Saint Peter's.

Q: They kicked you out?

A: Yeah, because they busted me. See these two girls there, they were working in the kitchen, and we used to sneak out to their rooms and go into their rooms and talk to them. So they finally busted us, me anyway. They finally got me out of there.

Q: What do you remember about staying at Saint Peter's?

A: Well, like for instance?

Q: Well, what do you think of your experience at Saint Peter's? Was it a good one?

A: Well, the reason why I think I didn't graduate—I used to be pretty educated in school, but I think I would have graduated in all these years if I would have stayed in a public school. I only went to schools like Catholic schools. You know, *puras hermanas*—all Sisters.

Q: You weren't in a Catholic school in Santa Fe, were you?

A: I was in San Gabriel.

Q: How was San Gabriel? What do you remember?

A: I never had any problems there. In school I used to get straight A's. But then later on I was still getting straight A's but I was skipping, and like I said, I was hanging around with older boys and they used to wait for me over there in school.

Q: Didn't your parents ever find out that you were ditching school?

A: Yeah. My dad—he used to whip me or something . . .

Q: I get the impression that your mom tried to cover up for you so that your dad wouldn't find out, because he was so strict.

A: Right, right. She was always—she didn't want to really cover up, because she really wanted for me to straighten out, but in the way of him whipping me, she never liked it.

Q: Thinking back to it, were these whippings really bad? Or were they reasonable?

A: They were bad. Sometimes they were reasonable but at that time I never saw it from his point of view. Whenever your dad whips you, you don't like him. I remember my dad used to get drunk and he used to be home. He would fall asleep, and I used to go in and he would set his pants there on the seat. I used to go and steal his money, you know, or whenever my dad and mom, you know, got mad and he would rent a room in town, I would always go see how he was doing. Even though he was always whipping me, I always used to go and see how he was doing.

So I used to go down there where he was staying and tell him . . . by this time I was just a little older and a little wiser so I would go and by that time he would give me his whole wallet and say, "Well, why don't you take what you need," and I would say "Well, okay. I'm going to take this for me and I'm going to take this for my mom and this for my mom."

And he would say, *"Llevale a tu mamá"*—"Take it to your mother."

Q: Who sent you to Saint Peter's? Was it the Welfare Department?

A: I don't know, I don't know how that happened. All 1 can remember is that I got in trouble with them burglaries and the next thing I knew I was in Saint Peter's orphanage.

Q: Who induced you to go into burglaries, friends?

A: *Los camarades. Todos los que eran camarades de mí*—friends, all the ones that were my friends. We used to make a little money on the side, *robando aquí, robando allá*—selling papers on the side, you know, and making a little money here and a little there. We were always hustling.

Q: Were they older than you?

A: Oh, yeah. I was like ten at that time and they were maybe fifteen or sixteen.

Q: Did you have much to do with your grandparents?

A: Well, my dad's grandmother—I never did meet her till 1963. She lived in Colorado.

Q: And the other one?

A: She's in El Rito. My mom would always take me to El Rito.

Q: Did you ever stay with your grandmother?

A: Yeah. I remember staying there once for about a week but I didn't last. I came hitchhiking back home. They have a big old ranch over there, you know, and there wasn't anything to do and nothing to steal, nothing like that, and so I just came back.

Q: How about aunts and uncles? Did you have any that lived close by, that you were close to?

A: No. No aunts and uncles that I could say I was really close to. As a matter of fact, see my dad was also married before he married my mom and so in his first marriage my dad had two daughters. *Ahora que murió mi* dad—now that my dad died—they brought me from prison for the funeral, and I didn't know her.

Q: His daughter?

A: Yeah. One of them, and my mom and my wife, they introduced her to me.

Q: When your dad got a divorce from his first wife, the girls stayed with—

A: With her.

Q: Did they live in Santa Fe?

A: No. In Colorado.

Q: You said your father used to be a teacher?

A: Well, as far as I know, my mom says he used to be a teacher.

Q: Did he have some college education or . . . I remember in those days they used to allow high school graduates to teach.

A: He was pretty well educated, my dad, *no más que, como digo*—except like I say, his only problem was drinking.

Q: He would drink every weekend or almost every day or—

A: Well, just about every day. As the years went by he started drinking more and more and more till it finally killed him.

Q: Why do you think he used to drink so much? What do you think started it?

A: I don't know. I couldn't say. Sometimes I think that it might be because of the love he had for my mother, or I more or less try and figure it out you know, *pero no puedo*—but I can't. I can't more or less balance it on that because when we were younger he was drinking and later on he was still drinking, so I couldn't say for sure what was his real reason.

Q: He didn't seem to get along too well with his parents, huh?

A: Well, my dad was the sort of person, *si le quería hablar, le hablaba, y si no le quería hablar, pues no más no te hablaba.* If he wanted to talk to you, he talked to you, and if he didn't want to talk to you, well, he didn't talk to you. If he didn't like you, he let you know it.

Q: So you didn't feel like he wanted to be around his family, or—

A: No. Well, I remember me and him used to have some real good times together. I remember once he bought me a BB gun and he took me to the arroyo to go shoot with the BB gun, and he bought me a glove and ball and played with me. When he got laid off for about a month or two months, he was always fixing the house, painting the house.

Q: So he was really good when he was sober?

A: Yeah. *Cuando andaba borracho*—when he was drunk—if he was in a good mood, well, he was real nice, but he used to talk a lot. He used to talk, talk, talk . . .

Q: Generally what I have seen with people like that, when they get drunk they cry about all their problems and all that.

A: That's what I was thinking, you know. That's what I was thinking of him, because when he got that way he never wanted us to stop talking. He started like at eight, ten, at two in the morning he was still there.

Q: Were you usually the one that was sitting there listening to him?

A: Well, I was more or less, you know *cuando le gritaba mi mamá, "Callate, Jorge, callate, ya duermete"*—when my mother shouted, "Be quiet, Jorge, be quiet and go to sleep." And he used to call me "Palo," "Stick," and he used to call my—

Q: Why did he call you "Palo"?

A: I don't know. That was just a name that he got. He used to call Juan "Indio," you know, "Indian," because he was a bit darker, and he call Nesto "Ojos Blancos"—"White Eyes." So when the kids were all together Nesto would call me "Palo Palito," and I would call him "Entelerido"—"Chicken." So we actually had some fun once in a while . . . So anyway, I left Saint Peter's about 1954, no, about 1955.

Q: You were maybe twelve, thirteen then?

A: Like I say, I don't remember.

Q: So you came out of Saint Peter's in about fifty-five?

A: Fifty-five or fifty-six, somewhere around there.

Q: How were the teachers down in Santa Fe, in school? Did you have any problems in school there?

A: I remember one time I was in San Gabriel.

Q: You said in San Gabriel there were mostly nuns?

A: Yeah. Well, I don't really ever remember having a problem.

Q: Were those teachers mostly Spanish teachers?

A: Spanish, *unas cuantas gabachas, gabachos*—some Anglos. I don't think I ever really had a problem with the teachers, especially there. Not until later at Saint Peter's.

Q: If I remember, you were always easy to get along with. Do you remember any teachers back in grade school that really stand out?

A: Well, actually, when I was that young, I was always doing my work and paying attention. I would always finish my work and I would go. I guess that's why I never really had a problem with any of the schoolteachers. I remember very well I used to do my work and I really liked school. At that time I used to like school very much. But in a Catholic school, I didn't get much of a kick out of it because in the morning we'd pray, go to mass, right after church, breakfast, right after breakfast, *rezar*—pray—and go out and play for a little bit.

Q: Was it a boarding school?

A: *Aquí* in Saint Peter's?

Q: No. San Gabriel.

A: No. That's not a boarding school, but more or less you know, you learn more about God and Jesus and things like that.

Q: What was your impression in Santa Fe of the police? Were you afraid of them?

A: I was afraid of 'em. I remember one time this cop, he picked me up, you know. I don't know how old I was *pero yo tenía mis papeles y mi* shine box—I had my newspapers and my shine box and this guy picked me up. I forget why but anyway he was gonna take me home, and I was afraid of my dad so he gave me a break and he let me off about two or three blocks from the house. They busted me at the drugstore.

Q: They found out you were stealing?

A: And he came and picked me up and instead of taking me to my parents he gave me a break. I was kind of shook up and he thought, "We'll give this guy a break."

Q: Were you ever in jail in Santa Fe, since they didn't have a D home there at the time?

A: No. They never had a D home there. That's why I guess he was taking me home because I guess I was too young to be in jail. *Pero* when I got busted, you know, for these burglaries, well I was way too young to be in jail and I was in jail, so they made me a trustee and I stole a key and opened these guys' door and we left.

Q: Is that right? You got straight out of jail and busted your buddies?

A: Yeah.

Q: How long were you in jail? Do you remember at all?

A: About seven or eight days before we got out again.

Q: Where did you go when you got busted out of jail?

A: Well, I wanted to go back home, you know, and get clothes, but those guys said they were going to Española and I was gonna go with them. So I wanted to go back home but I couldn't get there because my daddy was always around. The three of us went walking and I turned around the corner and there came my daddy. He chased me for about four blocks and then later on a policeman was after me. They finally busted me.

Q: So you weren't out very long when you broke out of jail?

A: I wasn't out very long. The others—they stayed.

Q: They got away?

A: Yeah.

Q: You went back to jail then? Is that the time you came to Saint Peter's?

A: Yeah. They took me back, you know, to jail and then they

took me to see a man. They wanted to send me to . . . I don't know where, Springer or whatever.

Q: You don't remember if that was your probation officer?

A: I don't know what he was, I just remember seeing a man. The next thing I knew I was in Saint Peter's.

Q: *Ellos te enseñaron como robar? Tus compañeros?*—They taught you how to rob? Your friends? Did they teach you or did you already know something about it? Say, remember the first time you went to a house. Is that what you were doing then—breaking into houses or shoplifting or what?

A: We were shoplifting commercial places, like that drive-in.

Q: What did you take from there?

A: This guy . . . *cómo se llama?* Junior was his name. We used to call him "Ham and Eggs." And the other—I forget his name, you know, completely. I only remember that they called him "Green Eyes." We were going to Española because there in Española, there by the river, where we would go swimming, were some phone booths. At that time *esos* phone booths *estaban muy simples*—phone booths were very easy. You just tore out the whole phone booth and carried it and broke it in the river. So we were going there for that, so someone gave us a ride, and they dropped us off next to Jim's Drive-in and one of them said "Let's give it a try here."

Q: Were you hitchhiking?

A: Yeah. So we just went in through a big old window—a big picture window.

Q: Was it in the daytime?

A: Daytime. Broad daylight; you know. So we just broke that window, we went in, and there was a ton of boxes where the popcorn was. We were opening all of the boxes and everything and then Junior opened a box and said, "Here it is," and took out the sack.

Q: Of what?

A: Money. *Pero* it wasn't that much, *pero* at the time, for us thirty or forty dollars was quite a bit, you know. And that son of a bitch, I didn't realize, they told me "take" and passed me five, ten dollars and they kept the rest.

I remember another time that we went on bikes, we went robbing. We stole a purse, but they didn't give me more than two, three dollars and they kept all the rest.

Q: Where did you steal the purse?

A: I don't remember. I think it was in a shopping center or

something like that, *en una tienda grande*—in a big store. They didn't
give anything to me, but like, I don't know, I guess I just wanted to be
like them, you know. *Robar como ellos*—to rob like them—or
something.

So we broke into that drive-in and we went to Española and we
broke in one phone booth over there. When we came back we had
money so we started spending. But then they tell us the cops are
looking for us. I think that's the way it went.

Q: Do you know the families of these boys who were with you
in jail?

A: No. I know who the mother of Green Eyes is. I've never met
her, maybe I did but I don't remember. And his little brother, he's
maybe a year or two younger than me. I met him *allá en la
pinta*—there in prison. And the other one, I never seen him again after
that. Junior, they called him Ham and Eggs, I've never seen him.

Q: Did you go back and forth between Santa Fe and Española?

A: Yeah. We used to. Not very much, but I remember we used
to.

Q: What did your parents think about you being gone so much?
Didn't they ever say anything?

A: Every time I come home my dad would knock the shit out of
me because I was always doing something. I never did anything right.
Como le digo—like I tell you—my dad used to hide my shoes, *y le decía
a mi mamá, "No vas a dejar a este salir"*—and he would tell my mom,
"Don't let this one go out." My mother didn't dare. And if I didn't
find the shoes, well, I would go out without shoes and go to the plaza
and steal some new ones, and there I went again.

Q: Seems like you learned pretty young, then, how to steal?

A: Yeah. And from there I go to Saint Peter's orphanage.

Q: It was mostly religion at Saint Peter's?

A: Religion . . . that's all it was.

Q: Were there any men working there? Did they have a dairy
farm?

A: Yeah.

Q: They used to raise alfalfa?

A: I think, I don't remember.

Q: You said that Nesto, Pancho, and Juan were all living at
Saint Peter's.

A: I think. I'm pretty sure they were. I don't know if Juan was
but I know that Nesto was. Pancho was.

Q: Did you like girls at the time?

A: Huh?

Q: *Te gustaban las niñas?*—Did you like girls, did you have any association with girls?

A: With girls? They don't have any girls there. It was just boys—some girls with babies but they don't let them go over there to Saint Peter's. Some kids, their parents placed them there when they were very little and now let's say like Joe, he's about forty, forty-two, and he's been there a long time working now.

Q: Were they pretty strict at Saint Peter's?

A: Oh, yeah.

Q: Did you miss your family when you were at Saint Peter's?

A: Well, my mom used to come. They never came very much, you know, but when they used to come I always wanted to go with them. But they had to take me to a room and two sisters stayed with me to see that I didn't leave the room. But I never ran away or nothing like that and I had the chance.

Q: How often did they visit you, once a year, once a month?

A: I don't really remember, maybe twice a year, something like that, *no me acuerdo.* I don't remember.

Q: Were your parents separated at the time?

A: Yeah.

Q: So did your dad ever visit you?

A: *Como le digo,* they separated and got back together.

Q: It was mostly your mom visiting you, then?

A: Yeah.

Q: Did they ever allow you to go home on visits?

A: Once. They let me go once and like they let me go on a Friday or Saturday.

Q: How did your mom get there? Was she driving? Or did she take a bus?

A: She was always . . . bus, walking, bus, walking. She really had it rough, you know. You know a lot of people would think that because we were in the orphanage they were going to forget about us. But no, she came back later when she could and got them all out—all my brothers. Not me because they had already kicked me out. She came back and took them all out. She tried her best. Whatever she could.

Q: What happened afterwards?

A: Well, right after I came out, I right away . . .

Q: Your mother was then living in Albuquerque?

A: Yeah. My dad was too.

Q: They were together?

A: Uh-huh. I used to go around stealing pigeons.

Q: Where did you live?

A: Right here in Vineyard. We stole pigeons from this guy and we sold them to Mr. Williams. You remember Mr. Williams? The old courthouse, right across the street on Fifth Street, right on the alley, he lived there, he used to have a lot of pigeons, all kinds. We used to sell them to him. So that's how I started again. No . . . because when I was in school also, when I was at Saint Peter's I stole some there too. I don't remember what I stole.

Q: Did you go to school after Saint Peter's?

A: Sí.

Q: You were still living in Vineyard and going to Hamilton?

A: No. When we were living in Vineyard I went to another school, but I don't remember what school. *Pero* when I came from Santa Fe I went to Hamilton. And there's where I really started—

Q: But actually when you got out of Saint Peter's, you went to another school and it wasn't Hamilton?

A: Yeah, right.

Q: Then you were probably twelve or thirteen when you got out of Saint Peter's?

A: Around there.

Q: In the fifth or sixth grade?

A: I think because I still couldn't go to Hamilton.

Q: You got kicked out of Saint Peter's? Why?

A: They caught us on the roof. We were going to see girls, two girls. We used to go there to their window and talk with these girls.

Q: It was always exciting to do something you weren't supposed to.

A: Right. It was always like a challenge or I don't know . . .

Q: When was the first time you got busted here in Albuquerque?

A: The first time? I really can't remember. I think it was a gas station. Me and this guy, we were riding our bikes. We got the gas station, he went out for a cup of coffee. When he went out, we went in and grabbed, and left. When we robbed that money we made it for the street first, and my dad used to hang around there. I went around looking to see if my dad was in one of the bars. I asked, "Do you have any money?"

"No tengo"—"I don't have any." He thought that I wanted some so I had all the money right there in my socks. I gave him some bills.

Q: Did he ever ask you where you got it?

A: No. By that time he didn't say anything to me—now I even stayed out till twelve at night and came home alone. I even came home drunk alone and went to bed. Now they didn't say anything to me. *Yo creo que se cansaron de andarme diciendo todo*—I think they got tired of telling me everything.

Q: How about school in those days?

A: In those days I never liked it that much. I did go. I went up to ninth grade in school. That's where I really stated to *robar más*, going into bigger things, going to sniff, going to marijuana, going to heroin, *y todo*—and all that, you know. I've already been through all that.

Q: When was the first time you came into contact with the police in Albuquerque? And the courts and the judges? What happened?

A: Let me tell you one thing . . . the first time that I went to court, being that it was my first time, I never got a break. It's right on the record. Once they gave me a break. Just once. I used to be in the D home constantly. I was out for thirty days, in for another sixty, sixty . . . They never gave me a break. I think maybe that's why I'm so bitter against the judges and things like that, and now I realize it's more or less like a political thing, election is coming and they start giving you a break. But I remember I used to go to the D home and do sixty days there, thirty days out, sixty days in. I passed my life there. They sent me to Springer—I spent seven months there.

Q: Wasn't Mr. Irwin your probation officer?

A: Yeah.

Q: Did he help?

A: Aw, man. That guy, he really did try . . .

Q: Have you seen him? He was at the state pen.

A: Yeah, but he quit *porque* he got into a bit of misunderstanding with Mr. Johnson.

Q: I remember you were involved and he was working with you and Nesto and—

A: All of us. All of us . . .

Q: He was really working.

A: I never did see him as a probation officer, you know. I always used to see him as somebody that I could go to and discuss any problem that I might have or something like this you know, with him. Money . . . when you needed money you could borrow money.

Q: It seems to me—wasn't he the one that kept you out of Springer for a long time?

A: Yeah. But they were always giving me time at the D home. I remember when he was working there. A lot of guys didn't like him. He'd go and look for them and say, "Get up, you tramp," and who knows what else, playing around, you know, a lot of guys don't like that. They got the trash can and put it on his head.

Q: Were you in the D home then?

A: I was in another cell while it was going on.

Q: What did you think of the detention home? What was it like—very frankly?

A: I don't know. I guess it was like home to me. *Yo no sé.* I think so because when I went there for good, they made me a trustee, and I was always buffing the floors. But I don't know why we've always liked it.

Q: Did you ever get in trouble by yourself?

A: Well, yeah. All the times that I went to the D home and they gave me sixty days. Maybe three or four times I got busted with somebody else but they never gave the other guy any time.

Q: Did you ever get in trouble with your brothers?

A: With Pancho once, I think. But you know, by that time I was eighteen or nineteen.

Q: When you went to Springer, how old were you then?

A: I was seventeen, sixteen.

Q: What happened that time, do you remember? Why were you in Springer?

A: Oh, yeah. There was a party and I wasn't at the party, *pero* these friends of mine, they were at the party. And there was this girl and everybody was screwing her there in the bedroom, and later this other guy and I got there, and the girl used to live about a block from my house. So now I wanted to screw her, too, so there was nobody at the house. My mom was in El Rito—she went to go visit her mother. So I took her in the house and by that time it was two or three o'clock. And I was like *como un* blackout, who knows how, and I wanted to screw her and she didn't want to so I think I slapped her once or twice, you know. Then I went into the other room and by the time I came back, she wasn't there. She went home *pero* when she went home she told her parents she was with me, and like, you know, she was something like thirteen, fourteen years old. Maybe younger, I don't remember. So anyway they charged that I had raped her. Something like that. So that's when I went to Springer. She was—what do they call it? Molest? When you hit a girl, or . . .

Q: They didn't charge you with rape?

A: No, it's something like that. It's there on my record.

Q: How old were you?

A: I was about seventeen.

Q: How involved were you during this time, going to the D home, with sniffing and stuff like that?

A: I never got busted for sniffing . . . more or less they realized that I was sniffing.

Q: Were you doing a lot of it?

A: Yeah, quite a bit.

Q: And drinking quite a bit?

A: Drinking a lot.

Q: Were you involved at all with marijuana?

A: A little later on. Four or five of us guys would get together and their brothers, they used to push, and we were always in the background. They would go and hide the grass and grow it or something and then we knew where to go. They would grow it and we would wait and then get it.

Q: Did they realize that you were doing it?

A: After a while they snapped to it once. They had a sack of griffa, a big old sack like that. I don't know what they were doing. They had a fire next to the ditch there in Barelas.

Q: Did you live in Barelas?

A: I lived on Silver at that time, but I got together down there in Barelas.

Q: When you were at the D home—would you go out and sniff in the garage? Or would somebody come to the window and hand in stuff? I remember several times when they found little bottles of liquor and stuff like that.

A: No, I never did that there. There in the detention home I never did anything, I don't know why, I never did anything wrong. Not really that one could say I wanted to much. What I'm telling you is that I . . . like if I was holding a job or something like that, I remember they left money in the office where I cleaned. I was curious, something like that, or maybe they left it open to see if I would take it, you know. I think those people wanted to test me. I've never stolen from a job while I'm holding it. If I wasn't holding it, and there was a chance . . . but not while I was working there, man.

Q: So you did time at the D home maybe what—five or six times?

A: No. More than that. Because I remember when they interviewed me in prison, your whole record is there. So I told the guy, "Can't you let me see?" I was curious about my record. It was already about thirty or forty pages and he was still turning over more pages where they had busted me, armed robbery, burglary, curfew, all that.

Q: You were involved in an armed robbery?

A: I was there but I wasn't involved in it. And I got busted. I was too drunk and I was seventeen, sixteen at the time. When they took me to the city jail, I was really drunk. Every time I was drunk the cops would really beat me up. They were always knocking the shit out of me. Maybe because I was too drunk and I purposely provoked them. This was a little, he was a Chinese man. We were in Barelas and we wanted a drink. We used to drink wine a lot and we wanted a drink if he was able to lend us fifty cents to go buy a pint of wine. We were already drunk, we just wanted to drink some more. We were with this guy, this guy was way too drunk. And they abused him, I seen it. I was there but we got picked up for that.

Q: Did they take his money?

A: And he didn't have any. We asked him and he told us he didn't have any. We just didn't believe him. We were gonna tie him down. So I stayed about eight days in jail. That was the time when they gave me a break, you know. They told me, how old I was, and I told them I was nineteen. I was only seventeen, sixteen.

I stayed seven, eight days in the city and then when they found out I was way too young to be there, they made me transfer over there about twelve o'clock at night. My mom came and picked me up about two or three days later. I went to court and the judge said to me, "Well, how did you like the City Hall?"

I didn't think it was all that bad, you know. But I told him, "It was really bad."

He told me, "Well, I think eight days in the city jail was enough for you. You can go."

Q: What was your impression of juvenile court? You went to court several times, I guess it was always the same judge?

A: Right. Judge Benson. I hate that SOB. I guess like a lot of times I try to run it down with him, you know, like sometimes guys like us, we get in trouble but we still want to explain, you know, something to him. And that old SOB never let me tell him anything. "Sixty days," he'd say. Just, "Go sit down over there." They had some benches. "Sixty days. Now go sit down."

Q: Was Mr. Irwin always your juvenile probation officer?

A: Well, not always, but the last time . . .

Q: Who was your probation officer before?

A: I don't quite remember. The only guy that I remember as probation officer was that Mr. Irwin.

Q: Mr. Marquez was working at the D home when you first started.

A: He was working there? I never liked him very well. Maybe as I was growing older I understood him a little, *pero* when I was here I never liked him because I always thought he was two-faced, you know. *Yo le digo*—I tell you—the worst thing you can do to a guy locked up is lie to him. He asks you a favor and you say "yes" and then you don't do it. You're just getting him more bitter than he already is.

Q: Were you bitter?

A: I don't think I was. Maybe I was, you know, I don't know what bitter is. That I really hate somebody, that's when I really get like that. I'm the type of guy that you can do something wrong to me *hoy*—today—and *mañana* I already have forgotten it. But if you do something to me today and tomorrow you still want to do it to me, then I'm going to try to do something to you.

Q: Did you ever feel that you were picked on because of your record or because you were a Chicano or—

A: No. At that time the Chicano movement wasn't what it is now. I thought that was just because of my record they would pick me up, or a burglar would rob a house and those people would say it was one of the Lucero boys. They wouldn't pick up my brothers, I was the one they picked up. I was always pretty bitter against the cops, I guess you could say.

Q: You felt they were picking on you?

A: They were, you know . . . cops. They bust you for something. Okay. You get busted, there ain't nothing you can do. Now there ain't nothing they can do. They already busted you. They did their job so now they gotta get you and turn you over to this guy and you're locked up and that's it. *Pero*, no. They get you, and they take you down, and they want you to say something you don't even know nothing about, you know. I turned myself in for two or three burglaries that I didn't have absolutely nothing to do with them. But I stayed because I was tired of them beating me up. I was pretty well, you know, it didn't just bother me in detention. The chances are slim that they will send me to Springer. So I'd take a chance that they'd give me sixty days and the other guy was on the outside.

Q: Do you think you had too many chances or not enough?

A: As far as chances, I don't think I had too many chances. I mean I wouldn't call 'em chances.

Q: You did time at the D home several times, you were on probation all along—was your mother on welfare at that time?

A: No, I don't think so.

Q: And all these people that were involved with you and your family, why do you think they didn't help in some way? Whatever they were doing, why didn't it help? Like you had a pretty good relationship with your probation officer?

A: Yeah.

Q: That didn't keep you from getting into trouble.

A: No. Ah, *yo no sé como.* I don't know how. Well, like I say, you know, we always used to look up to guys that were always on the move, always hustling or something like that. We were raised around them. We didn't know any other way to go, you know. I guess that's probably the reason.

Q: What kind of friends did you have?

A: All my friends, even up till now, they're all ex-cons. A lot of them are settled down now, *pero* all of them at one time or another, we were all the same. You know, many of them changed. *Muchos de ellos*, they were on the same kick and they just kept going and kept on going. Like me, I guess. I just kept on going.

I got a real good buddy who is working right here at this bank as a bank teller. And I remember we were kids, I used to, it's not that I want to say that I was pretty bad, but I remember I used to slap him around you know, take his money. And when he could, he'd get me too. We stole together once in a while. That's the way it went, you know. He changed and he went all the way through school.

Q: What was your experience at Springer?

A: Experience with Springer?

Q: You spent about six months there?

A: I don't know, for me it was like . . . I don't know.

Q: You always got along pretty well in institutions . . . you did pretty well at Springer, apparently, because you got out so soon. Like you do go along with rules and stuff, but you were never the kind of guy that was considered a rat by the other kids. You always got along well with them.

A: Yeah.

Q: Did you have good friends always—in every institution you went to?

A: Yeah, and still . . .

Q: Inmates and staff were always your friends?

A: Well, I don't know. I guess I just see it that you've got a job and you gotta do it and if I don't like the way you do your job, I can't say anything to you. But also there are times that you get fed up with me because I'm doing little things here or there or something like that. I wasn't as good as you think I was, you know. I just knew how to pull the strings, more or less. I've always been a pretty perceptive person and, more or less, I know how to act in front of so and so person and how to, you know—

Q: You know what appropriate behavior is for the staff and what appropiate behavior is for the inmates?

A: Right. You know like . . . now that I was in prison, we were taking group therapy and things like that, it's better to just be yourself and be the way you are and say the things you want to say, and if they don't like the way you act, to hell with them. They don't have to sit there and hear what you have to say. Like we used to have something like a "hot seat." Some of them would challenge in English, while I would in Chicano, and I told the guy: "Here, then you are playing games, why are you doing so, why don't you behave? You don't want to stop, just in order that they will not see you as you are." They got mad at me but the next day they were fine.

Q: You didn't make a lot of enemies?

A: No. But I always treated everyone the same, but if you don't like that I can treat you another way, and if you don't want that, well, I won't talk to you at all. Because it's not gonna bother me if you talk to me or don't talk to me. *Pero,* you know, like a guy that's been doing a lot of time and everything like that, well, like now I feel a little better *porque* I know you, you've known me so I can say anything the way I want, *pero* like other guys that have done a lot of time would feel very, very different in front of you. You know they would feel very paranoid, very—

Q: Persecuted?

A: Yeah.

Q: What was Springer like? Why don't you tell me something about it?

A: Well, always when I'm locked up my kick is sports. You know, I go for sports—basketball, softball, things like that and that's the way I've always done my time. Do my job, what I have to do, and then go and play whatever I want to do. Life in Springer, it was all right to me. We used to go to a movie every Sunday, walk in town, see girls, talk to girls, you know. We'd leave them a little note there in the theater where we were sitting. The girls, they were already waiting for us. We would just toss them notes and they would throw us notes too. There were times that there in the detention home we got somebody to cover up for us, and they'd be waiting for us like in a car or something.

Q Who would cover up for you?

A: Like friends, you know. Good friends. They would cover up for me. For two guys you need two guys to cover up for you. Like every time they come and count. The guy can get in your bed and play like he's asleep and when they pass there just crawl under the bed and go back to his. While we were in town riding around with some girls or something. I never did cut out on 'em or anything like that.

Q: You would just go into town?

A: Yeah. And we would go and buy some liquor and we'd drink it.

Q: Weren't the dorms locked?

A: Yeah. They had some pipes, they were dark brown, we'd saw 'em about that much space where we would fit. What do you call it, scotch tape? We'd tape the pipe, it was all the same color—you couldn't see anything. That's where we went through.

Q: So you would sneak out and be gone most of the night?

A: No. About two, three hours. I mean, what a guy learns that is doing time, whether it's Springer or wherever, he always knows when Mr. So-and-So is going to come and what time. Like, I know when Mr. X is coming in. I'd better hurry because this guy is kind of a lookout and it's better to go back or things like that. *Pero,* Springer was pretty good.

Q: Didn't you mind being locked up—at the D home or at Springer?

A: Well, how can I tell you? I said, "This guy is doing ninety days. Well, sixty isn't anything." Like in Springer, man! This guy's doing a year and I don't know when I get out. So it's better to play it cool and get out in six or seven months. You know, I was doing one to five, and some were doing natural life—one to fifty—and so I'd feel pretty good. I'd feel damn good and that's the way I do my time. That way I don't even think it's that much time.

When I was in Springer, I was still going around with the same girl that I married right now, so we've been going around together going on twelve, thirteen years, and I don't know how she's waited for me this long. See like I'm twenty-six and my wife is already thirty-four and we're still together.

Q: After you got married you continued to live the same way, or you changed, or what?

A: Well, I just got out of prison, I guess you could say more or less that I wanted to make a good living for myself and work and get a good job and just stay out and all that but my problem was, now it wasn't marijuana, it was heroin now. I was on heroin. I'd been involved in it for about eight or nine years.

Q: Before you went up to prison the first time?

A: Yeah. I was already involved.

Q: That was after you got out of Springer that you became involved with heroin?

A: Before, even before I went to Springer I was already messing with it but very, very slightly, you know, and after I got out I got more involved and I finally got hooked.

Q: How did it happen? How did you start into heroin?

A: Curious.

Q: Did somebody introduce you, give you a start or what?

A: Well, I used to hang around with guys that their brothers used to push it, you know. So their own brothers, they finally got hooked, and I used to hang around with them. At that time I used to go out and steal and make money and go sit in a bar and drink and play pool and have a good time. Always they had caps and offered them to me. I started with the cotton, then half a cap, and pretty soon I was pretty well involved with it.

Q: When your habit was worst, how much were you taking?

A: When I had the worst habit was in sixty-seven. I had a habit of about, oh—fourteen, twelve caps a day.

Q: A cap was costing you how much at that time?

A: Five dollars. About seventy-five to a hundred dollars a day.

Q: When you went up the first time, what did you go up on?

A: Burglary.

Q: You were already addicted?

A: When I went the first time? It wasn't a pretty bad habit then.
I had about seven, eight caps a day.

Q: So you had to hustle for about fifty dollars a day, anyway?

A: Yeah.

Q: You weren't married then?

A: No.

Q: You were living with your mom?

A: Yeah. Well, I stayed with my mom and I knew a girl here,
and . . . like I tell you, I've always hung around with older people,
and I've always gone around with older broads than me. I would go
and stay with one for two or three days . . .

Q: Who else was living at home then?

A: All my brothers.

Q: The Corregidors were all gone by then?

A: No. They were off and on, you know.

Q: Your dad was gone then?

A: Yeah.

Q: Was your mother aware that you were addicted?

A: I don't know. My mom, I think she more or less probably
knew. She used to bust me *con* marijuana. Things like that. Like one
time she found a roll about that big of joints in the house. I was selling
pot then, like in school. Like in Candelaria High.

Q: Did you go to Candelaria High?

A: No.

Q: You just hung around there?

A: Yeah, like during noon hour and everybody goes out to eat
and the guys already knew where I was and they would go and buy
grass from me. I was around fifteen, sixteen, seventeen, somewhere
around there.

Q: Right around the time you went to Springer?

A: Yeah.

Q: Were you selling before you went?

A: Yeah. By that time I was more or less messing with junk. But
like I say, very slightly. I liked marijuana very much.

Q: But you were having to raise the money for the stuff?

A: No. When you take it very slightly like popping twice a
month, you're not really hooked. This is when I really started
aprendiendo how to hold it, because it's hard to hold *cuando* you've
never been lit, it's pretty hard to hold it in your system because you
feel like throwing up, you know.

Q: Do you remember the first time you used heroin?

A: Yeah. This guy, he was already an addict . . . I was going around with my wife then, and I asked him, you know, and he said he was gonna go score and said if I wanted some. I said "no."

He says, "Yeah. It is better that you don't try this damn stuff—it isn't worth anything." So when he said it like that I more or less felt a challenge so I told him to pass me a little bit.

The guy says "I'll pass you, but I don't know why you're gonna let yourself fall. And it's gonna be your first time and you're not gonna feel very good."

"No," I said, "that's my problem. Are you gonna give me one or not?"

So he said *"Bueno."*

So we went into this house and there was a bunch of guys around. I was the youngest. You know, like these guys, they were about twenty-six, twenty-seven. This guy tells them that he's gonna give me a fix and that I've never let myself fall and finally they let me come and they tell me, "Don't let yourself fall."

"Give me the fix." They were already hooked, man. So there! So then I did want to.

So that was the first time I took it and boy, I remember I really got sick. You know, the first time it seems like—from my feet up, just went up like that. I had to open the door and throw up and everything.

Q: When you throw up like that does that mean that you lose the kick?

A: No. It's just . . . if you learn how to hold and not throw up, you enjoy the kick, but if you have to throw up, you don't feel good; like you can't eat. That was in the early sixties and I mean early sixties because I met my wife the last part of fifty-nine, sixty and we were already going around together, so I already had it maybe a year, two years with her, when I started messing around with it.

Q: Where did you get the stuff? Downtown? Were there some people that would sell it to you?

A: Yeah. I already knew where to go. Anywhere, any part of town, I knew where it was.

Q: Did you ever mess around with anything else besides pot and heroin?

A: Well, like what?

Q: Pills and stuff.

A: Well, I've experienced pills. I've experienced LSD, speed, all that. *Pero* you know, like pills, like barbiturates, I never did quite like 'em.

Q: How was it in those days, when you had a habit of, say, twelve caps, how would you get the money? How would you proceed?

A: What I used to do to get the money? Well, like I used to . . . sneak thief. Do you know what sneak thief is? Well, sneak thief is when . . . like you're standing right there, let's say a girl is standing right there and she's in her office. And you notice the majority of the time the door is open and she's standing right there and her purse is right there. I come and go inside and open the purse and take out the little wallet.

And I would have a car, you know. I would go up to the Heights or anywhere and pull some burglaries, I always used to get enough money, you know, to get me going for two or three days. I was always a little ahead.

Q: I figure, though, you said you had a habit of twelve, fifteen caps per day so you were having to raise seventy to a hundred dollars a day, and if you were burglarizing—

A: But you know, it's not as bad as you think it is. Like you were saying seventy to a hundred dollars a day. Well, you know, like if you score a gram, a gram was pretty big. The guys know me as a guy that keeps his word. I can go and ask them, "Can you give me about five caps and I'll come right back and pay you?" They would give them to me and I would go steal and take them the money and score some more. So it wasn't really that bad. If you're scoring with a lot of guys, scoring like three, four caps, you're paying fifteen dollars, twenty dollars. But say, this guy is coming with seventy-five, a hundred dollars a day, well, he's practically taking it all from you so the next time around you give him a break.

Q: Yeah, "You're my best customer." How long does it take to sell the stuff you get from burglaries?

A: Well, let's say like me. I usually already had the fence.

Q: Did you sell most of your stuff to one person?

A: No. I had different kinds of fences. Like this guy gets TVs. This guy gets appliances, things like that.

Q: Are the fences out of town?

A: No. They're in town.

Q: What would they give for a TV valued at two hundred dollars?

A: Let's say that I would have a TV worth three hundred, a

portable color TV. I would get about seventy-five dollars for it. About a fourth of the price.

Q: You were never caught in any of those burglaries?

A: I never been busted inside, except on one commercial burglary. *Pero* in residential burglaries—I've never gotten busted inside. *Me han torcido*—they've busted me—for fingerprints or something like that.

Q: How would you select the house to go into? Let's say we're walking together and I don't know anything. How would you explain to me, how to select a place? How would you go about it?

A: Well, I'd take a look at the place, a good look. *Miro las salidas, miro la entrada y miro la salida*—I look at the exits, I look at the entrance and look at the exit. How I'm going to go in through this door and leave by that one.

Q: How do you know there are no people inside or what time they come in, what time they go out?

A: Well, you never know at what time they come in. You never know when they left. You just go and knock. And you knock hard and if nobody answers the door, I guess that means nobody's in there. So the way I used to do it, I used to get me a little rock about so big and if you throw it right at a window, it just goes "pop" and doesn't make noise. It just makes a little hole about so big. So I just take out the little pieces to put my hand in and I open the window, or a little hole in the door and I open the door.

Q: Are there any times during the day that would be the best?

A: I never did 'em during the nighttime. I used to do them during the day.

Q: How about the neighbors?

A: Well, that's a chance and I just took it.

Q: So you parked your car in front of the house, close to the house?

A: My car, I would park it about a block away and walk. I already knew where the house was.

Q: You passed by first?

A: Yeah.

Q: You would observe, a little before, the area?

A: Yeah. And then I would park the car and go to the house and go in and get all the stuff together outside where, more or less, they couldn't see very well, and then I would come in the car and just park it and put the stuff in it and go.

Q: Were you by yourself most of the time?

A: The majority, yeah.

Q: What would you guess is the number of houses that you burglarized?

A: I couldn't count, because they haven't busted me. They busted me for, let's say, two, three house burglaries. Let's say like I've done about three hundred, four hundred burglaries.

Q: Three hundred, four hundred in how many years?

A: In one year.

Q: Which area of town would you burglarize? Any area?

A: Any area as long as you pick a good neighborhood where you know that you're gonna get something that you're gonna take out.

Q: What would be a good neighborhood, the Heights?

A: The Heights is about the best, I guess.

Q: Is there any competition?

A: There's lots of competition. There's guys going every day, every day going all over town. If you notice now, you've never seen burglaries up so high, especially in this town. In burglaries you see something like one hundred and thirty-six in a week. Maybe that's why they raised *el tiempo* so much—the time. Like if they bust you now for burglary, you get two to ten. You used to get one to five.

Q: Do you suspect at this time there are a lot more addicts, is that the reason for the increase?

A: Yeah. And there are a lot of people that aren't even addicts, but they've used junk once or twice. They say that they're addicts because they feel that they might get a break this way and actually what they're really doing is messing up the addicts more.

Q: They think they might get a break in court?

A: They say it's like to treat them differently, because they're an addict or something.

Q: You got sent up, you were out, you got paroled, you violated and went back, and you got out and you got sentenced again? The first time you went up what did you go for?

A: Burglary.

Q: Then, you violated again for—

A: Burglary.

Q: And then the other time you went up—

A: Burglary. Just burglary and that's all.

Q: Suppose we would decide to go and burglarize a place. Are you sure that you could detect a house in which we could go?

A: Like if we were to do it now?

Q: Yeah. Are you confident that you could identify a place, select a place—*escoger, elegir un lugar?* That would be no problem?

A: That would be no problem.

Q: It is for me, because I wouldn't know which house to select.

A: Well, you know, the majority of the time that I've gone and burglarized a place, the people have never been there. I don't know, I guess I just sense it or see it real good or I don't know why.

Q: It is intuition. The same way you feel about persons, you feel about houses. You go and get a feeling there is nobody there.

A: I don't say that it hasn't happened cause I have gone . . .

Q: What do you do when they answer the door?

A: I'm looking for so-and-so, you know, or I'm from so-and-so. Something like that. When you go knock you always have to have a good reason.

Q: What would be a good reason? Let's say you knock at my door and I say "What do you want?" What do you say?

A: Well, I'm a pretty perceptive person. Say it was just a little old man. I would say, "Hello, sir. My name is so-and-so (another name) and I need a job very badly. Would you like for me to cut your grass or do something for you?"

And he would say, "Well, not today," or something.

"Well, I'll leave my name and number here with you and if you should need someone, would you call me?" This way they feel more confident *que* you're not a burglar. You're leaving your phone number and you're leaving your name, you see?

Q: I remember that's happened to me two or three times.

A: But you know, that's an old story. But like a good story would be, since there are a lot of people they don't like you to knock on their doors, *pero* you wanna make sure that nobody's in there, so you're making a lot of racket and finally *ella o él se aguita*—he or she gets fed up—and finally they go and answer the door, "Yes?" *Bien aguitados*—really fed up—and you say, "My name is so-and-so and I was noticing that you have a fireplace and I'm selling firewood, and I could deliver whenever you want."

Q: Do you always play the role of the poor guy?

A: Either that or you play the role of you're selling appliances or something like that. You always play the part of something.

Q: Would you return afterward to the same place?

A: No, never.

Q: Never. So a place is disqualified as soon as you knock on the door and somebody comes.

A: Right. If you catch 'em there and like I said, you're pretty perceptive, you see 'em the way they're dressed and everything and you can tell if they're housewives or they're men that they're there all the time.

Q: Do you ever go back to burglarize a house that you burglarized before?

A: No. Well, I have.

Q: Would you carry a gun or is it customary or never?

A: No, never. I don't carry a gun or nothing like that. You'd have to kill somebody and you sure as hell don't want to do that. But there are a lot that do, you know, they do carry guns.

Q: What happens if you get caught in the house?

A: That's how I got this right here. [Scar over eye] Me and this other guy, we were going along, we see this girl, woman really, and she got her purse, and she got in the truck and she went. So naturally we figured at two-thirty in the afternoon or evening, she can't possibly be there. She's got to be at work. So, there's nobody in the house. This is what we figure. But to make sure, we go and knock. Nobody answers, you know.

So I tell my buddy, "You keep on knocking and I'll see if anybody is at home." So he keeps knocking and I go around the house, around the block and then come around the house and the back door is open, so I walk in and my buddy, he's still knocking so I open the door for him, so everybody around there thinks that the people inside opened the door. So he comes in.

So we go in and he goes into the other room and starts looking to see what there is and I see the color TV there. I'm gonna get the damn color TV right away. So I start to pick up the portable color TV. So while I'm bent over like this getting the TV, my buddy, you know, he passes by and he says, "There's a guy asleep in the bedroom, let's get out of here." I don't hear very well, and I didn't see him very good.

Q: You didn't hear him?

A: So I was grabbing the cord, you know, and I get up and there's a big old cowboy like this, see. So this cowboy, he says, "Well, you little son of a bitch," and he had something, a board or something, you know, hit me right there with it.

We were by a table and the door was right there, like the back door was there and the front door was here. So he was way too big for me to even fight with him and you don't want to stay and fight. You want to cut out before someone comes to help him out, you know. You don't want to get busted. So he's on that side of the table and I'm on this side of the table and I'm kind of trying to fake him.

He was covering both sides of the table because he was a big son of a bitch, you know. So he was there and I can't make it out, you know, so I'm thinking of the window right here, you know. When you're like that, bloody like that, blood was coming out of me, you're liable to do anything, you know. This is why I say when you have a gun you might shoot somebody or something, *sin querer*—without wanting to. So in my situation, I guess I was lucky.

Mi camarade, my friend, saw that I didn't come out so he came back through the back door and grabbed an iron and gave it to him right in the nape of the neck. He fell down to his knees, so I just got a chair and hit him with the chair.

Q: You didn't take anything out of that one?

A: Nothing. But he left me really messed up.

Q: What happened to the fellow?

A: We don't know what happened to him. We know he wasn't hurt that bad because when the other guy hit him with the iron he just fell down on his knees and I just pushed him with the chair just to lay down there.

Q: Is that the only time you were ever caught in a house?

A: Yeah.

Q: So you were busted how many times, would you say?

A: I've been busted about three times for burglary and I've been picked up for burglary a lot of times.

Q: A lot of times, but not charged?

A: *Nunca me haceron, nunca me puderon proba*—they never got me, they never could prove it.

Q: Were the police rough on you any time, just to get information?

A: Well, let's say you got busted for burglary. They'll get you and they'll knock the goddamn shit out of you. It's pitiful. They will. One thing the cops, they don't like *a un tecato que anda robando*—an addict who steals. They don't like an addict.

Q: And the police know you as an addict?

A: Right.

Q: Were you on methadone afterwards?

A: Yeah. I was on methadone like for a month. Then I got sent
up.

Q: Is that the last time you went up?

A: Yeah.

Q: Did you get on methadone after you got busted?

A: No. See, like for these burglaries, they didn't bust me in
there, you know, or nothing like that. But they were looking for me
and I got busted. I was hooked then and I got busted and I had to, you
know, cold turkey *en el conda'o*—in the county jail—and I got out on
bond. Then they picked me up for another burglary which was about
a month old *pero levantaron los* fingerprints—they picked up the
fingerprints—so then I had to cold turkey again.

So, the last time that I did get out on bond they put me on
methadone so I started methadone, started working, just when I was
really getting started really neat—at that time methadone had just
come out, it hadn't been out very long. That was about sixty-nine. So
by that time they called me to court, they found me guilty and gave
me two nickels—one to five for burglary, one to five for larceny.

Q: How much time did you spend in Santa Fe that time?

A: Two years. I've just been out about a month and a half,
maybe two months now.

Q: The first time you went up, you spent how much time?

A: The first time I did a year. I went to board in six months and
I made it within six months . . . setup.

Q: A projected parole date of six months?

A: Yeah. So actually I did a year. So I got out and I stayed out
about a year. Then I went back and did fourteen months that I had
left. Did that, and got out and stayed out for about seven, eight
months. Got busted again.

Q: So you've been up there about four and a half years?

A: Four and a half altogether.

Q: You said the police mistreated you. What did they do?
Suppose that you were busted today—is there mistreatment or just
harassment or is it physical?

A: Harassment and physical you know. And the thing that really
bugs me more sometimes, *son los mismos* Chicanos—it's the very
Chicanos, you know, *los juras*—the cops. Of course, they got a job to
do, but it's the very Chicanos that give it to you. La Raza.

Q: What did they do to you?

A: They took me over there to a ditch, there in Armijo. The one that got busted that was working for the county, that detective, what's his name? Remember he got busted because he was trying to make out with that broad *aquí en la mesa*—here on the mesa?

Q: Oh, yeah, yeah, yeah.

A: He was just a young kid, but that guy was always messing around with us. He always used to stop us in front of all the people and say, "Put your hands up," and he would take out his pistol and who knows what else. But this guy took me to the ditch, and he and another guy, and they really gave it to me and then they brought me and left me at home.

Q: Trying to get information from you or what?

A: Oh, like if I wanted to go score from you and then set you up, you know. They were trying to get a sale on him. Like if you were pushing stuff, if I wanted to go score from you and give him the stuff and that way they would have a sale on you.

Q: In other words, trying to force you to agree to set someone up?

A: Right.

Q: How about when you get picked up for something else?

A: The same thing happens.

Q: Say, they pick you up for suspicion of burglary.

A: The same thing happens. See, they get a burglary and they go and investigate you for burglary and everything, and then suddenly they say, "You wanna make a little money? Five, six hundred dollars? Why don't you get a sale from this guy and this guy and this guy, and we'll give you this much money and you can blow out of town." See, they don't give a shit if you've got a family or not and they don't know that if you squeal on these guys you put your whole family in jeopardy. You're not going to live right for the rest of your life.

Q: Are there a lot of guys that do it, though?

A: Oh, yeah.

Q: They agree to set somebody up?

A: Well, it's happening now. All them guys they been picking up in raids and all that, well, somebody's setting them up. It's not a cop all the time that they make a sale to.

Q: You read in the papers about these undercover agents buying—

A: Yeah, undercover agents. That's what they call them. Because at the time when he's making the sale for the cops he is an "undercover agent." But that's the way they put it because they're not gonna put his name there. Because for the simple reason that if they put his name there, these guys can get out on bond and they know who the guy is already, see. But if they don't have his name there, well, they're curious to know who the hell it was and then when they get to court, he's right there. He has to testify.

Q: In Santa Fe were you able to get heroin?
A: Well, yeah. About fifteen, sixteen caps a day.
Q: That's a pretty heavy habit.
A: Not compared to some guys I've known that are taking a hell of a lot more than that.
Q: Is that right?
A: Yeah.
Q: But they also have to go and burglarize places and get the money out of some place.
A: It doesn't specifically have to be burglaries. Some of the guys, they have different ways of making money. Like armed robbery, strong-arm robbery, or they've got a girl *que* she's addicted *también.* She goes and gives the guy some bread.
Q: She'll prostitute?
A: Yeah. She goes and gives the guy some bread. Or she goes and takes a guy to the side and the guy is waiting and they bash him on the head *y agarran su dinero*—and get his money.
Q: How about . . . do a lot of the guys that are addicted make money by selling the stuff? Selling heroin or any other drug?
A: Yeah.
Q: When did your teeth get knocked out?
A: *Ya me faltan como siete*—I'm missing about seven already.
Q: Did they get knocked out or—
A: Yeah, well I already had them in, *no más que ahora para el* riot *me agarraron unas juras y me las chingaron todos*—except that during the riot, some cops grabbed me and screwed them all up. So now I have to buy them, you know. Maybe I will do it if I get in school. And if I don't find another job within a month I'm gonna have to do something. Get in school . . .
Q: What school?
A: Well, I got some hours in carpentry.
Q: Did you take it in Santa Fe?
A: Yeah. *Pero* very, very little and not that much interest. I took it because I had to, you know. They didn't want to give it to me and they didn't want to change me, and they told me, "You better go, and if you don't go . . ." Right now, I'm having a problem. See, I need

glasses. Like right now I'm driving without a driver's license and they don't want to give me a license. Because I need glasses. And I want to get a job but if I do get a job I need a driver's license, you know, to drive. So *ahora* I've got more or less like a permit . . .

Q: Does your wife work?

A: Yeah. No. But right now she is working, because we need the money. *Estamos medio atracados*—we're half broke—so she's working. She's doing housework.

Q: You have one daughter?

A: One daughter . . . Well, they say that any ex-convict can't work in a federal job or a job like this. You know, we had some . . . like the program that we got now, Esperanza, *es puro* group therapy. They're trying to help ex-convicts, the penal institution, or whatever, and for once we got some guys who are really good and really know how to get across to these kids. Because these kids, they would rather listen to a guy like me than to a guy with a cap or with a big ole star. They feel very nervous *cuando miran una jura asi que* he's talking to them—when they look at a cop like that, that he's talking to them.

Q: So there has to be some way to arrange a program—

A: We got this program from here in Santa Fe, they came and they're gonna give 'em two hundred and fifty, two hundred and sixty thousand dollars for housing projects of New Mexico government. So it's already approved and they're gonna get this money by the end of May, I think, and they want to spread this money around so they could get halfway houses *para pintos*—for convicts, halfway houses *para chavalas*, for girls, and for young kids . . .

Q: Who's working for it?

A: The guys from Santa Fe. They came down to talk to Martin, these guys that head Esperanza.

Q: Do you know their names?

A: *Son pintos*—they're convicts. He's the only ex-con on the board, on their board. So I think they're just gonna have to think it over and see what happens. Because whenever we start out a good program like that, now it's called "Esperanza," afterwards it will be called something else, pretty soon the city wants to take over and that's the way it goes. Like the Colony.

Q: You were telling us something about Santa Fe.

A: In prison? What do you want to talk about?

Q: Let's talk about when you went in there first. Some of your impressions and experiences.

A: When I went in I was nineteen years old, gonna be twenty. I didn't think it was a big deal but I thought it was something like . . . you better be cool, you know.

Q: Were you scared?

A: No. Fear no, because fighting for my principles and all that, I've always done that, you know. But I don't know . . . to walk into a penitentiary when you're not sure if you know anybody there, five or six guys could jump you. I'll just put it this way, when you're that young there are guys that have been inside for eight or nine years and they wanna screw you, in other words. But like now, in my situation, I already had guys that were in the reform school with me. I already had guys that would help me. *Pero no me baqueaban*—but they don't back me—unless I stand up for myself. But I already had all that, so I never had much of a problem in that way.

One time I did. This guy, this guy tried and I had to, you know, straighten him out. Like I was a friend, you know. These guys, they can really con you. So I thought this guy was a pretty good friend *pero como te digo*—but like I say—I'm pretty, you know, perceptive, and I realized more or less what was going on. He just started talking and everything, so I took him out to the day room and we really gave it to each other.

But these guys that are getting busted now for anything, eighteen years old, there's some dudes that are sixteen years old. Guys here outside think they're really tough SOBs, but outside they can grab a gun. When they get inside, that's where they really show how they really are. So these young dudes, now they're not like that . . . *no son jotos ni nada de eso*—they're not queers or anything—but they make them that way.

Like they go tell a dude this way: "You're doing two to ten years. You're going to be here three, four years." They scare him right away. "You're going to stay about three, four years here and these guys, they wanna screw you."

They tell him, "I'll give you what you want and I'll protect you and these guys aren't going to get to you. And you just give me a break and these guys aren't gonna screw you. And if you don't like it this way, these guys, they're all gonna get you and I'm gonna get some there too and we're all gonna do it any time we want to. Now, if you wanna rat, well, go ahead, but they're gonna lock you up and that's where you're gonna have to stay."

So that's what's going on with these young dudes. There's some guys in there act like girls. The wives of the guards, they send clothes to be washed in the laundry. The guys steal bras and panties and a lot of guys wear them and, oh, man, all that shit is going on in there now. And like there's a lot of fighting going on between races, there is *mucho.* The Chicanos and *mayates*—blacks—mostly.

Q: Are there a lot of *mayates?*

A: Oh, yeah. Lots. *Que bárbaro!* Man! There's a ton of blacks. There are more blacks and Chicanos than anything else.

Q: Do they mix them in the cell blocks?

A: Oh, yeah. They have to mix 'em because if they don't, they'll really mess them up. You can't do that in an institution. You can't keep them in one place and the Chicanos in another. You gotta, you know, like they say, this is the United States and you all gotta live together and you might as well make the best of it. That's against the law. *Pero,* there is a lot of fighting going on, *y* harassment from the screws, all that you know. This is the reason why the riot started, you know.

Q: The *mayate* was a *pinto?*—the black was a convict?

A: Yeah. But he didn't say nothing. He just walked up to the TV and changed it. A Chicano stood up and says to him, "Hey, man. You just been here like a month. You better learn how to respect your fellow convicts. You can't be changing the goddamn TV any time you want to or just doing anything you want to around here," he said.

The black thought he was really tough and they gave it to him. So the next morning, that Chicano, they went to eat in the morning, and right after breakfast about eight or nine blacks came, and like they say these *mayates* are thirty-one, thirty-two, thirty-three. They came in and they got this guy in bed and knocked the shit out of him.

Q: The Chicano?

A: Yeah. There weren't many Chicanos inside because they were all eating breakfast. So we started a big old thing right there in the hall, you know, and nobody wanted to get locked up back in the dormitories. We all wanted to go and straighten out that thing right there. The Chicanos there are very united, and the blacks are very united, and we were gonna have it out. So we arranged that and they locked up two blacks and five Chicanos.

So the blacks got together, they know what the hell's going on. So now they're thinking *que* they want us to get together—*los* Chicanos *y los mayates.* So now we get together and we plan a riot. So that's what we did, we planned a riot, against the administration. So that's the way it goes. *Pero* the thing that I'm pretty strong on—poor guys, you know, especially the young ones. You can just imagine what happens to a guy. He's a pretty cool guy but he's young. He's not a snitch or anything and they take him there and they do sodomy to him or something like that, and that is gonna change his whole life.

Q: Does that happen at Springer, too?

A: Oh, yeah. But very, very rarely.

Q: Why does it happen so much more at the pen?

A: Well, like you're sleeping right next door to a guy like that and the screw's not here all the time. Like the screw's way over there all the time. And they all watch out for the other guy. They put a lookout there because I'm gonna go in and give it to this guy. The guy don't fight for himself so what is anybody else going to do? So a guy comes and he lets him and another one comes and another . . . and that's just the way it goes. You know, pretty soon the guy gets so used to it that he starts being like that, like I tell you, it changes his whole life.

A lot of mothers—their sons, you know, have had the courage to tell their mothers what the hell is going on and yet their parents, they don't wanna do anything about it because they don't want to get involved with a political thing like that, because eventually it would get into a political thing. And that's the way it goes. *Chavalos*, poor guys, and you know their parents send 'em money and they have to give the money to the guy. They gotta pay for protection and things like that.

The administration is like, I come and ask, "Mr. So-and-So, why don't you let me work here because I feel better if I do this type of work than this type of work."

You ask me why and I tell you, "Because I feel better."

Then you ask, "Don't you get along with those guys over there?"

And I'll say, "Yeah, I get along with them but I'd rather work over there."

Q: Because you don't want to tell him the real reason that you want to move out of there?

A: Yeah. Still I feel that they should put me there if I feel that it's gonna be better for me. But no. There they just tell you, "You're gonna work at the laundry, and if you don't go to the laundry you go to a kangaroo court," where they tell you, "You lost six months and you're going back to the laundry."

Q: They don't give you any way to defend yourself?

A: No way. Like you go to court and the school makes a report on you, and you ain't got no—no authority to talk for your rights. No nothing. You know, they're just gonna do whatever they want to do and that's it for you. That's the way it is. There's a lot of tensions there right now, you know. There's a lot of bitterness. *Todo hay*—there's everything.

Q: Do they allow you to see your wives there?

A: Visits every Sunday, you get five visits a month.

Q: Do you get any privacy?

A: No privacy. *Nada.*

Q: Is it your wife on one side and you on the other?

A: Right.

Q: So they don't have conjugal visits? Where you can have relations with your wife?

A: Nothing like that. You can only kiss her when she comes in and kiss her when she leaves. That's it.

Q: Must be pretty hard on the guys that are there for ten years?

A: Yeah. Yeah, them guys are really . . . well, a lot of them have sense enough to forget sodomy and all that, you know, and if a guy is doing life, he's got to look forward to doing ten years, and that's what he's gonna do before he even goes to the first court. Like there's a lot of dudes in there that educate themselves, learn this trade and that trade. They already know when they're going to the board. They might make it, they might get out. It gives them something to look forward to, whereas these other dudes, they don't want to learn a damn thing. They go around bullying these young kids, they're taking advantage of young kids, and that's their kick, you know. They figure, "Well, I'm doing life and I'm not gonna be out anyway. I might as well get what I can *aquí.*"

Q: Is that the worst thing you see going on?

A: I think that is the worst thing that is going on, but the food is bad. People think it's not because when people go to visit or eat, they always know when these people are coming, you know. So in other words they always prepare special food so it looks good. But when these people leave it's back to corn that's not worth a damn and meat that, you know, you can't eat it. It's like rubber. The guys get fed up. They get there with the tray and just throw the tray and leave. And things like that, you know.

When a tour gets there, they lock all the grills and they lock us up. We could never talk to them. And if we would try to talk to them, when they left, they would lock us up and they'd take us to the hole and knock the shit out of us. So that's why everybody was pretty—*todos estaban espantados.* Everybody was afraid. They had everybody afraid. And now that this riot broke out, if you notice, there's a lot of guys that what they're saying, they're telling the truth because they have grown out of that *espantado que los tenían*—the fright that they had. Now they're talking. They're not afraid to talk because they know that they're gonna be protected now. But before, no one said anything. They had us pretty well *controlados*—under control, you know.

Q: Did you talk to the grand jury?

A: No. The guys they took to the jury, maybe two or three of them were good guys. The other guys were planted. They had planted them there.

Q: What did the other prisoners feel about the guys that were planted?

A: *Esos vatos salieron*—those guys got out.

Q: They're out?

A: The majority. Those guys are like snitches. They know something is wrong but they don't have the courage to say it because they're doing too much time and they want to get out. If they have to lie for the administration, they'll do it. Just so long as the administration puts in a good word for them when they go to the board, and that's the way it goes.

Then, something would break out between races, that the blacks are going to have it out with the Chicanos. There are some gringos that are going with the blacks and some are going with the Chicanos. The Chicanos control the whole prison if they want. All in all, they're not that united but now they can control it whenever they want to. *Pero* as far as deadly weapons or things like that, they could get them in like that. They got knives and everything. They just go out into the yard and grab bats, switchblades, and everything. They say that the penitentiary is secure, but you can make it out. If you want to escape, you can. If you're a guy with sense enough to know how to do it, you could get out, you know.

They got 'em all mixed up, you know . . . *a los jotos con todos acina*—the homosexuals with everybody else. The homosexuals are running around all over the halls. "Hey, man, I'm playing poker. I'll give you some and you just give me two or three dollars," you know. They go around like that.

Q: Do you get money, and how do you spend it?

A: As far as money—it's like Hi Hos, Fritos, things like that. Things that you buy at the store.

Q: Do you get paid for some of the work you do?

A: Well, I was working in IBM. You know, keypunch, and I was getting paid for that. They've got two or three jobs where they pay you to work. But they never had that before. The reason why they admitted all that now is because it was looking too bad for them, you know. They had to do something to make it look good.

Like these furloughs that they have now. You gotta have a year's clear record and you might get a furlough and come and visit your family and go back. But they started that because of the riot. They looked bad when that riot broke out. They looked real bad, you know. The way they handled the whole situation. Because that riot wouldn't have started because we told that guy, "Okay, you're gonna come talk to us because *todos eramos* spokesmen, *vez?*—all of us were spokesmen, you see?" We had two guys from each dormitory and we all went and talked to the warden. There was about sixteen, seventeen guys.

So we went over there and we said to him, "We don't want to start anything. We just want you to do this and this." We weren't asking for nothing. We were just asking for the rightful things that, you know, that they were supposed to be there and they weren't. "Or if you don't want to do it this way, we'll tear this whole place down." We had to act like that.

So then he decided, "I'll talk to you guys tomorrow." So he didn't come. He sent Contereas, Contereas came and we went and talked to Contereas, and he told us, "You guys tear the place down but you guys know you're gonna lose." Well, why in the hell is he talking to us that way for? If he really knew how to handle his job, he would say, "Well, you guys play it cool and you guys are making it hard on yourselves." But no, he says, "Go ahead and tear it down."

So we told him, you know, "Okay, by tomorrow, by one-thirty, nobody is going out to eat." There was already one day that we hadn't gone. "By tomorrow at one-thirty, we want to see some people from the free world. We want to talk to some people from the free world with authority. We want to talk to them, and let them know what the hell is going on. And if you don't have them here, we're gonna tear it down. Whether we lose or whether we don't."

He says, "Well, I'll talk to you guys tomorrow at one-thirty." So he waited. He was there all the time, and you know what he did? He went and gave gas masks to all the guards, and he gave them clubs and everything, when all he had to do was call us at one-thirty and talk to us, you know . . . try to cool everything down some more. So at one-thirty we started throwing the whole place down. And that's where it went worse for them than for us.

Q: Did you spend any time in solitary confinement?

A: I was in solitary four months.

Q: After the riot?

A: I was one of the fifteen to get out. When I made the board now in February, I had about a week out of solitary.

Q: How come you made the board?

A: I don't know. I figure it was time, I guess. I didn't think I was gonna make it, you know. I was planning on getting my GED. My wife had already wrote a letter to the board and well, I don't think that helped or nothing . . . I don't know. I went to the board and they gave me parole. Like another guy that was messing up, they let him out too—

Q: Were you considered maybe a troublemaker?

A: No.

Q: Why did they keep you in solitary confinement?

A: When that riot broke out, yeah, I was considered one of the instigators.

Q: Was that a good way to get rid of you?

A: Yeah. It was. Like you get mixed up in a riot and they want to say that you're an instigator and they don't have no proof. Now, they can't go to the board and say, "Don't give parole to this guy because he's an instigator." No. Because if they do that to me, I can't get in any deeper than I already am, so I'm gonna fight 'em all the way, you know. I'm gonna put prejudice and everything against that board if they do something like that to me. Or if I even think that they're doing it, that's what I'm gonna do. Now, I'm a lot wiser in law. I know more or less my constitutional rights, things like that, you know, so I know more or less how to go about it. And I'll throw writs at them with my attorney, you know, to turn me loose. But they can't go to the board or they can't say to any member, "Well, this guy, we think he's an instigator."

I'm not saying that it don't happen because it does. But when the riot broke out, they would have looked very bad with all that publicity goin' on. They would of looked very bad if they would of said anything against anybody.

Q: What kind of difficulties have you found since you got out? You were out last time for a year. What were the main problems you think you had?

A: The main problem that I had was being married. I wasn't the kind of guy that was used to being married, staying home, fixing up the house a little, water the grass. I never was that kind of guy.

Me and my wife, we argued a lot. She's forever, she's trying to do good for me, *tú sabes?* She's always trying to help me out, but you know, the way she does it, I tell her that I don't appreciate the way she does it. I appreciate what she's trying to do but I don't think much of the way she's doing it. Even now we get into some bad arguments, and sometimes I just get disgusted and I get in my car and take off like a stupid ass sometimes, you know. *Pero* then I just ride around and I'm thinking about it. I just go off and cool off and then I come back. But before I used to tell her, "I'll see you go and get yourself a divorce if you want, and I don't give a damn what you do." Things like that.

Q: She waited for you while you were in prison this time?

A: She's waited for me three times already.

Q: But before—you weren't married.

A: Yeah. Right.

Q: Except the last time when you got sent up, were you married?

A: Yeah.

Q: Did you get married when you were out on parole last time?

A: Yeah. I got out in sixty-seven, got married in sixty-eight, went back in sixty-eight, she waited for me; went back in sixty-nine and she waited for me up till now.

Q: Then actually most of the time you've been in prison?

A: I've been locked up. I'm out for a while, and sometimes it just seems like I'm doing pretty good *y* everything just goes haywire, you know. But I know the problem now, if I can stay *como* now without heroin, they're not gonna get me again. I'm not taking any methadone . . . I'm not taking anything.

Q: You feel okay?

A: Uh-huh. I get methadone there whenever I want it, whenever I want it, I get *cómo se dice?*—priority to get it right away and I don't have to stand in line or nothing. *Pero,* you know, like my parole officer told me, I thought I was gonna have to go on methadone but he told me, "If you feel like you can make it without methadone, there's no sense in even taking it if you're not hooked on anything."

And you know, well, this is what I was thinking while I was locked up. That I wasn't gonna take nothing. Since I got out I'm not taking nothing. I've been out two months.

Q: So, two months then with no problem?

A: Two months and nothing yet. *Ando muy bien*—I'm doing very well.

Q: *Muy bien.* What would be the kind of circumstances in which you feel that you might have problems? That you might start feeling a need for heroin again?

A: It's not a need. It's like somebody took something to relax. Let's say that I have a bad argument with my wife. Let's say that I get into a very, very bad argument with her and that I get mad and everything, because this is what happened before.

Q: That's the reason you might go back?

A: Yeah, right now that would be about my only reason because I don't have a problem with going around stealing anymore. I don't get a kick out of that.

Q: How about financially?

A: Financially? Well, like I don't pay any rent and—

Q: Where do you live?

A: Well, right now we're with my, you know, mother-in-law. When we got married they gave a house to my wife, see, so she's gonna move out now—

Q: Your mother-in-law?

A: Yeah, and she's going with, ah, my wife's brother. So I mean right now I don't have any, like I don't pay any rent, there's very little bills. They're not mine. They're my mom's and they're my wife's but I'm gonna pay them off because she's been helping out my wife since I was locked up, so I feel that it's only right that I pay her bills, which isn't very much—about two, three hundred dollars. But I don't have any bills. I never realized what it was to have bills. In other words, responsibility and all that jive.

Now, I feel if I have something that I owe, bills or something like that, I go and do it, and I have to pay it—well, then, I know that this is something that I have to do. I'm thinking about that every time that I feel kind of run down. Man, if that's the way to keep out of trouble, that's great by me. So far I've been doing pretty good.

Q: How do you think the probation officer or the parole officer—what effect has he had on you?

A: Nothing. I just go out and I fill out my report. I know one thing, before when I used to have a problem, I never asked anybody for anything. My way out was that if I had a problem, I used to smooth it out with the burglaries and get a little money and go have a little fun and that's the way I'd always forget it. The way I feel now, if I have a problem now, I'm gonna ask for help, you know, and try to get some kind of help from someone or something.

Q: So you're saying that you might see your parole officer if you have a problem?

A: Yeah, well, not long ago when I got out I had a problem. I have a car. So I got this job, see, and I gotta drive at four o'clock in the morning to work, which was right here at a bakery, you know, way over there from the South Valley. That's a long ways. So, I tell him I'm driving without a license because I got a job and I got a damn good job, you know, they're paying me two thirty-five an hour, and I just got it but the problem is that I need a driver's license and they won't let me have a driver's license unless I get my glasses. So I ain't got no money to go and get my glasses, so he referred me to DVR. And they were trying to help me, so finally they told me that they would help me if I would get into some kind of trade school. *Pero* they won't pay you to go to school and I got a family that I have to support, and my wife, she's not getting any more welfare since I got out, so now I have to do these things.

So I told him, "I can't get in school. I gotta find a job one way or the other." Maybe if I would get ahead on my bills and everything, well, maybe I could start going to school. So then, you know, DVR couldn't help me so they referred me to these people. So now I got my glasses. I just went for the frame and the lens and everything so in about eight or nine days I'll get my glasses, and I can get my license. Then I can get me a good job right away and I don't have to worry about anything.

Q: You lost your job because you couldn't drive?

A: No. The car broke down one morning, and any bakery that you work, small bakeries, all them bakeries are strict, you know—you got to be there on time. Well, anyway I called up on a Saturday morning, I was supposed to go in at six, and I called up and I told them, you know, that my car didn't want to start and, well, I am a long way from there and I don't got nobody around here that I could call or somebody that could come and bring me—not at six in the morning anyway.

So he said, "Well, are you sick?" and I said "No, not exactly, but my car is . . . you know, just don't want to start."

He said, "Come in Monday." So I went in Monday and they had my check there and I just went and got my check.

Q: How long did you work there?

A: I hadn't been out more than three weeks. Right after I got out, that same week I started working there.

Q: Did they know you were—

A: No, see, that's the hell of it. I can't do, you know, too much trouble because they don't know that I'm an ex-con.

Q: Do you think if they knew it would be different?

A: They wouldn't even hire me if they'd knew. But Mr. Weems's bakery, I was working there and I had about a week there so I finally told him, you know, what I was and everything. He understood very . . . *muy suave*—very nice.

Q: Was that the last time?

A: Yeah, before I went to Santa Fe. Just a little before I went to Santa Fe I started working for him. They started giving me methadone then and I wasn't shooting anymore or nothing, and he gave me a job and I was doing pretty good on methadone, but they called me to trial. I went to trial and they gave me a sentence.

Q: How did you feel about the trial? How do you feel about going to court?

A: Well, before I never did take it very serious, you know. It all depended on the charge that I was charged, like if it was in a city jail or something like that, I was sent to one of them small courts. I wouldn't take them serious at all. I knew that I was gonna get out in a couple of hours or something like that, that they would come and bail me out or something. *Pero* these district courts . . . I don't know. I guess I always took it like "what the heck," now I realize that it's pretty serious. I know when they got me busted cold and I know when I'm gonna be found guilty even if I plead not guilty. Even before I go to court I know what's gonna happen. I already know how much time I'm gonna get.

Q: Did you ever spend much time in city jail or county jail?

A: Well, in sixty-four, that's when I really started getting busted to city jail. If you recall 1964, they used to pick us up a lot for illegal use of narcotics. Remember that they were forever picking up guys for this illegal use of narcotics, and that's what I was getting busted for—illegal use and things like that.

Q: You usually bailed out?

A: Yeah. I did a little time, about sixty days, something like that.

Q: In city or county?

A: City, and then in sixty-five like every three months I got busted for something. A lot of times, and the majority of those times I was not even supposed to be in jail, *pero* they just locked me up because they couldn't really catch me. If they felt that, you know, that they had something on me that they could keep me for a while. They would just do it to harass me. So they would bust me up with a bum rap like illegal use of narcotics.

One time they busted me for that and *este—comó se llama?* —what's his name?—Luna, it seems to me that he was a detective, Luna, and he said, "Okay, I'm gonna give you a break, why don't you go." And when I was walking down the stairs, I just left and this other detective came and he got me and booked me back up again. Well, what kind of a deal was that? Of course, they got me, they were already after me for anything they could catch me. But even yet I mean they wanna go by the law. Well, shit, you know, if they want you, why don't they get you while they have you? I mean when they can really get you. But if they want to go by the law, well, they should go by the law, you know.

Q: Did you hire your own attorney or were they appointed?

A: Both times that I've gone up, I've hired my own attorney.

Q: Your mom would help you out?

A: My mom, my mother-in-law, my wife, even before I was married to my wife, my mother-in-law, my mother, and my wife were always helping me, even seven, eight years before I married this woman.

Q: How about your experiences in city jail? What kind of place was it? I guess you were in the old city jail?

A: Yeah.

Q: You were in Montessa Park?

A: No. Oh, no. They never took me there.

Q: They didn't feel they could trust you?

A: They never wanted to trust me, I guess, because you know at the city jail when you're doing thirty days, they ask you if you want to go to the Park. Well, they take you over there and if you're doing thirty days, over there you only do fifteen. But now if you stay at the city jail, you've got to do thirty. Always half of your time. But they never took me there. *Pero* as far as the city jail, it's a, you know—if people . . . I feel if people could really see what the hell goes on in there . . .

Q: What do you mean?

A: At the city jail, especially with old people, you know, with old men, what you would say, winos. If people could see what is happening to these poor old men, they're old now and they're really in bad shape. Well, you and I know how an old man—drunk like that—is gonna act. He's gonna act all stupid *y todo*. They should excuse him a little, but no, they get him and knock the hell out of him and then when he goes down to court they say, "assaulting an officer," and all this, you know. An old man, I can't see how an old man, drunk, is gonna assault a guy twenty-two, twenty-five years old. In what way is an old man like that gonna assault a cop?

Y pobrecitos—and poor guys stay for sixty, thirty days with their eyes all messed up, they throw them inside and leave them there. They never took them to the hospital *ni nada*. They really had to be dying.

Like you remember Juan Arellano. He's around your age—you're around thirty-seven, thirty-six?

Q: Thirty-three.

A: Thirty-three? Well, he would have been around thirty-seven now.

Q: Was he a wino?

A: No. This guy wasn't a wino. This guy wasn't nothing. This guy he would take pills. That's all, that's all the guy used to do. To me that's nothing.

Pero like this guy he was with me that night, you know. This was in sixty-four, somewhere around there, and me and this guy we were together and we went and we stole a big old jack, you know, a big old hydraulic jack, from a filling station, and we went and sold it for twenty-five dollars. So there we went, you know, and like I said before I never took any pills, I never had a problem like that. But he did, but not much. Anyway he told me to drop him off by his house, at this apartment, so I dropped him up there. Then his landlady came out and told him, "I'm not gonna let you take your clothes and you're not going in there until you pay me the rent." You know, it was five dollars and by that time he didn't have no five dollars and I didn't have anything either.

So he said take me to Pajaro's house. Do you remember a guy they used to call Pajaro?

Q: I remember the name but I can't recall—

A: Yeah, he was always getting busted. So anyway I took him down *a casa el Pajaro*, somebody opened the door for him, well, I said, "Okay, he's all right, everything's all right."

Then when I went home, this other guy came for me, so we went to a dance and everything. But before we went, we decided to pull a burglary, which was, you know, what I went to prison for the first time, except that I stayed out about two years before I even went to trial. So anyway while we were out pulling the burglary we didn't know that this place had a silent alarm. It was, you know, a commercial place.

So now we got cops looking all over for us, and by this time this guy that I took over there . . . he's walking nearby.

Q: Arellano?

A: Yeah. He's walking, oh, about two or three blocks nearby, eh? And the cops are all over there, because they're looking for us, eh? They don't catch me but—

Q: They busted Arellano?

A: I took him down to Pajaro's, see? And somebody else came and picked me up, another friend. So we went and pulled a burglary. But Arellano didn't go into Pajaro's house, he started walking back to town. So while we were pulling all this shit over here, he was walking way over here, see. So when I got out, you know, they busted my friend and I got away clean. And now they were looking for another guy all around there. So Arellano, they picked him up, and he had a straight razor in his pocket . . . so right away they said, "Drunk and carrying a deadly weapon," so they lock him up.

So when my friend is busted I'm over there getting a bondsman and everything *para sacarlo*—to get him out, so by the time I took him out, we arranged everything with a lawyer and I got him out and everything, Arellano had already been put in the city jail. He was already in bed *asina*—like that. The next morning they found him dead.

Q: They found him dead? Why?

A: Uh, they said because he was sleeping . . . there in the cell they ain't got no bunks, they ain't got no nothing, you know. Like if you have to fall asleep you're gonna fall asleep flat—you know, just flat *y se ahogó*—he suffocated, he threw up and he suffocated.

Q: He was drunk?

A: Well, very little, he wasn't that drunk, because he knew where he was going. He couldn't have been that drunk. So maybe, you know maybe, if they would get some of those bunks or something in there . . . Who knows how many guys have died there, and they don't do very much about it? *Se han colgado vatos allí*—guys have hanged themselves there.

Q: You know of cases *que se han colgado?* They have hanged themselves?

A: Do you remember Cristobal's brother? What was his name? You know which one, he was always in the detention home. Well, this was Cristobal's brother, the youngest. I don't know, but every time they used to take him to the D home, they used to have to lock him up in—wasn't it number fifteen?

Q: For raising hell?

A: He was always raising hell, yeah. He was in city jail and he was banging on the doors *y todo el pedo*—and everything. "You better come get me out of here or I'm gonna hang myself."

"Go ahead and hang yourself," *le dijeron*—they told him, and that's what he did.

Q: How old was he?

A: Shit. I think I was older than him. I'm twenty-six so he would have been about twenty-five now.

Q: How many years ago was that?

A: This was about two or three years ago. Not too long ago.

Q: How about the county jail? Did you ever do any time there?

A: Yeah. In the county jail I've done about four, three months, you know. But the times I have done it, it was always on my way to Santa Fe, waiting to be transferred over there and all that. I've never been locked up for drunk or nothing like that.

Q: Was the county jail easier than the city jail?

A: Oh, yeah. They feed you a hell of a lot better at the county jail than the city jail. In the morning they give you mush. You know what mush is? They just throw two weenies inside and—

Q: In the city jail?

A: Yeah, and some jelly on all that mush, and then the bread right on top of everything *asina*. Everything like that. All stuck together.

Q: How about the county?

A: Oh, the county, *Agarras un* tray *acina*—you got a tray, like this, like on Sunday morning you get eggs with potatoes and, well, things that you can eat, you know, chicken and everything. At city jail you don't get nothing like that. At the last before I got sent up, they were only feeding them once.

Q: Are you serious?

A: Yeah. Like, you know, they feed you in the morning and they won't feed you any more. They would transfer you to Montessa Park.

Q: Oh, yeah. But you weren't there?

A: No. I was in the old place. In the old place they were already doing that. They were only feeding you once, and then in the evening they would transfer you over there and I guess you would eat there. I don't know. I just got to the city and I just stayed there about three or four hours. Then I got transferred to the county jail.

Q: Is there any difference between the police in the county and the police in the city? Do you think there is a difference, what kind of difference?

A: Well, the city goes more by the book, well, not more by the book. Let's say that they want to be more strict.

Q: They know the law better?

A: Yeah, they know. I can't say but it seems like they just want to show you something. But the county, they don't go by the book. *Pero* I guess anybody like me, I guess they would tell you that the county treats 'em better. You know, they're more considerate towards any man, I guess, or whoever gets busted. City jail, they pull you in and if your mom's there they also pull her in and lock her up. Like that guy they shot. Now *porque lo mataron?*—why did they kill him?

Q: Did you know him?

A: No. They just learned his real identity. I know damn well that if I would be a cop and I would stop two guys like that and tell them, "You're under arrest," and turn around and search them, and then make a call, you know, but I wouldn't panic or nothing like that, and that's exactly what that cop did. Then that cop, he shouldn't even be a cop because if he's gonna panic like that, he's gonna go around shooting people. They're supposed to be training them, so why in the hell don't they train them to be, you know, perceptive and know their job the way they should? They don't have to go around shooting people.

Q: Francisco, do you think the police of the city know about all of these fences in town?

A: Oh, they know. What they know, they know. But what they get them for is something else. Like they just bust some guy for something. As soon as they bust him they ask him, "Who are the fences," you know, "do you know them?"

Like let's say they had somebody under suspicion and they ask the guy *"Cómo la está haciendo aquel vato?"*—"How is that guy doing it? Are you selling him a lot of shit?"

And he says, "Who?" and they say, "So-and-so."

And they ask him, "Have you sold him anything lately?"

"No. Not lately." Well, right there they know he is a fence, man.
So, there they go and they watch the place and if they're looking for
him, eventually they're gonna get him.

Q: Do you know of some fences that have been busted?

A: Yeah. Oh, yeah. And like I say eventually they're gonna bust
'em. They don't have to go out and really try and get 'em *pero* they
know now that the guy's a fence *y* eventually he's gonna get busted
because they're gonna investigate another guy like that, and they're
gonna tell him, "Well, why don't you go sell him this for us?" And
while he's selling that *le pegan*—they nail him—and they got him.

Q: Setting him up?

A: Another rat, yeah. And that's the way they do it. And like if
you don't want to rat, well, "I'll just take you out back and I'll whip
the goddamn shit out of you and then I'll take you back upstairs and
in about two or three hours, well, I'll bring you back and what do you
feel like saying to me now?"

Q: Does this happen often?

A: It happens every day. Well, let's not say every day but
something like this is always going on, you know, especially if the
guy's an addict. Like a guy's an addict *y lo encierran*—he's been
locked up. Well, they know he's hooked. They already know that if
they take him back up there and lock him up, in three or four hours
that guy's gonna get sick. You know, he's gonna start craving for it and
all that, so in about three or four hours they call upstairs and they say,
"Bring that guy down here. We want to talk to him," the detectives.

So they go and they bring him. Now they already have him in
bad shape and everything and they're ready. "Well, what do you feel
like saying? We'll let you off and give you this fifty-dollar bill, you
know. You go fix and everything, just tell us this."

And that's the way it goes. *Y salen las ratas*—the snitches leave—
and pretty soon they have to make it out of town, see?

Q: Francisco, why are there so many fences in town?

A: Why? Well, because some fences are pretty . . . they've
been fences for years and years and years.

Q: How come they are able to stay in business?

A: Why? Well, because . . . uh, well, I'm gonna put it this way.
To start with they have a business.

Q: A legitimate business?

A: Right. A legitimate business. So secondly, he's just making
more money, a hell of a lot more money on the side and, you know,
not any cop is gonna go over there and try to bust him, because he

already has a legitimate business and "You mess around with me too much and I've got the money to back myself up."

So, "We're not gonna mess with you." That's the way the cops think. You're just gonna have to find somebody to set him up, and I will admit to find somebody to set him up is gonna be pretty hard, because you know not everybody wants to go over there and snitch on that guy. Especially if that guy has money, he's gonna . . . you know, I mean he can send somebody out to kill you, knowing that you set him up. So not anybody is gonna want to do something like that.

Q: When you were getting rid of the stuff you were stealing, did you know the fences, did you actually know the people who were in charge of them?

A: Yes. I knew. I knew the people that owned the place. As a matter of fact, I used to borrow money from them all the time. I used to borrow two hundred, three hundred dollars and pay it about a week later, something like that.

Q: If you needed some money, they would give you the money knowing that later on you would repay it?

A: Yeah. Well, let's say like you would lend a hundred dollars. Maybe two, three, four days later I stole a big old color TV and I say, "Well, I owe you a hundred—here. I'll see you." And you're paid, see? That's the way it went.

These people, even if they get a little bust on them, they can afford it, because they got the money. See, they could get some of the best lawyers in town. I say that if they can do that and get away with it, what they call little is buying hot stock from somebody. That's what they call little. So if we get busted for something like that, we get a two to ten or a one to five in the penitentiary. But if they get busted for something like that, they get away with it because they got the money, right?

That's how it goes. You know, a lot of people don't believe it like that, but it runs like that. A good lawyer, let me put it this way. The district attorney owes a good lawyer a favor, and this lawyer, he's defending me, so this lawyer says, well, "You owe me a little favor. Why don't you, you know, a little lecture by the judge and turn him loose?" *Para que no se mire muy mal*—it doesn't look real bad—and that's exactly what they do.

Q: How do the fences, the guys you were selling your stuff to, how do they get rid of it?

A: How do they get rid of it? Well, let's say like we sell it for thirty percent or forty percent, usually thirty-five, thirty percent is what we sell it to them for. Well, they got their business, right? They could either sell it there for a top price or like, let's say you're the fence and this guy has another business. He's a fence, too—well, you can just sell it to him for let's say fifty-five percent and he's gonna sell it for eighty-five percent, so you gave me thirty-five percent. You sold it to him for fifty-five and he's gonna sell it for eighty-five percent, so everything's cool. And it just goes all around like that. They know how to go about it, how to get a top dollar for it.

Or they already got people, you know, that they've never been busted before or nothing like that. Well, them people once in a while they like to buy a real nice big old console TV and record player and everything. They like to buy something like that for two or three hundred dollars and they'll pay cash, you know. Like if you go to a store you pay about nine hundred dollars for something like that. But they'll pay about two or three hundred dollars for it.

Q: No questions asked?

A: No questions asked—not even a receipt. If anyone asks them for a receipt, they say, "We had it right here," and that's it. *No hay recite, no hay nada*—there's no receipt, not anything.

Q: So the thing is just to get a good lawyer with good connections?

A: No, that doesn't have to be it. But if you get busted, you need a good lawyer, especially a guy like me. Like if I was to get busted now, I know that I would need a damn good lawyer to get me out, because you know that I am an ex-con and everything. You know they're not gonna turn me loose just like that—they're gonna try and send me back up as soon as possible. But then a guy like you, you wouldn't need a good lawyer. You'd just need any lawyer. He'd be able to win. See, a guy like me, I already know even before I go and do this burglary, I already know that if I get busted for that burglary, I'm gonna get sent up. They're not going to give me a break or nothing like that. They're gonna send me up right away. But if I would do this burglary, and I wouldn't have a record, well, I'd stand a hell of a chance to make it.

Q: Francisco, there are some people who are expert in burglarizing—some good people in town. How would you rank them?

A: You mean rank the burglars?

Q: Right. Expertise, knowledge; beginners, others who are professionals . . .

A: Well, we're all beginners, I think, because we're not really good. I read some books, you know Reader's Digest and some things like that that are going around. In—*cómo se llama?*—what's it called?—*en* New York, *en* Chicago, you want to talk about good burglaries, them guys are really good. Them guys . . . you could lock that door real good and they could open that door just like that, you know, without even breaking anything. Whereas, we have to break something to get in there.

Q: So, here it's very simple?

A: Yeah. It's more like—

Q: Well, then you have to have a knowledge of . . . a feeling for how to do it. If you don't have that feeling will you get caught?

A: Right. Well, you know, like these burglars here, they've got a little experience. I mean, I'm not saying that they don't have a little experience. They've got a little experience, because that's all they've been doing all their life, but they just learned one day and they just kept on doing it the same way, you know. Now, if they would really get interested in, you know, burglary and maybe put their heads to it, well, shit, they could open the door instead of breaking the window to the house or something like that.

Well, maybe one of these days if you want to, I'll take you out for a little ride and I can show you what, more or less, I would do if I would ever do it again.

Q: That's what I don't know, you see, what to look for—this one, the next one, and so on.

A: Oh, well, let me put it this way. You see like if you go to a rich neighborhood, to a very rich neighborhood, *no pueden hacer mucho*—you can't do much, for the simple reason *que* them rich guys, everybody's watching this house and everybody, you know, like "Mrs. Anderson, I'm gonna be leaving to so-and-so state and I won't be back till about a week. Would you mind watching the house for me?" or something like this, eh? And besides that, them houses are pretty hard to get into. But, let's say you go to a middle class neighborhood . . .

Q: You would call the northeast section of town a rich area or the Four Hills area or what?

A: Right. Them big old houses like that, there, and those are the ones you could really make some money out of. But these, you know, like middle class, well, you just find something there right away like a portable color TV. Something you can take right away—a record player, something you can take right away, and go open the door. They might have a mink or something like that you can take. Things like that. I never did stay in a house longer than fifteen minutes.

That's all I stayed. I would stay just a little more if I couldn't find anything, but I just had to take something because I had already pulled it, you know. But that's the way it was done. Not longer than that *porque* if you stay longer than that . . . remember what we were talking about, you know, that you never know when the people are gonna come back or nothing like that.

Q: What are the hours that you would select? Hours in the morning, lunchtime, the evening, or it depends—

A: I used to pick it like one-thirty, two. Maybe in the morning, but late in the morning, about ten-thirty, eleven-thirty, you know. But about twelve don't ever do it because they just might come and have lunch, you know. And then at one-thirty, you know that if they're not in by one-thirty at their work, well, they're not working.

Q: Is there something outside that gave you the idea that the house is empty or occupied?

A: Right.

Q: Like what, for instance? If there are no cars there and—

A: Well, yeah, that—no car. The windows—the curtains are closed.

Q: If the curtains are open would that be an indication that somebody's in?

A: No, no. If the windows are open and well, you know, I have to look at it to really . . . but like if the windows are open and I take a damn good look, you know, and the windows could be open, and I could still go and try it and nobody would be there but them are . . . should I say careless people . . . that just leave their house like that.

Q: You see some people leave their lights on outside . . .

A: The doors open, even. I've walked into some houses where the door's wide open. Just go up and open the door—

Q: So—it would be protected if they have the lights on the outside and the inside . . .

A: Oh, if they would leave a light inside, just a couple of little lamps, so that light could be seen, maybe the burglar would get cautious and go to the door and really knock and say, "Well, they got dim lights on so they're probably taking a nap or something." And you know, they start to think like that and once they start thinking like that, they'd just rather forget it and go somewhere else, where they're gonna feel better doing it.

Q: So, it's a matter of feeling—

A: Right.

Q: If there are any indications of something just not right, it's better not to touch that and go to another place? And how about commercial places? How do you select a commercial place?

A: Commercial places? Commercial places, the way I used to do it, *como* it was sitting right here you know, when I went around, maybe once around the block, just once . . .

Q: Walking or in the car?

A: *En el carro, y* I look at the place but I wouldn't go around another time, because if I went around another time and a cop passed by and then I would burglarize it, well, maybe this cop remembered that car or something and he would stop me there or something. So I'd just pass once and then go park the car and then I'd walk and I would wait, like in the alley, and look at the place for a while, you know. If you pull a job in a commercial place, it's gonna have to be done at night, regardless, because during the day they're always open, right?

So I would go and hide there and I would just look at the place, and then *me figuraba cuantas veces un jura era pasa por alli o por la calle cuarta*—I'd figure how many times a cop was going to pass by there on Fourth Street or you know wherever you're at, because at nighttime a cop is always gonna pass by. So, I was way over there for a while, and then I would run over, break the window, take out all the pieces and everything. Then I would run back and just sit there for about fifteen or twenty minutes.

Q: So first you broke the window. In other words, to see if there was an alarm—

A: Like a silent alarm or something like that. Just go over there and break the window, or like if anybody heard me, I already went back to where I was and I'm hiding there . . . just looking at the place to see who's seen me and who's gonna call the cops on me or if they had a silent alarm. And I'd just wait about fifteen or twenty minutes.

Q: Were you nervous at the time? Very nervous?

A: Well, you're always a little shook up but yet—

Q: Your heart beat fast?

A: Like I was always ready to make a big run for it in case the cops did come, you know. *Pero* I used to feel better when I was inside than outside.

Q: Then what do you do inside? Do you go to the counter or a special place?

A: Yeah. You go around looking for money and things like that, you know. And if you don't find any money, well, you just take about six or seven TVs or something like that.

Q: How do you carry the TVs through the window?

A: No, well, you already went in through the window, so, you know, why go out through it when you're already inside, when you can open the door from the inside, right? So you just use the door or the garage door or wherever you're at. Like I pulled it at this place there on Second. And they have a truck in there. And I was gonna take the whole truck and fill the truck with TVs.

Q: And then what happened?

A: We got busted.

Q: You got busted inside?

A: Well, you know the first time I got busted, the cops came—

Q: The cops?

A: Yeah.

Q: Were you alone?

A: No, I was with another guy.

Q: You were really gonna pull a good one there?

A: Oh, that would have been a good one, you know. We would have, well, *una trocka de esas*, two-ton, *llenandola de puros* TVs *todo eso*—one of those trucks, two-ton, filling it up with just TVs and all that—then we were gonna take it out, we already had plans and everything.

Q: In a commercial place like that, a big supermarket would be the ideal place, or a small one, or what?

A: In a supermarket I'd never—

Q: Why? The policemen patrol there or—

A: No, a supermarket is always . . . I don't know. I've always thought of it that way—always a sure bust. If you pull a burglary in it, you're gonna get busted. If you rob, if you rob a place, you know, armed rob it, you're gonna get busted.

Q: I suppose that in a supermarket there's not that much stuff that's of large value—

A: What are you gonna take, food? There ain't nothing you can do. I used to pull burglaries by myself, and I used to steal about six, seven, eight, nine TVs by myself. And when I used to do that I used to even go and steal a car. I didn't have no car but I would go to a lot, you know, a parking lot. And I would find a car that I could use and I'd just take that car and pull the burglary and get all that stuff and take it and bring the car back to the parking lot and go home.

Q: Nobody would notice that you had taken the car from the parking lot?

A: Not unless I got busted or something.

Q: Did you ever get busted with a stolen car?

A: No. I've never been busted for that. I got busted once with Frank, I know you remember him too. We got busted, and see I got out on a Thursday and this guy he got out on a Wednesday.

Q: From the D home?

A: Yeah. And like he came for me on a Friday, and he told me this was his car. Well, I didn't figure he was gonna lie to me, you know, so we were all riding around and everything, and a cop stopped us and he found out that the car was stolen, and the cop opened the glove compartment. There was a jar in there filled with money, and Frank he didn't even know that jar was there. You know, he had barely stolen the car.

Q: When you are going to burglarize a place does it come suddenly to you or do you plan things carefully? Or is it more that you "feel" like this is the place?

A: Well, I don't know. I never liked to plan very much. I'm just gonna do it this way, this way, this way, because I've found out that if you start planning every detail, well pretty soon you start thinking, "Well, no. What happens if this happens over here?" or something like that. Or you start planning, you know, too much for it.

Q: Francisco, how many times do you recollect that you burglarized homes, in relation to the times you have been busted? It's almost minimal—the times you have been busted. It appears that you have a "feeling" for the place and the situation and you have absolute control of the situation.

A: I don't follow you.

Q: How many times did you get busted for residential burglaries?

A: For residential burglaries? Let's see, one, two, three, four, about five times, but I've been, you know, convicted three times.

Q: If you could give me a number, just guessing, of the number of times—

A: *Entre todo?*—In all?

Q: Absolutely all, *entre todo, todas las veces.* In all, all the times. What I think is that you have a great feeling for it—they've caught you two times, three times, how many times have there been—

A: *Las que no me han pescaron?*—The ones when they didn't catch me?

Q: Yes. How many?

A: Uh-huh, *como* seven hundred, eight hundred *que no me han pescado*—that they haven't caught me. Because I didn't just burglarize here, you know, I used to go to Santa Fe, Española, Belen.

Q: It's that easy?

A: Well, it's not always that it's easier there. It's more that you're already too hot here, you know.

Like me and my cousin, this morning, we were way out here on Montaño Road. We were looking there for work and we would go in the truck, stopping to inquire about work. I tell him, "Do you remember how we used to be? Why in the hell didn't they kill us over there?" Right now he's got his own house, he's got a truck, a car, a motorcycle, *todo*.

Q: Who is your cousin?

A: Pete Anaya. He's never been . . . I mean he's been busted *pero* he's always got him a damn good lawyer and he's gotten out. He's already aware. He's not getting in trouble anymore. Of course he's taking methadone. He's been on it around, you know, two or three years, but hell, look what he's getting in two or three years. He's got his own house. He's got a hell of a lot of property, and he's got a car, a truck—not new, but—

Q: You could do the same, Francisco. You are a brilliant man, a man of real intelligence. Everything you would do, you would do very well. Out of eight hundred "investments" you only lost on two or three. If you had put all that money to work on a business, my God, you would have made a fortune. With all the burglaries you pulled, you would be rich. Don't you think so?

A: Oh, like I used to—this was when I really got involved with heroin, we used to invest money *y traibamos onzas de carga de heroin*—and we would bring ounces of heroin. I used to make a hell of a lot of money.

Q: Where did you get it?

A: From over there.

Q: You went to Mexico?

A: I never went. We had a guy that he used to be a runner, we would give the money to him. In other words, we would just take a chance that he would return. Well, like it was about four or five guys. He would take about twenty-eight hundred dollars with him. At that time an ounce cost like four hundred and fifty. So, we'd bring about five or six ounces with that.

Q: What do you get out of an ounce?

A: Well, they—I'll put it to you this way. Like let's say you pay four hundred dollars for an ounce. You make something like thirty-three hundred out of that ounce if you sell it cap by cap. That's what you get. Because when you get it there, it is almost pure, you know. So when you bring it here you actually make about three or four ounces out of it because you cut it with sugar. You can get rich right away.

Like I used to know a guy that had a big old trailer, paid for with cash. Had a brand new car, paid cash for that. You know. But the dude started paying cash for everything so they realized, what the hell he was doing? He wasn't working, and of course he had a little business of his own. If you recall, you might remember the name but I'd rather not say it.

Q: No, there is no need to mention any name.

A: *Y asina va*—so it goes. Sometimes you make it, and sometimes when you're making it you get a little greedy and you get busted.

Q: You mean the times when you have such a large amount of money in your pocket?

A: What I've had . . . the most money that I've had that I could say was mine was about thirty-six hundred dollars. All at the same time, in small bills, *también*.

Q: Is that when you were pushing?

A: Yeah.

Q: To support your own habit?

A: Well, I was pushing, and then I had some other guys pushing for me too.

Q: I see, then you were dealing?

A: Right.

Q: Is that less risky than pushing?

A: Well, I consider dealing like when you're pushing—

Q: I thought dealing was if you're selling to guys who are pushing.

A: No, you don't sell to them. You just give them the stuff and you tell them, like you give them so many caps and you tell them, "Okay, six are for you and the other ten you sell for me."

Q: Where would these guys go—to bars?

A: No, they'd stay home. The guys come around by themselves. They go and score by themselves.

Q: Yeah, the addict knows where to get his stuff. Are you still associating with people that are addicted now?

A: Uh, I see them almost all the time, and the way I see it, I don't associate with them in that way, you know. That I'm going to go get hooked with them, go score or something like that. I don't associate with them that way, *pero* I talk to them because they're my friends. They've been my friends for years and years, you know. I know what they are when they're sober *y todo.* In other words, I know the kind of people that they really are. They just have a problem, you know. I mean I'm not gonna turn my back just because they're using stuff, they're addicts and I'm not supposed to talk to them. I talk to them and if I don't want to do something with them, I tell them, "You know what? I don't want to. I'll see you." If they get mad I tell them, "Just get mad," and I leave.

But we only get mad just for like—*no más por un ratito, eh? Te dicen "culón"*—just for a little while. They call me "you big ass," because they've asked me for a ride *y* every time they ask me for a ride I ask them where and they tell me. They tell me the name of the guy, and I don't want to go there because I know that if I take this guy there then everybody's gonna think I'm on it again. So I'm not gonna go and risk getting busted like that so they can violate me back, send me back to Santa Fe, you know. I'll give him a ride home if that's where he wants to go, to his house. I'll give him a ride then. If I don't want to go, I'll just tell him, "I can't give you a ride."

Q: You're still pretty familiar, then, with the drug culture and people that are involved in it?

A: Well, no. Not now, now I wouldn't know where to go.

Q: *Han cambiado muchas cosas,* Francisco?—Have many things changed?

A: *No han cambiado.* They haven't changed. Just that now they're in different places—here and here and here. *Pero,* like if they tell me the name or something like that, I snap to it right away and I can more or less, you know, figure it out what type of guy this guy is.

Q: Is one of your parole rules that you don't associate with ex-convicts?

A: Well, see, nowadays they can't take specifically that rule seriously anymore, because ex-cons want to help ex-cons, you know, so they're gonna be together trying to get you familiarized with the rest of the convicts, you know.

Q: Francisco, *tú piensas que la gente no quieres emplear a un ex-con?*—Do you think that people don't want to employ an ex-con?

A: Well, it's a lot better now than it was before. Before, you couldn't do it. *Pero* now people are trying to help an ex-convict, and he can help a young kid. Because, you know, this young kid is gonna listen to you better than a cop with a cap on with a star and a gun on his hip. What happens now also is that these young kids, there isn't much you can tell them because they know it all. They know the score already. There isn't much you can tell them.

Q: I used to say that when I was a kid.

A: See, like now I've got a little girl, you know, and she's telling me the other day, "Where are you going, Daddy?"

And I said, "Well, I'll be right back." And she is like her mom, the same as her mom.

"How long are you gonna take?" And she looks at the clock, you know.

I say, "Oh, about fifteen or twenty minutes." I don't know why I've got the habit of saying fifteen or twenty minutes, so when I say that my wife already knows it's gonna be an hour, an hour and ten minutes, an hour and five minutes, somewhere around there.

So when I come back she says, "I thought you were gonna take fifteen minutes—fifteen to twenty minutes. That's what you said. And mama said you already been gone an hour and a half."

You know that kind of makes me feel bad because I lied to her and you know a young kid like that, you don't wanna get her started on things like that, you know. And they're more—they know everything. There's not very much you can do. Like I stopped, you know, and I talked to a real old friend, and it was a girl, you know, and my little girl was there. As soon as we got there, you know, to the house the first thing she said was she told my wife about it.

Q: So you had a lot of explaining to do—

A: No. My wife knows that if I would do something like that, she knows that I wouldn't do it in front of Rita like that.

Q: Is that your little girl's name?

A: Yeah.

Q: Do you feel, Francisco, that a lot of things that have happened to you, have happeed to you because you're a Chicano?

A: Uh, some, yeah. Some. Before, you know, when I was getting busted, the Chicano movement wasn't as much as it is now, and I guess that's why I never thought that I was gonna say, "Well, you're doing this to me because I'm a Chicano." My impression was always like, "You're doing this because I ain't got no money, you son of a bitch. Because if I had money you wouldn't do what you're doing to me now," which is still true right now.

Q: So you wouldn't think in terms of being Chicano or not Chicano? It's the matter of having money or—

A: Now I would. Now, I would because now I've seen it all. Like when you're in the penitentiary, all you do is—I used the read the paper every day and I used to see the guys they were sending up. Every year I used to write that down—*los gabachos,* the Anglos, I used to write 'em on this side, *y los* Chicanos, I used to write 'em on this side. And like I had a little list of names of *gabachos* about that big and of Chicanos about *that big.* Well, goddamn, something's wrong there.

Then later on you hear like Ken Baker's son, Paul Rye's son, Titarelli's son—they're getting in trouble now, see. So now they are approving of ex-convicts trying to help these guys out and the program that we're starting now, and everything, see. That's the way it's going. Everybody wants to help now. Because their sons started doing it now.

I tell you one thing, there in prison, I've seen guys that got money, you know, and in other words their families have money, they're pretty well educated and they just got busted for something that . . . a cruel crime. Like in a small town, rich people, they like to live way out in the country in a small town, and they get busted—well, that small town is not gonna turn this guy loose because he did one of them crimes. Money is not gonna take the cake, you know. He's just gonna have to do a little time before he gets out.

Pero what I'm talking about is the majority. The majority that have money, they don't go up as much as the poor Chicanos do *y* the white guys that are up there are not Chicanos but they're poor—ain't got no money. So that's the way it is. *El hijo de* Titarelli—he got off on his own recognizance. *El hijo de* Paul Rye got out on his own recognizance. So why can't a guy like me get out on his own recognizance? Or another Chicano without a record—why can't he get out on his own recognizance? And even if he does, why does it take about two, three weeks, a month before he can even get out on his own recognizance? Why? When this guy gets out right away, they're telling you right then that you're no good. That you don't qualify for any of that stuff.

Q: *Y que han hecho esos que has nombrado?*—And what have those that you named done?

A: *Matado.* Killed.

Q: Which one?

A: Well, if you might remember a guy that his name was Lindholm. He did ten years *aquí* in Santa Fe. He was from a small town. I forget where he got busted. Anyway his dad is a doctor. Got a lot of money, you know. So what this guy did—he went and killed another doctor and his wife, I think. He killed the doctor and his wife. So they gave him life. When they give you life imprisonment, you get to go to the board when you have ten years . . . you start going to the board every year thereafter.

So he went to the board in his tenth, eleventh year and he made it straight out. He's already gonna graduate from college.

Q: Were you able to, if you wanted to, read or anything in prison, could you take books, magazines, everything?

A: Well, for literature and things like that, I've always tried to get books from out here, from the free world, you know, the kind of book I like to read and things like that. I used to go, see, because when you go to get something that you want from the outside that you're gonna pay for it, you've gotta talk to your caseworker. And when you go talk to your caseworker, man, those guys you go talk to them and they tell you, "No, you can't. Why don't you just get the hell out of here?" Something like that. And that's it. We used to get a little literature there but not that much, you know.

Q: Your people can't send it to you?

A: Even that, you could only do that at Christmas time. If they sent you something like that—

Q: Were you very anxious to get out, Francisco?

A: This last time I was very anxious to get out.

Q: Did it seem like you couldn't bear it any longer there?

A: Oh, no. I know I can do it, you know, but like every time you're getting near to the board, you started thinking about the free world and things like that.

Q: The day you came out, when you were out, two months ago for the first time—coming home to see your family, what came to your mind?

A: *La primera cosa que quería estar con la familia, jugando con mi chavalita.* The first thing that I wanted was to be with my family, playing with my little girl, because she is already four years old now,

see, and I've only been with her like seventeen, eighteen months out
of all that. I don't know, I guess; I remember thinking, too bad that I
was doing the things I was doing, keeping me away from my family.
So I try to think of Santa Fe, every once in a while I put my mind
back over there.

Q: Why?

A: Makes me feel better, like I don't want to go back to that
place anymore but still I want to face the problem like I should.

Q: Thinking back, can you think of what might have been done?
Or what are the things that might have kept you out? Do you have
any idea on it?

A: All I needed, I think all I needed was somebody to help me
the way I'm trying to help young guys go the right way. You know,
when you are going to help a guy, you don't have to tell him off. You
gotta rap to him like you know it all—you gotta rap to him like he
knows it too, you know. "But why don't you see this point for a
minute, then if you wanna go back to whatever you were doing, well
go back and do it—it's up to you." And things like that, you know.

But like I'm talking now, like if I needed somebody to help me
out the way I see it now, I think I might have made it . . . if
somebody might have paid more attention to me and really tried to
help me out, get me started in something, something, you know. At
that time they weren't doing it. Well, of course, I never—they never
took me to any place where I could . . . and if somebody's gonna help
you, you've gotta like him. You gotta like him, specifically that
person, you've gotta like that person.

Q: You said you had a really good relationship with Irwin, you
know, the probation officer.

A: Well, Mr. Irwin, he was always helping me, you know. I
mean I'll admit it. That guy always helped me with everything.
I would go once in a big while, you know, like, "Mr. Irwin, can I
borrow about two or three dollars?" Something like that. He'd let me
have them and I paid him back.

And pretty soon I got to thinking, "Well, this guy, he is all right
with me, and I just can't go around taking his money, so I better go
pay him and not bother him anymore." So, like I told you before, if I
had a problem, I just never discussed it with anybody or never, you
know, tried to get any help.

Of course, I was too young to think about anything like that, but
I think if somebody would have really . . . *como* I used to do the right

things. And then later on when I was out, I was always coming back, you know, I guess that was something that I could not understand very well . . . something very complicated for me sometimes.

Q: Do you think that any institution ever helped you?

A: No. About the only place that I would say—the only place that I could more or less say that I've got something like a good feeling out of was this place—*aquí*, you know, the D home. I don't know why. But if you notice there's a lot of young guys *que* got out and they kept on, you know, getting in trouble and still came to see Mrs. Helen. I guess it was the way Mrs. Helen and everybody here always treated me. I guess it was that, because they treated me real nice. I know that Mrs. Helen gave me what was coming but I always respected her.

Pero in the penitentiary, in the reform school, I can't say a thing like that because you can never communicate with a guy that is working there because he's forever—he's always standing, like on his guard all the time, looking at you in a real mean way, so you're gonna feel like you've gotta be on your guard all the time. In prison you just walk into the mess hall, the captains and everything, they're always trying to bust you for something or it's always "shake down," "strip, shake down," or report something on you.

Q: What is going to keep you out is the fact that you hated some of them?

A: No. I wouldn't say that I hated. I would just simply say that was a bad life if you're gonna be locked up all the time. But I wouldn't say that you have to hate it. And I guess I say that because even right now, I feel sure that I'm not going back, but even yet you never know. Someday something can happen and sometime I'm gonna have to go back, and I wouldn't . . . I sure as hell wouldn't like to go to a place where I would say that I really hated it and really be that bitter about it, you know, because you wouldn't do your time good.

Q: *Me parece que tú eres incapaz de odiar*—I think that you are unable to hate.

A: Well, like I said before, you know, maybe today I can't talk to you, today you make me mad and you cuss me out and I cuss you out and tomorrow, well, if you want to talk to me, well, sure, why not? That's it.

Q: What you haven't told about—I think that you love your mother very much, that you love your mother very much and that you also love your father lots. What do you think about it?

A: Yeah. What my dad is, that's what he is. He liked wine, see, and when I was older I would see my dad and I asked him, *"Que no tienes dinero,* Daddy?"—"Don't you have any money, Dad?" He'd say, "No." I would say, "Well, come on with us." And we used to take him out to the house and used to take him out to eat, then I would take him back home. When I got back to the house I bought a pint of wine so that . . . he was already at home anyway. And that's just the kind of guy I am, you know?

In other words, my dad, I saw his point and he saw mine, but he used to feel very bad when he tried to give me advice because he always knew that I knew it but I didn't want to face it the way it really was. We had a very good understanding as far as that goes.

Q: How do you feel about your brothers?

A: We're very close—*todos.* As a matter of fact, last Sunday we were with Juan and his wife and we took the kids out to the park, out to playland, and the week before that, we were—*yo,* Pancho *y* Juan *y* Nesto, we got together. We like to play around together a lot.

Q: Your friends that helped you in the burglaries, were they ever Anglos?

A: *Gabacho?* Never.

Q: You never had *gabacho* friends?

A: Well, I've had a lot of *gabacho* friends, *pero*—they're not . . . they're ex-cons, but they're not, I don't know why, there are very few that I feel good with. Then there are others that, I don't know. There's something *que,* well, I'm doing it now, we see them there at the meetings—*gabachos* with long hair and we just get into a rap session and things like that, you know.

Q: Did you ever have the feeling, when you were involved in all this, that you were trapped? Like this was your way of living, and it was gonna be and that you couldn't get out of it?

A: Well, I tried to see it that way. I tried to see it, I used to explain to my mom, to my wife, to everybody, whenever I got just a little drunk, and I knew that they were worried about me or something. I would ask my mom, "Mom, they say that God is real big, huh? And they say that God is the one who gives you your destiny, so I think this is my destiny—do time . . . get in trouble, and always be involved in this kind of thing. So I think this is my destiny, so I don't know why you worry."

I would more or less try and make 'em feel better that way. I don't know. I guess that was my way of showing them *que* I was trying to make them feel better or something. My mom, she's been the type of woman—she's been a very strong woman, you know, because *yo* and Pancho and Juan, we were at the D home all the time, and we were young as hell, man.

Q: Did Pancho and Juan ever make it to Springer?

A: No. *Yo y el* Nesto, but Nestor, when he went to court the first time, they sent him to Springer, and he got out and after that he's never been in trouble, *no miento*—no trouble. Once, once in a big while he goes into some pretty bad hangups, you know, gets to drinking a lot and anything he can do, he does it. Always in trouble he gets like that, *pero* when he's sober he's okay for two, three years, and then he just goes out on one of them bad ones. Sometimes they get him and sometimes not.

Q: Is he married?

A: No. Nesto and Raul are the only ones that are not married now.

Q: How old is Raul?

A: He's about eighteen, seventeen. No, he's seventeen because he was at the D home about two, three months ago.

Q: I guess I didn't see your mother when she came to pick him up. Why was he here?

A: They got busted in a car and they were drinking or something, I mean they were drunk. Or something like that, I don't know. Raul *dijo que* the cops tried to mistreat him so he wouldn't let them and they locked him up. That's what he said, you know, but of course sometimes when they're that young, they're used to the cops mishandling them all the time *porque* they figure *que* if they lie a little, well, that's good because you're doing them a little wrong or something, see? I don't know, I might be wrong.

Q: But he hasn't been in too much trouble?

A: No. Not bad. Not serious trouble.

Q: Are you happy now? Or do you have a—how do you feel now?

A: *Yo me siento en buena salud*—I feel well. Like before, I—*siempre me sentía* rundown, how I always felt. I never had time enough, you know, to put a clean pair of pants on. I'd just wear them for two or three days and put on another and I would just dress any old way and go out and shoot up and I didn't even shave, you know, things like that. Now I'm in good health. I go out and I play basketball just about every Sunday because, you know, that's my favorite sport.

Q: You look very well.

A: Oh yeah. Sometimes I feel like, you know, to go out and have a little party or something like that. But I get that off my mind.

Q: Are you allowed to drink?

A: Well, I'm not supposed to drink but I have a beer, two or three beers at home and I take my wife out and my mother and her mother and I take them out for a drink once in a while. That's all.

Q: What do you think are some of the things they should change, based on your own experience with police, courts, with detention homes, and the whole works? What do you think are some of the things that we should work on to change?

A: I don't know. You know, a lot of recreation is good. I know that because I used to enjoy it a lot. Recreation, basketball, and if you remember *el* trampoline when they used to have it at the D home, well, everybody wanted to go. That's one of the things that everybody enjoyed a lot.

You know, things like that—when someone is in his room, instead of giving him . . . well, a deck of cards is pretty good because they can play rummy *y todo*. But that's where they start learning how to play poker and then they start thinking, "One of these days I'm really gonna be a gambler and I'm gonna gamble like, you know, like my father's friend—he's a gambler that makes his living just gambling and he always has a lot of money, so maybe one of these days I'm gonna do it." And as he's playing along he's got that thought back here, you know, subconsciously he's got all that there.

I say things like, just give them a book, you figure that they won't be interested or nothing like that and when you leave them alone for a while and they can't find anything to do—eventually they'll get that book, and they'll start going over it. They might just get interested in it, and start turning all the pages through it. Because I remember I never used to read or nothing like that. I never knew what the hell was, what was really going on, but as I was beginning, when I started to read more, and I started learning new things and all, then I started getting more interested in reading.

Pero as far as changing things, I don't know, I couldn't say . . . I guess I'm just the type of guy, if I would be there I would know how to handle the situation. If something would start, I would know how to handle it. Of course, you know, don't let them run over you, more or less have a very good understanding.

One of the things that I feel they should really change *ahora que me acuerdo*—now that I remember—is the system . . . the system, because no matter what rules you make, at one time or another you're gonna have to break that rule. You're gonna have to change it, and as far as that goes right now, it seems that the citizen is the one that's changing the rules and coming out with new ones all the time. So they got everybody confused.

Like you got a guy in an institution for five, six, seven years, well, he's always known this rule and then all of a sudden he does the same thing. Well, they changed that rule. In other words, he broke a rule that he thinks he's abiding by, and someone comes and tells him, "Well, you broke a rule—I'm gonna write you up."

Well, goddamn, *que va a pensar ese vato*—what's a guy gonna think? They taught him that rule and he was going by that, so now he broke it and they got him all pissed off again *y todo*. They should show more interest, more interest because the way I see it, now, young guys, you know, they're killing their mothers, they're really going way out. These days you stop by a stoplight *allí en* Central and they bump into you and you get out of your car, "Well, what the hell is wrong with you, you son of a bitch, you kids," and so forth. Well, they'll just take a gun and shoot you right there. Because that's the way it's going on right now.

Ahora at the park, I don't think you heard of it because I don't think nobody found out about it. They were young, these guys, they were about nineteen, twenty years old. They were out there in the park—they were shooting at each other, there between the trees. This was about two weeks ago.

Q: Roosevelt?

A: Yeah. Lucky nobody got hurt, but still, I mean, playing around with guns is a pretty serious thing . . . just shooting at each other. *Está cabrón*—this SOB, you're walking in the park and you're just, you know, behind a tree and somebody else is shooting you. Then at nighttime you never know when some other SOB will go up there and kill you.

Q: Well. One of my ideas is that an institution is not where your problems were, your problems were out there.

A: Right. But an institution is a place where not too many people belong. But an institution is made to correct the wrongs that these people are doing. Any institution, they put it to rehabilitate a guy and not to make him bitterer than what he already is.

Q: What happens in the institution is that people get more bitter and—

A: I know a guy now, you could check in the paper about

nineteen or twenty years back and you could find these articles by him because they ran for about six months. This guy's about fifty-eight, fifty-nine years old. He shot three guys, you know, and before that he had already done time in Texas for shooting another guy. This guy's been there nineteen years and when he got out he was fifty-eight, fifty-seven years old but, of course, when a guy is in jail that long, well, he might look a little old but he don't really feel old.

And he got out after doing nineteen years, he got out and he came back, seven months later, and they violated him for something that was really not necessary. What they should have done is looked and, "Damn, well, this guy's done a hell of a lot of time, you know, this guy needs a break. He just might make it, you know." So now he's back after doing nineteen years.

And you see it all the time. You see guys that do seven, eight, nine years *y salen*—they get out—and a week later they're back. The guy ain't got no prerogative at all. Any little thing that he might do, he just might get busted for it, you know, just any little thing, and he will go back for another three, four, or five years.

Q: It doesn't seem to worry you—that you're . . . you know, any little thing you're gonna do you're gonna get busted?

A: Oh, me? I mean it doesn't worry me *porque* I don't feel that I'm doing anything that they'll be able to bust me for again. The only thing that I feel they can bust me for is if they catch me with another guy, like let's say that I'm talking to you right there and a cop comes and catches you with caps in your pocket. Well, I was with you, I'm gonna be violated right there. You damn sure can't be talking to a guy and telling him, "Are you sure you don't have anything, nothing in your pocket that, you know, in case a cop comes or something?" You don't feel right asking a guy things like that. I was just talking to him because he's a friend of mine and things like that. *Pero* as far as me going out and being out there with them or me going out to a bar by myself and, you know, drinking my ass off or something like that, no.

Q: Were you involved with the Y here or Boys' Club or—

A: The community center—I used to box for them. I started boxing when I got out of Springer, when I was at Springer that's when I started boxing. Then when I got out I got involved with them and I started boxing for them *y todo*.

Q: And did you find, Francisco, that when you were in *la pinta*, did you change in one way or the other, the way you think in—

A: Well, like a lot of people feel that a guy, if a guy is gonna change, he's not supposed to associate with this kind of people, and if he's supposed to be . . . *su trabajo, su cantón, su familia*—his work, his home, his family, and that's the way it is, and that's the way it really is. But you know you can't turn against your own people just like that, just because you want to make it this way. You know you can talk to them, rap with them, whatever you want and yet—

Q: Be your own—

A: Right.

Q: Your own people. Do you mean by your own people *los pintos*—ex-cons?

A: *Pintos*, my *raza*, things like that. *Gabachos, mayates, no hay pedo*—gringos, blacks, there is no problem. See, like there's a lot of *mayates* that I don't like *pero también* there's a lot of Chicanos *que* I don't like either and they don't like me, *pero también* there's a lot of *gabachos también*, and that's the way it goes. And I—that's one thing about me, that I don't think I could ever concern myself, you know, prejudice against *mayate* or gringo, you know.

Q: Do you feel that La Raza . . . I kind of have the impression that—

A: Well, I got more feeling for my *raza* than for any other race.

Q: You mentioned that guy that used to work for the sheriff's office.

A: Oh yeah.

Q: You were talking about him and you were feeling like he's a guy *que se boltiado a* La Raza—he's turned against the race.

A: No. I mean—I said it in a way, like *el vato* is Chicano and yet this guy is still messing around us more than what he would be a *gabacho*.

Q: In other words, he is being prejudiced against the Chicanos, and not treating them like he does everyone else?

A: Right, right, right.

Q: Do you think there should be some changes in society?

A: *No, pues, cambios*—well, changes . . .

Q: If you were in conditions to make some changes, not only in the system but in the world, in the society, what would you do?

A: Well, in the first place I wouldn't . . . I don't think I would be qualified to speak or anything, but in order for something to change like an institution, any kind of institution . . . now I'm going back to perception again. You yourself have to go and look at the situation and balance it, but really do it, but like these guys—there's something wrong over here and you know the higher power guys up here, they say, "Yeah, we'll do this. We'll do that," and you have orders and that's it. There's no more to it. Of course, they might send somebody down but goddamn, they send someone that, I don't know—

Q: What are some of the changes you'd like to see in your own life?

A: What I'm doing now? I guess as far as changes goes I see them still as they were, but I feel like in a way, like I'm doing it, and I'm facing the whole problem at the same time. You know what I mean? You know, like the changes in my life.

I'm still the same guy. I'm still what I was years ago, like *un tecato*—that's an addict. I don't consider myself an addict. I wouldn't say that—I would say that I consider myself an addict because I was an addict for so long that I know that any time that I would get involved with it, I would fall right in with it just like that. Somebody else, you know, he would take quite a bit to drop into it, but a guy like me, I could fall into it right away, and this is what I mean that I haven't changed. My ways—I've changed the things that I used to do, the way that I used to do them and things like that, but as far as *robando* that's one thing about me—

Q: You don't have any more feelings like that? Why?

A: Just . . .

Q: It looks like something has passed in your life—that the thing doesn't interest you any more. The same as if you'd had a wife and now she didn't interest you.

A: Well, you know, how I used to think there in the walls and I'd say, "What the hell, here I am in the hallway" and I wouldn't have a penny in my pocket, you know what I mean? Not a goddamn penny in my pocket, but always happy with my tennis shoes here in my hand and there I went to the gym and would say, "Why the hell can't I be outside and why am I going to rob?"

Porque el addiction problem, I wasn't addicted anymore. I had already thought that over and I knew that I wasn't gonna do that anymore. *Pero* like I said, there's always the possibility of falling backward.

When I was out here and going around broke I would feel bad, you know. I just feel—well, I feel very bad when I don't have money. So I used to go out and steal it. But now, I don't have a cent in my pocket but I feel pretty good.

Like they say, my mom says, *"Hijito de mi vida, vale más un pájaro en la mano que cien volando"*—"Little son of my life, a bird in the hand is worth a hundred flying." And I guess that's just the way it was. I guess, if that was the way to solve my problems, well that was a way out, you know.

Like a lot of guys, they look for a way out and they look for it in a real, you know, complicated way. They look at it, they say something like *"Bueno.* I'm not gonna shoot up any more, now, I'm just going to smoke marijuana," so I say that if they see it as a way out for them, well, the hell with it. You know the burden to be messing around with heroin is pretty goddamn heavy shit. *Y la marijuana,* you pay fifty cents a joint and that'll last you, well, about a day. You don't pay anything for that and then it could be that eventually you get tired of marijuana and you say, "I'm getting tired of marijuana, too," and there it goes. People like you couldn't see it, you know, *pero* a lot of guys think like that because they've been on heroin for twenty years, nineteen, eighteen years.

THEORETICAL APPENDIXES

Appendix A

On Criminal Careers and Typologies

Introduction

The conceptual and theoretical analysis of deviant and criminal careers has received considerable attention in contemporary criminological literature. Of particular significance are the works of Becker, Clinard and Quinney, Erikson, Gibbons, Goffman, Glasser, Lemert, Scheff, Szasz, and others, who have stressed the crucial role of societal reactions in the inducement and stabilization of deviant and criminal careers.[1] "However," Milutinovik says, "serious criticisms have been directed against the idea of regarding crime and deviance as lacking an objectively given characteristic in itself; deviance and crime depend on the way in which a certain behavior is viewed by others and their reaction to it neglecting the fact that the legal norms concerning criminality and the positive incriminations are socially determined, that they are supported by the social reality which objectively gives them force and might."[2]

Hall confirms this:

> The surest single generalization available is that all societies proscribe behavior that runs counter to their preservation. Group preservation requires not only prohibition of indiscriminate killings and of the lesser batteries and mayhems that lead directly to such homicide; it also requires protection of infants and consequently of institutions that provide, as well, for care of females during the childbearing period and afterwards. Thus the generalization that crime "is relative" does not aid understanding; it merely points to the variations of criminal behavior and implies a total failure to recognize any common characteristics. Yet, these are the *sine qua non* of any science.[3]

Later he adds:

Criminologists may consider the fact that while some laws (and *pro-tanto crimes*) may be arbitrary or archaic, most of the serious ones (barring despotism) have intimate relationships to social harms, to moral attitudes, to ethics, to the affective nature of man, to culture and to custom. If the approach is by way of "violation of group values against which the group reacts positively" we are confronted by the whole sweep of social life, which we can penetrate only by partial insight. Or suppose our starting point is "social disorganization" or "social pathology." Can we understand these without knowledge of "social organization" which, in other terms, also involves the whole of social reality, including actual criminal laws?[4]

We fully agree with Hall. While there are "crimes and deviant acts," products only of "labeling" and "insiders' reactions," the criminal law is closely tied to the cultural, ideological, and socioeconomic history of a given time and place.

There is no denying, however, that criminal definitions many times describe behaviors that conflict with the interests of the segments of society that have the power to shape public policy[5] and that, quite often, "criminality is a construct, beyond the quality of specific behaviors, that is formulated and applied by the power segment of society."[6]

An integrative approach to deviance and crime should articulate, we believe, the interactionist perspective with the view that recognizes that deviance and crime are grounded, at least in Western law and societies, on certain common basic characteristics of the actions involved beyond "insider" reactions.

As Lemert has indicated, the concepts of *individual, situational, and systematic deviation* are central to the study of the nature and structure of criminal careers. In effect, initial actions of deviant behavior are frequently instances of risk-taking, representing tentative flirtations with proscribed behavior patterns. Whatever the reasons for these actions, many become subject to societal reactions. Societal reactions have more influence in subsequent career experiences than anything else that occurred to the initial offender prior to his involvement in disapproved conduct.[7]

At this point, social reactions and agency contacts may be of major significance. One of the major factors that may drive juveniles toward delinquency as a systematic role revolves around the extent to which the individual has been defined as a "delinquent" and "bad boy" by community organizations and agencies.[8]

Situational structural opportunities could provide additional incentives to the initial offender, and finally, at the end of the continuum, the criminal role has been confirmed to a given social actor by society and its formal and informal organizations.

The operation of criminal justice systems in this process could well function to provide for stabilization of criminal careers.

Intervention techniques, then, should take into account the relative stage of involvement of a given social actor in an *individual, situational, or systematic pattern*, that is to say that variations in techniques are a natural outcome of the adjustment of intervention strategies to individual actors.

Common Characteristics of Career Criminals

A number of common characteristics of career criminals have been exposed by Clinard and Quinney:

> *First,* persons engaged in career crime usually *pursue crimes of gain,* mostly property crimes. Career criminals either supplement an income through property crime or, as with organized criminals and professional criminals, *make a living from criminal activity. In comparison to persons in legitimate occupations, career criminals make part or all of their living by pursuing activities that have been defined as illegal.* One of the occupational hazards for the career criminal, however, is the risk of being arrested and convicted. Since only about 20 percent of all property offenses (and only those that are *known* by the police) are cleared by arrest, *the risks are not exceptionally high.* For many career criminals, the often-quoted adage that "crime does not pay" is fiction, a myth maintained by and for law-abiding members of society.
>
> *Second,* criminal activity *is a part of the way of life of the career offender.* A career in crime involves *a life organization of roles built around criminal activities,* which includes *identification with crime, a conception of the self as a criminal,* and *extensive association with other criminals.* In career crime there is a *progression in crime which*

includes the acquisition of more complex techniques, more frequent offenses, and, ultimately, dependence on crime as a partial or sole means of livelihood.

Third, persons in *career crime tend either to develop a pattern of property violations or in some cases to specialize in a particular kind of offense.* A professional criminal, for example, will specialize in one of a number of violations, such as picking pockets, sneak thieving, passing illegal checks, or shoplifting. Career criminals also develop over a period of time special skills and techniques for committing offenses.

Fourth, career criminals are engaged in *systematic behavior that requires both personal and social organization.* In contrast to noncareer crime, the violations of career criminals are not the result of personal conflicts and immediate circumstances. *Career criminals commit their offenses only through awareness of the situation and after planning the offense.* Career criminals depend upon the assistance of other criminals and may be involved in an organization of criminals. Because of the involvement of career criminals in crime, there is the prospect of a lifetime career in crime with increased isolation from the legitimate work patterns of society.[9]

There is thus a consensus today in criminology that "a useful conception in developing sequential models of various kinds of deviant behavior is that of a *career.*"[10] Gibbons has said that "offenders' roles can be also analyzed profitably in longitudinal terms as *role-careers.*"[11] In some criminal roles, role performance is represented by a single isolated illegal act intruding into an otherwise exemplary life history, while in others involvement in sustained deviance continues over several decades, as in the instance of professional criminals.

Gibbons has also made the point that some delinquent patterns lead to adult criminal careers, while others do not.

On the basis of assumptions concerning criminal role careers, Gibbons has constructed a criminological typology that we shall examine in relation to Clinard and Quinney's multidimensional and integrative typology.

On the basis of both attempts we shall consider finally our five criminal lives, subject of this book.

Property Offenders and Criminological Typologies

A number of attempts have been made in recent criminological studies to develop a systematic typology of property offenders. Gibbons[12] says, "Professional heavy criminals who engage in robberies and burglaries of various kinds are distinguished from semi-professional property offenders and 'one-time loser' property criminals who also engage in robberies and related offenses. One major basis for separating these offender role careers is that the three vary markedly in terms of the criminal expertise demonstrated by the respective role incumbents." However, Gibbons continues,

> . . . it ought to be made clear at the outset that the distinction between professional "heavy" criminals and semiprofessional property offenders is actually one of degree rather than kind. The dividing line between professional and semiprofessional property offenders is somewhat arbitrary. On the whole, professional "heavies" are highly competent lawbreakers who reap large sums of money from their illegal activities and work at this occupation full-time. Semiprofessionals tend to be relatively unskilled, poorly paid for their criminal endeavors and work at crime in some cases on a part-time basis. Doubtless many offenders would fall clearly into one or another of these types, but there would be some criminals who might be difficult to categorize, in that technical skills, amount of profit from crime, and involvement in criminality are matters of degree rather than different qualitative attributes of offenders.

Gibbons then proceeds to define the professional heavy role career in terms of *offense behavior, interactional setting, self-concept, attitudes,* and *role career.* In addition he discusses background—*social class, family background, peer group associations,* and *contact with defining agencies.*

In relation to offense behavior, he notes:

> Professional heavies engage in armed robbery, burglary and other direct assault upon property. They are highly skilled at crime, so although the element of coercion and threat of violence is involved, actual force is rarely employed. The *modus operandi* of professional "heavy"

criminals involves a relatively lengthy period of detailed planning prior to the execution of the criminal offense. The semiprofessional property criminal also engages in strong-arm robberies, holdups, burglaries, larcenies and similar direct assaults upon personal or private property. They employ crime skills which are relatively simple and uncomplicated. For example, strong-arm robbery does not involve much detailed planning and careful execution of the crime, but rather application of crude physical force in order to relieve a victim of his money. This is referred to as semiprofessional crime, because even though technical skill is not characteristic of these offenders, most of them attempt to carry out crime as an occupation.

In terms of interactional setting, most activities of professionals are carried on as team or "mob" operations. Although robberies can on some occasions be carried out by a single offender, most burglaries and robberies by professionals use a number of crime partners involved in specialized roles. The semiprofessionals, in contrast, operate without a complex interactional pattern. The criminal act tends to be direct and unsophisticated; many of the offenses of semiprofessionals are two-person affairs involving an offender and a victim. On occasion, Gibbons says, semiprofessionals operate in groups of two or more, as in instances of burglary and safe robbery.

Self-concept in the heavies implies that they define themselves as criminals and as professionals in crime. They are proud of their specialized skills and view crime as a lucrative and satisfying way of life. Semiprofessionals do not view themselves as professionals in crime; rather, they see few alternatives to their criminal behavior, and regard themselves as victims of a corrupt society in which everyone has a "racket." They blame the "system" and so feel no personal guilt.

In their attitudes, the professional heavies do not exhibit great hostility toward the police, who are regarded as necessary persons with a job to do. The attitudes of semiprofessionals toward the police tend to be more hostile and antagonistic than is the case with professional heavies. In the same way, semiprofessionals' views of the courts and correctional agents are more hostile than those of professional heavies. Semiprofessionals also denigrate conventional occupations as a way of life, holding that "only slobs work."

Gibbons examines at length the role career of the heavies. They normally come from urban, lower-class backgrounds. Most of them began their criminal careers as predatory gang delinquents. The heavy usually goes through a process of increasing differential involvement with older professionals from whom he learns the necessary crime skills. Persons who engage in professional property offenses tend to continue criminal activities into middle age, whereupon many of them ultimately retire into noncriminal occupations. Most adult semiprofessional offenders exhibit juvenile backgrounds of predatory gang behavior, and many juvenile gang offenders continue in criminality as semiprofessionals. As adults, semiprofessionals rapidly accumulate extensive "rap sheets," or records of crimes and institutional commitments. Because of the low degree of skill involved in semiprofessional crime, the risks of apprehension, conviction, and incarceration are high. Many of them spend a considerable part of their early adult years in penal institutions, where they are likely to be identified as "right guys" or antiadministration inmates. It does not appear that conventional treatment efforts are successful in deflecting many of these persons from continuing in crime. On the other hand, many of them ultimately do withdraw from crime careers upon reaching early middle age.

In social class and family background, Gibbons recognizes great similarity between heavies and semiprofessionals. Both types of offender have usually resided for long periods in working-class neighborhoods in urban areas. They frequently lived as youngsters in deteriorated neighborhoods in which patterns of adult criminality were often readily observable. As adults, some of them have moved into more "respectable," middle-class neighborhoods, while at the same time maintaining their previous social ties to working-class friends.

As juveniles, both kinds of offender experienced family backgrounds of parental neglect and exposure to delinquency patterns. The family structure was not usually characterized by intense interfamily tension. Family members were on relatively good terms with each other, but the offenders commonly did not receive close parental supervision. Some belonged to families in which their siblings were also delinquent or involved in crime, and some parents were on occasion involved in crime, so that differential association with deviant family members played a significant part in career development.

Adult heavy professional offenders are usually involved in stable marriages with close ties to offspring. Their deviant behavior tends not to disrupt family relationships, for "heavy" criminals are rarely caught up in the correctional machinery which might break up families.

Heavies and semiprofessionals experience similar peer-group relations. However, semiprofessionals have usually associated mostly with other relatively unskilled offenders.

Gibbons describes the peer-group experiences of the heavies:

> As a juvenile, this type of offender was involved in interaction within the structure of delinquent gangs or differential association with delinquent peers. In some cases these delinquent peers form a recognizable gang, whereas in others they represent a loose confederation of offenders. In either case, the offender exhibited differential avoidance of nondelinquent juveniles in his community. Commonly, this type associated with a group of youths known in the area as troublemakers and delinquents, all of whom shared such characteristics as expulsion from school and unemployment. The peer structure provided him with group support for his hostile and cynical attitudes. The peer structure also provided social rewards for prowess in delinquent acts, in that peers often accorded high status to the most delinquent boys.
>
> Adult "heavy" professional criminals continue to associate differentially with criminal peers. They may number among their friends a large number of other "heavy" professionals. However, these individuals do not usually constitute a stable "mob" carrying on repeated acts of criminality. Instead, "mobs" or groups of lawbreakers are formed on the occasion of a specific criminal offense and disbanded at its conclusion. The constituent members of these "mobs" vary, so that professional "heavies" are only loosely organized into a criminal confederation.

The contact with defining agencies is also similar in both types, according to Gibbons:

> The "heavy" . . . usually exhibited early involvement with the police. In many instances, his police contacts are considerably more common than indicated by his official record. This type was also well-known to the juvenile court. His record is likely to show several juvenile probation

experiences, culminating in placement in a correctional institution. The usual view of persons who dealt with the offender as a juvenile was that he was a "tough kid," lacking in insight and concern over his delinquent conduct. In turn, the offender's usual view of law enforcement and correctional agents was that such persons are "phonies."

The early adult history of this offender is likely to show several commitments to penal institutions. Commonly, some of the criminal skills exhibited by the person were acquired in this learning environment. As the developing professional acquires expertise in deviance and becomes more enmeshed in the world of professional criminality, prison becomes an occupational hazard which he infrequently encounters. Accordingly, the correctional machinery has an insignificant effect upon mature professional "heavy" criminals.

The adult semiprofessionals spend major portions of their lives in penal institutions. Contacts with defining agencies play a contributory role in their criminal careers. Gibbons has distinguished, in addition, fifteen adult types and nine juvenile types, among them, the opiate addict role-career.

Clinard and Quinney's Typology

An important step toward the construction of an integrative and multidimensional typology has been formulated by Clinard and Quinney.[13] According to these authors, the phenomena associated with crime include: (1) the formulation and administration of criminal law, (2) the development of persons and behaviors that become defined as criminal, and (3) the social reactions to crime.

These theoretical assumptions are contained in the five dimensions of the typology, being each type conceived as systems of behavior. The dimensions are:

1. Legal aspects of selected offenses
2. Criminal career of the offender
3. Group support of criminal behavior
4. Correspondence between criminal and legitimate behavior
5. Societal reaction and legal processing

Included in these five dimensions are the diverse phenomena

associated with crime, that is, the formulation and administration of criminal law, the development of persons and behaviors that may be defined as criminal, and the social reactions to the behaviors. Together the five dimensions with their specific assumptions form the theoretical basis for our typology of criminal behavior systems.

Legal aspects of selected offenses. Crime is a definition of human conduct that is created by authorized agents in a politically organized society. *Criminal laws are formulated by those segments of society that have the power to translate their interests into public policy.* Criminal laws thus consist of behaviors that are regarded as threatening to the ruling class. The social history of particular criminal laws is a reflection of changes in the power structure of society.

Criminal career of the offender. The behavior of the offender is shaped by the extent to which criminally defined norms and activities have become a part of the individual's career. The career of the offender includes the social roles he plays, his conception of self, his progression in criminal activity, and his identification with crime. Offenders vary in the degree to which criminally defined behavior has become a part of their life organization.

Group support of criminal behavior. The behavior of offenders is supported to varying degrees by the norms of the groups to which they belong. Those who are defined as criminal act according to the normative patterns learned in relative social and cultural settings. Group support of criminal behavior varies according to the associations of the offender with differential norms and the integration of the offender into social groups.

Correspondence between criminal and legitimate behavior. Criminal behavior patterns are structured in society in relation to legitimate and legal behavior patterns. Within this context persons develop and engage in actions that have relative probabilities of being defined as criminal. Criminally defined behaviors thus vary in terms of the extent to which they correspond to legitimate patterns of behavior in society. The behavior of the offender is viewed in relation to the norms of the segments of society that have the power to formulate and administer criminal law.

Societal reaction and legal processing. Criminally defined behaviors vary in the kind and amount of reactions they receive from the public and from the society in general. The social reactions range from the degree of approval or disapproval to the official sanctioning procedures. Different policies of punishment and treatment are established and administered for each type of criminal behavior.

Social reactions are also affected by the visibility of the offense and the degree to which the criminal behavior corresponds to the interest of the power structure of society. Finally, the types of criminal behavior vary in the ways that they are processed through the legal system. Patterns of detection, arrest, prosecution, conviction, sentencing, and punishment exist for each type of criminal behavior.

On the basis of these five theoretical dimensions a typology of criminal behavior systems is constructed.

Nine types of criminal behavior systems are constructed by Clinard and Quinney in relation to the five theoretical dimensions. The types are:

1. Violent personal criminal behavior
2. Occasional property criminal behavior
3. Public order criminal behavior.
4. Conventional criminal behavior
5. Political criminal behavior
6. Occupational criminal behavior
7. Corporate criminal behavior
8. Organized criminal behavior
9. Professional criminal behavior

Without going into a detailed discussion of the nine types of criminal behavior, we shall describe "conventional criminal behavior," "professional criminal behavior," and "organized criminal behavior," the types in which Clinard and Quinney have included characteristics relevant to the analysis of our five criminal lives (Tables 1–5).

The conventional criminals of Clinard and Quinney are similar in many respects to the semiprofessionals of Gibbons, already discussed. They began their careers early in life as juvenile delinquents. Their early lives show a pattern of truancy, destruction of property, street fighting, and delinquent gang membership. By the time they are young adults, they have an extensive history of contact with the law and possibly have had institutional experiences. As juveniles they become involved in a culture that is either neutral or opposed to the law of legitimate society. Their acts are not isolated and personal, but rather are often part of the way of life and norms of a local slum community.[14]

As juvenile offenders progress into conventional career crime, they become more committed to crime as a way of life and develop a criminal self-conception. "Conventional criminals, in comparison to

TABLE 1

Legal Aspects of Selected Offenses

Criminal Behavior	Legal Considerations
Conventional	The laws that protect private property include such crimes as larceny, burglary, and robbery. Since the primary interest is in protecting property, general laws regarding property do not need to distinguish the career nature of many property offenders.
Organized	Many traditional laws have been used in the attempt to control organized crime, especially those regarding gambling, prostitution, and drug traffic. The government has more recently enacted special criminal laws in order to infiltrate organized criminal activity in legitimate business and racketeering. But since organized crime is closely tied to the general business economy, these laws tend to invade the privacy of all citizens rather than to control organized crime.
Professional	Professional crimes are distinguished by the nature of the criminal behavior rather than by specific criminal laws. Such professional activities as confidence games, pickpocketing, shoplifting, forgery, and counterfeiting are regulated by the traditional laws that protect private property.

From Clinard and Quinney, *Criminal Behavior Systems: A Typology.*

organized and professional criminals, are more likely to be eventually arrested and imprisoned."[15]

Typological Profile of Our Cases

Life always exceeds the rigid limits of intellectual tools or constructions—in this case, the neatness and "purity" of types. This is not to argue against the validity or desirability of type construction;

TABLE 2

Criminal Career of the Offender

Criminal Behavior	Career Description
Conventional	Offenders begin their careers early in life, often in gang associations. Crimes are committed for economic gain. There is vacillation in self-concept, and partial commitment to a criminal subculture.
Organized	Crime is pursued as a livelihood. There is a progression in crime and an increasing isolation from the larger society. A criminal self-concept develops.
Professional	There is a highly developed criminal career. Professional offenders engage in specialized offenses, all of which are directed toward economic gain. They enjoy high status in the world of crime. They are committed to other professional criminals.

From Clinard and Quinney, *Criminal Behavior Systems: A Typology.*

TABLE 3

Group Support of Criminal Behavior

Criminal Behavior	Group Support
Conventional	Behavior is supported by group norms. There is early association with other offenders in slum areas, and status is achieved in the groups. Some persons continue primary association with other offenders, while others pursue different careers.
Organized	Support for organized criminal behavior is achieved through an organizational structure, a code of conduct, prescribed methods of operation, and a system of protection. The offender is integrated into organized crime.
Professional	Professional offenders associate primarily with other offenders. Behavior is prescribed by the norms of professional criminals. The extent of organization among professional criminals varies with the kind of offense.

From Clinard and Quinney, *Criminal Behavior Systems: A Typology.*

rather it is an argument in favor of more comprehensive and exhaustive typological analysis.

Soledad, Modesto, Ralph, and Francisco are a *mixture of types*, property offenders and drug-addicted role careers. In their lives, property crimes, mainly burglary, and addiction to either heroin or cocaine are two sides of the same coin, inextricably linked. If we examine in detail that interrelation it is easy to conclude that drug addiction was their "master" role, and burglary the "subordinate,"[16] if we consider just the criminal side of their lives. Jack, on the contrary, the "heavy" property offender, is, from that perspective, characterized by the "centrality" and "salience" of his professional criminal role: burglary at the beginning of his criminal career, later armed robberies. He was not involved in drugs. There are additional

TABLE 4

Correspondence between Criminal and Legitimate Behavior

Criminal Behavior	Relationship to Legitimate Behavior
Conventional	Conventional criminal behavior is consistent with goals of economic success, but inconsistent with the sanctity of private property. Gang delinquency violates norms of proper adolescent behavior.
Organized	While organized crime may be generally condemned, some characteristics of American society give support to it. The values underlying organized crime are consistent with those of the free enterprise system.
Professional	Professional criminal activity corresponds to societal values that stress skill and employment. Some of the offenses depend upon the cooperation of accomplices. The operations of professional crime change with alterations in the larger society.

From Clinard and Quinney, *Criminal Behavior Systems: A Typology.*

TABLE 5

Societal Reaction and Legal Processing

Criminal Behavior	Reaction and Processing
Conventional	The societal reaction to conventional crime is a series of arrests and convictions, with institutionalization and rehabilitation (attempted) of the offender. Agency programs preserve the status quo without changing social conditions.
Organized	There is considerable public toleration of organized crime. Offenses are not usually visible to the public. Immunity of offenders, as provided by effective organization, prevents detection and arrest. Convictions are usually for minor offenses.
Professional	There is considerable public toleration of professional crime because of its low visibility. Offenders are able to escape conviction by "fixing" cases.

From Clinard and Quinney, *Criminal Behavior Systems: A Typology.*

implications in being a mixture of property and drug offender, mainly the likely possibility of their participation in patterns of organized crime, through the "fence" and the pusher or drug dealer.

According to the typological analysis of Gibbons, one of the subjects of our research, Jack, then is a paradigmatical example of a "heavy."

The rest of the cases are of "semiprofessional" offenders. However, there are differences of degree among them. Soledad and Modesto are clearly semiprofessionals. Ralph and Francisco are in the middle of the continuum between heavy and semiprofessional. However, both the heavy and the semiprofessionals of our research have many traits in common.

The burglars self-described here, with the exception of Jack, may be considered "semiprofessional property criminals" in terms of Gibbons's typology:

Semiprofessional property offenders are one illustration. This pattern begins at the onset of minor delinquency acts in early adolescence. Such a career life frequently leads to more serious forms of delinquency with advancing age: repeated police contacts, commitment to juvenile institutions, "graduation" into adult forms of illegal activity, and more contacts with law enforcement and correctional agencies. Over this lengthy development sequence, the social-psychological characteristics of offenders also change.[17]

Appendix B

Toward an Integrative Criminology

The Nature and Content of Criminology in an Integrative Perspective

No attempt is being made here to indulge in traditional polemics, which have plagued both the social sciences and criminology, concerning the "cultural" versus the "natural" model of explanation and its pertinent methodologies, or more recently, the "clinical" versus the "sociological" model in the study of crime. We strongly believe in the adequacy of an "integrative criminological model" by which a variety of methods and perspectives could be fruitfully combined in the study of human conduct as an integration or coalescence, as Hall has suggested, of facts, values, and norms.[1]

According to Hall:

Criminology should be integrated with existing disciplines: economics, sociology, ethics, social psychology, biology and others. These disciplines can be reconstructed much more rapidly than the social realities they explore. Increase in knowledge in criminology, as in each of the social sciences, consists in the very exploration of the interrelationships of phenomena relevant to questions about certain social problems, i.e., in the construction of a total significant social configuration.[2]

Canestri recommends, in the same order of ideas, the creation of interdisciplinary scientific teams in criminology.[3] An integrative criminology has its foundations on a balanced perspective of human conduct—integration of facts, norms, and values—and is one of the "regional ontologies" of a "humanistic" legal sociology.

Hall, speaking of his "humanistic" legal sociology, makes claims for the integration of the actually fragmented spectrum of the social sciences. Thus he contends that the anthropology of law, political science, and of course the sociology of law may actually constitute a single social discipline.[4]

Legal sociology, for Hall, is a comprehensive denomination with humanistic concerns. His classic work, *Theft, Law and Society,* one of the outstanding contributions of the present century to the area of the sociology of law and legal institutions, is also a paradigmatic example of such a discipline. Criminology, in addition, is tied to cultural legal history, and would deal not only with legal concepts, but with relevant social problems, values, contexts, and functions. "Since existing institutions have grown from past ones, our knowledge of them is a correlative affair. . . ." Later, Hall adds: "We may conclude that, although events can be fully understood only if their general patterns are also considered, such general knowledge may supplement, but it cannot displace, historical knowledge."[5]

Criminological knowledge has to include consideration of values. "Values are of paramount importance in understanding of the rule of the law from Plato's statement to XX century dictatorships"; and "this has been the focal point in the quest for equality, security and justice; and all of this is incomprehensible unless the ethical significance of the rule of law is understood."[6] In relation to the current perspectives of the law, that is, logical positivism, natural law, and sociological jurisprudence, the latter in the American legal realism or Scandinavian version, Hall has emphasized continuously the need for an integrative perspective in which law is conduct that realizes values, expresses norms, and in cases of deviation is and ought to be met by sanctions.

In this construction, the sociology of law plays an important role, and "when constructed will be a theoretical social science consisting of generalizations regarding social phenomena insofar as it refers to the contents, purposes, applications and effects of legal rules."[7]

The subject matter of an integrative criminology should include:

1. Penal law viewed as rules (the normative perspective including doctrines and principles)
2. Penal law in action, that is, certain actions of legislators, judges, law enforcement personnel, penal and correctional administrators, and the like
3. Conformity and violation toward which official penal law, as

      action, is directed. The above dimensions of penal law as action include ideational, factual, and valuational aspects

4. Social problems that center on violation of actual penal laws[8]

Lay action and behavior are also part of the area covered by an integrative criminology. It is important to distinguish between *conformity*, where there is no awareness of relevant rules of law, *obedience*, where there is such awareness, and *compliance*, where there is not only such awareness but approval of the rules.[9]

Law as action should be distinguished from other types of action.[10] "The . . . dimensions of law as action—its ideational, factual and valuational aspects, do not comprise a mere addition or collection of features separately treated in particularistic legal philosophies; action is a vital unity."[11]

"Criminologists," according to Hall, "study those phases of social reality which irritate, produce tension, run counter to accepted values, constitute social problems. Specifically, their concern is those social problems that center on violation of actual penal laws. . . . Understanding these social problems depends on knowledge of social realities, which not only defy actual division, but which can be comprehended only as integers. Hence, criminology and the other social disciplines can be differentiated in terms of the types of questions asked concerning social phenomena. . . . Ideally, each social discipline would, therefore, represent the incidence of all social science upon distinctive questions."[12]

The integrative criminology has to reckon with the problem that "in many scientific discussions of crime, we have long been made victims of scholastic oversimplifications, even of fads that, in abortive efforts to surmount the real difficulties, limited the range of investigation to muscular movements, with talk and thought either ignored or labeled 'oral behavior' as though that aided understanding."[13] Further, "one major problem concerns the adequacy of legal concepts. It must be recognized that there is a constant, practically inevitable lag between the legal categories and actual behavior patterns; this lag increases in proportion to the acceleration of social change. Indeed, there is little factual content in any legal definition of crime that is entirely invariant over a long period of years."[14]

"Theory, research and practice are concerns of an integrative criminology. . . . Legal theorizing and the judge's practical knowledge intermingle in the decision making."[15] Legal sociologists try to increase knowledge of legal practice by vicarious participation in the action of officials and by observation. The knowledge acquired by a sensitive "participant" must be checked and supplemented by what he observes and it must be coherent with his jurisprudential perspective, including his theory of social action.[16]

Penal and Criminological Reform

It has been said that "the penal system of any given society is not an isolated phenomenon subject only to its own special laws. It is an integral part of the whole social system and shares its aspirations and its defects. . . . There is a paradox in the fact that the progress of human knowledge has made the problem of penal treatment more comprehensible and more soluble than ever, while the question of a fundamental revision in the policy of punishment seems to be further away today than ever before, because of its functional dependence on the given social order."[17]

This quotation points out the relative neglect of the sociology of penal systems, perhaps due to the influence of normative penal theory as a main approach to the problem.[18] We may add that the concentration on penal rules rather than on study of factual and valuational content has delayed, when not discouraged, the analysis of penal systems as the product of ideological, economic, and social forces at a given time and place. If crime "is a reflection of social conditions, it is to these conditions that we must turn our attention if we wish to transform the original scene."[19]

According to Hall, "The salient twentieth century fact about criminal law is widespread skepticism of punishment. . . . In sum, what merits consideration in twentieth century criminal jurisprudence is not the thesis that justice is obsolete but that it should be tempered by compassion and sincere efforts to rehabilitate."[20] Denis Szabo believes that the crisis in values of Western civilization is reflected primarily in the area of justice.[21]

The penal law itself, especially regarding the incrimination of the criminal receiver, has been the concern of serious scholars. There is no possibility of expecting gains in the fight against property crime and drug addiction without minimizing the rewards and increasing the likelihood of penal incrimination for successful fencing activities.

Hall has noted that:

> The only adequate approach to the criminal receiver is that which deals with him as an established participant in the economic life of society, whose behavior has been institutionalized over a span of more than two centuries in Anglo-American experience. . . .[22]
>
> The dealer in stolen goods must know the sources where the merchandise he wants can be had, and he must be able to get it.[23]
>
> Most analyses of criminal receiving emphasize the fact that the thief depends upon the receiver, that without the latter, the former could not exist. What has not been appreciated is the fact that the receiver is in precisely the same position as the thief as regards his dependence upon a market for stolen goods, which is, in the last analysis, a phase of the market in general.[24]

Indeed, the history of stolen property might be written in terms of the difficulties of convicting these offenders. "The receiver has not only obstructed the operation of the law where it was aimed directly at him, he has also been the traditional protector of the criminals associated with him. . . . The receiver is the natural rallying point for professional criminals."[25] It is clear that at every crucial stage in the administration of criminal law prior to the imposition of the sentence, the licensed dealers fare better than do general receivers.

The most serious aspect of the situation is that the worst offenders, who probably engaged in professional receiving, are only rarely brought to trial and when they are tried, under laws which indiscriminately provide the same penalties for all criminal receivers, their chances of escaping entirely unscathed are excellent.[26]

For the criminologist advocating an integrative perspective, community and social prevention of crime should become a top priority. New alternatives to crime, other than the institutionalization of the offender, should be implemented. Institutionalization of the offender should be the exception, not the rule. Instead, probation and parole should gain new effectiveness by being community oriented and structured.

Penal rules should be reexamined, to delete much of what tends to result in "overcriminalization" of the offender, especially with respect to minor infractions punished, with the consequent stigmatizing effect of law enforcement and the legal process.

Law is not the law of the books, but "law in action." Reflection should be directed also to the effective functioning of the criminal justice system to render its operations in tune with the needs for *individualized justice* and *effective rehabilitation.*

In sum, what is needed is a new criminological approach for a healthier community.

Notes

Editor's Introduction: On the Offender's Perspective

1. Enmanuel Levinas, "Reflexiones Sobre la 'Technica' Fenomenologica," in *Cahier de Royaumont-Husserl* (Buenos Aires: Edit. Paidos, 1968), p. 90.
2. Abraham Maslow, *Motivation and Personality* (New York: Harper and Brothers, 1954), p. 27.
3. Jerome Hall, *Studies in Jurisprudence and Criminal Theory* (New York: Oceana Publications, 1958), pp. 202–3.
4. Cited by David M. Petersen and Marcello Truzzi, *Criminal Life: Views from the Inside* (Englewood Cliffs, N.J.: Prentice-Hall, 1972), p. viii.
5. Marshall B. Clinard and Richard Quinney, *Criminal Behavior Systems* (New York: Holt, Rinehart and Winston, 1967), pp. 254–55.
6. Alfred Schutz, *On Phenomenology and Social Relations* (Chicago: The University of Chicago Press, 1970), p. 282.
7. Hall, *Theft, Law and Society*, 2d ed. (Indianapolis: Bobbs-Merrill, 1952), p. xvi.
8. Ludwig Biswanger, *Selected Papers of Ludwig Biswanger* (New York: Harper and Row, 1966), p. 204.
9. As Victor Frankl has expressed it: "To put it in Augustinian terms, man's heart is restless until he has found and fulfilled, meaning and purpose in life." Victor Frankl, *The Will to Meaning: Foundations of Logotherapy* (New York: Plume Books, 1970), p. 55. Later Frankl adds: "I have said that meaning cannot be given arbitrarily but must be found responsibly. I could have said as well that it must be sought for conscientiously. And in fact man is guided in his search for meaning by conscience. . . . Conscience could be defined as the intuitive capacity of man to find out the meaning of a situation" (p. 63).

Appendix A: On Criminal Careers and Typologies

1. Howard S. Becker, *Outsiders: Studies in the Sociology of Deviance* (Glencoe, Ill.: Free Press, 1956); Marshall B. Clinard and Richard Quinney, *Criminal Behavior Systems: A Typology* (New York: Holt, Rinehart and Winston, 1973); Kai T. Erikson, *Wayward Puritans* (New York, London, and Sydney: John Wiley and Sons, 1966); Don Gibbons, *Society, Crime, and Criminal Careers* (Englewood Cliffs, N.J.: Prentice-Hall, 1968); Daniel Glasser, *Social Deviance* (Chicago: Markham Publishing, 1971); Ervin Goffman, *Asylums* (New York: Anchor Books, 1961) and *Stigma* (Englewood Cliffs, N.J.: Prentice-Hall, 1965); Elmer H. Johnson, *Crime, Correction, and Society*, 3d ed. (Chicago: Dorsey Press, 1973); E. Lemert, *Social Pathology* (New York: McGraw-Hill, 1951); Thomas J. Scheff, *Being Mentally Ill: A Sociological Theory* (Chicago: Aldine, 1971); Thomas S. Szasz, *The Manufacture of Madness* (New York: Dell, 1971).
2. Milan Milutinovic, "Main Trends in Contemporary Criminology," *Seventh International Congress of Criminology* (Belgrade, 1973), pp. 12–13.
3. Jerome Hall, *Studies in Jurisprudence and Criminal Theory* (New York: Oceana Publications, 1958), p. 206.

4. Ibid., p. 213.
5. Quinney, *The Social Reality of Crime* (Boston: Little, Brown, 1970), p. 16.
6. Ibid., p. 233.
7. Lemert, *Social Pathology*, p. 23.
8. Gibbons, *Society, Crime, and Criminal Careers*, p. 237.
9. Clinard and Quinney, *Criminal Behavior Systems*, pp. 131–33.
10. Becker, *Outsiders*.
11. Gibbons, *Society, Crime, and Criminal Careers*, pp. 230–37.
12. Ibid., pp. 252–63.
13. Clinard and Quinney, *Criminal Behavior Systems*, pp. 13–21.
14. Ibid., p. 133.
15. Ibid., p. 135.
16. Becker, *Outsiders*, pp. 31–34.
17. Don Gibbons, *Changing the Law Breaker* (Englewood Cliffs, N.J.: Prentice-Hall, 1965), pp. 51–52.

Appendix B: Toward an Integrative Criminology

1. Introduction to Jerome Hall, *Theft, Law and Society* (Indianapolis: Bobbs-Merrill, 1952). Also, on the integrative perspective in the social sciences, law, and jurisprudence, see: Renato Cirell Czerna, "A Dialectica de Implicação e Polaridade no Criticismo Ontognoseológico," *Revista Brasileira de Filosofia*, vol. 11, p. 248; Cirell Czerna, "Notas Sobre o Problema de Certeza no Direito," *Revista Brasileira de Filosofia*, vol. 7 (1957); Pedro R. David, "El Integrativismo, Las Ciencias Sociales," *Eighth Interamerican Congress of Philosophy* (Brazilia, 1972); David, "Bosquejo de la Jusfilosofía Integrativa de Jerome Hall," *La Ley* (Buenos Aires: January 16, 1961); David, "Perspectivas de Dos Filosofías del Derecho Integrativas: Hall y Reale," *Anais do III Congreso Nacional de Filosofia* (São Paulo: November 1959), pp. 257–63; David, *Sociología Criminal Juvenil* (Buenos Aires: Edit. Depalma, 1968); David, *Instituciones Jurídicos Sociales* (Buenos Aires: Edit. Omeba, 1962); David, *Conducta, Integrativismo y Sociología del Derecho* (Buenos Aires: Edit. De Zavalia, 1970); Werner Goldschmidt, *La Ciencia de la Justicia* (Madrid: Aguilar, 1958); Jerome Hall, *Comparative Law and Social Theory* (Baton Rouge: Louisiana State University Press, 1963); Hall, "Reason and Reality in Jurisprudence," *Buffalo Law Review* 7:351 (1958), translated into Spanish by Pedro David under the title *Razon y Realidad en el Derecho* (Buenos Aires: Edit. Depalma, 1959); Hall, *Studies in Jurisprudence and Criminal Theory* (New York: Oceana, 1958); Hall, *Theft, Law and Society* (Indianapolis: Bobbs-Merrill, 1957); Hall, *General Principles of Criminal Law* (Indianapolis: Bobbs-Merrill, 1947); Hall, *Living Law of Democratic Society* (Indianapolis: Bobbs-Merrill, 1949), translated into Portuguese by Paulo Dourado de Gusmao; Hall, *Foundations of Jurisprudence* (Indianapolis: Bobbs-Merrill, 1973); Miguel Herrera Figueroa, "Delito Formal," in *Enciclopedia Jurídica*, vol. 6 (Buenos Aires: Edit. Omeba, 1957); Herrera Figueroa, *Jurista*, vol. 15 (Buenos Aires: Edit. Omeba, 1962); Herrera Figueroa, "Miguel Reale, Filósofo y Jurista," *Revista da Faculdade do Direito*, vol. 1 (São Paulo, 1955); Herrera Figueroa, *Psicología y Criminología* (Buenos Aires: Edit. Omeba, 1967); Herrera Figueroa, *Sociología del Derecho* (Buenos Aires: Edit. Depalma, 1968); Herrera Figueroa, *Justicia y Sentido* (Buenos Aires: Edit. Richardet-Tucuman, 1948); Herrera Figueroa, *Sociología del Espectaculo* (Buenos Aires: Paidos, 1974); Miguel Reale, "Estructura a Fundamento da Ordem Jurídica," *Eighth Interamerican Congress of Philosophy* (Brazilia, 1972); Reale, *Pluralismo e Libertade* (São Paulo: Edição Saraiva, 1963); Reale, *O Direito como Experiência Libertade* (São Paulo: Edição Saraiva, 1970); Reale, "Aspectos de Teoria Tridimensional do Direito," *Revista dos Tribunais Ltda.* (São Paulo); Reale, *Filosofia do Direito*, vol. 1, t. 1 and 2 (São Paulo: Edição Saraiva, 1953); Reale, *Horizontes do Direito e da Historia* (São Paulo: Edição Saraiva, 1956); Luis Recasens Siches, "Imperativo y Norma en el Derecho," in *Estudios de Derecho*, vol. 20, no. 60 (Facultad de Derecho y Ciencias Políticas de

la Universidad de Antioquia, Colombia); Recasens Siches, *Sociología* (Mexico: Edit. Porrua, 1958); Recasens Siches, *Tratado do Filosofia del Derecho* (Mexico: Edit. Porrua, 1959); Recasens Siches, "La Naturaleza del Pansamiento Jurídico," *Eighth Interamerican Congress of Philosophy* (Brazilia, 1972); Irineu Strenger, "Contribução de Miguel Reale a Teoria do Direito e do Estado," *Revista Brasileira de Filosofia*, vol. 11 (1959); Strenger, "Contribução a uma Teoria Geral dos Modelos Juridicos," *Eighth Interamerican Congress of Philosophy* (Brazilia, 1972); Glaucio Veiga, "Sobre um Livro de Miguel Reale," *Revista Brasileira de Filosofia*, vol. 6 (1956); Luis Washington Vita, "Miguel Reale, Historiador de Ideas," *Revista Brasileira de Filosofia*, vol. 11 (1959).

2. Hall, *Studies in Jurisprudence and Criminal Theory*, p. 214.

3. F. Canestri, "Personnalité Criminelle et Tipologies de Délinquants," *Seventh International Congress of Criminology* (Belgrade, 1973), p. 6.

4. Hall, *Comparative Law and Social Theory*, pp. 111–12. See also Herrera Figueroa, *Sociología del Derecho.*

5. Hall, *Comparative Law and Social Theory*, pp. 32–42.

6. Ibid., pp. 120–21.

7. Hall, *Studies in Jurisprudence and Criminal Theory*, p. 45.

8. Hall, *Foundations of Jurisprudence*, pp. 157–58.

9. Ibid., pp. 157–59.

10. Ibid., pp. 156–57.

11. Ibid., p. 159.

12. Ibid., pp. 212–13.

13. Hall, *Studies in Jurisprudence and Criminal Theory*, p. 202.

14. Ibid., p. 211.

15. Hall, *Foundations of Jurisprudence*, p. 153.

16. Ibid., p. 154.

17. Georg and Kirchheimer Rushe, *Punishment and Social Structure* (New York: Russell and Russell, 1968), p. 207.

18. Ibid., p. 3.

19. Nils Christie, "The Delinquent Stereotype and Stigmatization," *Seventh International Congress of Criminology* (Belgrade, 1973), p. 12.

20. Hall, "Justice in the Twentieth Century," *California Law Review*, vol. 59, no. 3 (May 1971).

21. Denis Szabo, "Evaluation des Systèmes de Politique Criminelle," *Seventh International Congress of Criminology* (Belgrade, 1973), pp. 3–30.

22. Hall, *Theft, Law and Society*, p. 155.

23. Ibid., p. 158.

24. Ibid., p. 161.

25. Ibid., pp. 195–96.

26. Ibid., pp. 198–99.

Bibliography

I.   Crime and Deviance: Prevention, Theories, and Methods

Abrahamsen, David. "Family Tension, Basic Cause of Criminal Behavior." *Journal of Criminal Law and Criminology* 40:339–43, September-October 1949.

Adams, William T. *Delinquency among Minorities in Rural Areas. Studies in Sociology,* Vol. IX, pp. 82, 90. Buenos Aires: Edit. Omeba, 1965.

Alexander, Franz G., and Sheldon T. Selesnick. *The History of Psychiatry.* New York: Harper and Row, 1966.

———, and Hugo Staub. *The Criminal, the Judge, and the Public: A Psychological Analysis.* Rev. ed. New York: Free Press, 1956.

Aftalion, Enrique R. *El Impacto de las Ideologías Económico-Sociales en lo Penal Económico. Studies in Sociology,* pp. 228–34. Buenos Aires: Edit. Omeba, 1965.

Arnold, David O. *The Sociology of Subcultures.* Berkeley, Calif.: Glendessary Press, 1970.

Barron, Milton L. "Juvenile Delinquency and American Values." *American Sociological Review* 16:208–14, April 1951.

Bean, Philip. "Social Aspects of Drug Abuse: A Criminological Study of a Group of London Drug Offenders." *Journal of Criminal Law, Criminology and Police Science* 62:80–86, March 1971.

Becker, Howard S. *Outsiders: Studies in the Sociology of Deviance.* Glencoe, Ill.: Free Press, 1963.

Blake, Judith, and Kingsley Davis. "Norms, Values and Sanctions." In *Handbook of Modern Sociology,* edited by Robert E. L. Faris. Chicago: Rand McNally, 1964.

Bloch, Herbert A., and Gilbert Geis. *Man, Crime and Society.* New York: Random House, 1962.

Bonger, W. A. *Race and Crime.* Translated by Margaret M. Horduk. New York: Columbia University Press, 1943.

Bordua, David J. "Delinquent Subcultures: Sociological Interpretations of Gang Delinquency." *Annals of the American Academy of Political and Social Science* 338:119–36, November 1961.

———. *Sociological Theories and Their Implications for Juvenile Delinquency.* Washington, D.C.: U.S. Children's Bureau, 1960.

———. "Some Comments on Theories of Group Delinquency." *Sociological Inquiry* 32:245–60, Spring 1962.

Brecher, Edward M., and the Editors of *Consumer Reports. Licit and Illicit Drugs.* Boston, Toronto: Little Brown and Co., 1972.

Brown, Julia S. "A Comparative Study of Deviations from Sexual Mores." *American Sociological Review* 17:135–46, April 1952.

Bullock, Henry Allen. "Urban Homicide in Theory and Fact." *Journal of Criminal Law, Criminology, and Police Science* 45:565–75, January-February 1955.

Burgess, Robert L., and Ronald L. Akers. "A Differential Association-Reinforcement Theory of Criminal Behavior." *Social Problems* 14:128–47, Fall 1968.

Caldwell, Robert G. "The Juvenile Court: Its Development and Some Major Problems." *Journal of Criminal Law, Criminology, and Police Science* 51:493–511, January-February 1960.

Canestri, Francisco. "Estado Actual de la Investigación Criminológica en América Latina." Valencia, Venezuela: *Relación Criminológica,* No. 5, November 1973.

Cartwright, D. S., G. W. Kelling, G. P. Taylor, and C. B. Cameron. "Measuring and Predicting Juvenile Probation Outcomes," *Criminology, An Interdisciplinary Journal* 10:143–61, August 1972.

Cavan, Ruth Shonle. *Juvenile Delinquency.* New York: J. B. Lippincott, 1964.

Chambliss, William J. "A Sociological Analysis of the Law of Vagrancy." *Social Problems* 12:67–77, Summer 1964.

Cicourel, Aaron V. *Method and Measurement in Sociology.* New York: Free Press, 1965.

———. *Social Class, Family Structure and the Administration of Juvenile Justice. Studies in Sociology,* Vol. IX, pp. 27–49. Buenos Aires: Edit. Omeba, 1965.

Clinard, Marshall B. *The Black Market: A Study of White Collar Crime.* New York: Rinehart, 1952.

———. *Sociology of Deviant Behavior.* New York: Holt, Rinehart and Winston, 1968.

———. "Contributions of Sociology to Understanding Deviant Behavior." *British Journal of Delinquency* 13:110–29, October 1962.

———. "A Cross-Cultural Replication of the Relation of Urbanism to Criminal Behavior." *American Sociological Review* 25:253–57, April 1960.

———, and Richard Quinney. *Criminal Behavior Systems.* New York: Holt, Rinehart and Winston, 1973.

Cloward, Richard A. "Illegitimate Means, Anomie, and Deviant Behavior." *American Sociological Review* 24:164–76, April 1959.

———, and Lloyd E. Ohlin. *Delinquency and Opportunity: A Theory of Delinquent Gangs.* New York: Free Press, 1960.

Cohen, Albert K. *Delinquent Boys: The Culture of the Gang.* New York: Free Press, 1955.

———. *Deviance and Control.* Englewood Cliffs, N.J.: Prentice-Hall, 1966.

———, Alfred R. Lindesmith, and Karl F. Schuessler, eds. *The Sutherland Papers.* Bloomington, Ind.: Indiana University Press, 1956.

———, and James F. Short, Jr. "Research in Delinquent Subcultures." *Journal of Social Issues* 14:20–37, 1958.

Cooper, David. *Psychiatry and Anti-Psychiatry.* New York: Ballantine Books, 1967.

Cressey, Donald R. *Delinquency, Crime, and Differential Association.* The Hague: Martinus Nijhoff, 1964.

———, and David A. Ward. *Delinquency, Crime and Social Process.* New York: Harper and Row, 1969.

———. *Other People's Money: A Study in the Social Psychology of Embezzlement.* New York: Free Press, 1965.

———. *Theft of the Nation: The Structure and Operations of Organized Crime in America.* New York: Harper and Row, 1969.

David, Pedro R., and Joseph W. Scott. "A Cross Cultural Comparison of Juvenile Offenders, Offenses, Due Processes, and Societies." *Criminology* 11:183–205, August 1973.

DeFleur, Lois B. "Ecological Variables in the Cross-Cultural Study of Delinquency." *Social Forces* 45:566–70, June 1967.

DeFleur, Melvin L., and Richard Quinney. "A Reformulation of Sutherland's Differential Association Theory and a Strategy for Empirical Verification." *Journal of Research in Crime and Delinquency* 3:1–22, January 1966.

Del Olmo, Rosa. *Penología, Textos Para Su Estudio.* Carabobo, Venezuela: Universidad Central, 1972.

Dentler, Robert A., and Kai T. Erikson. "The Function of Deviance in Groups." *Social Problems* 7:98–107, Fall 1959.

Diana, Lewis. "The Rights of Juvenile Delinquents: An Appraisal of Juvenile Court Procedures." *Journal of Criminal Law, Criminology, and Police Science* 47:561–69, January-February 1957.

Douglas, Jack D. *Deviance and Respectability.* New York: Basic Books, 1970.

Dubin, Robert. "Deviant Behavior and Social Structure." *American Sociological Review* 24:147–64, April 1959.

Durkheim, Emile. *Suicide: A Study in Sociology.* Translated by John A. Spaulding and George Simpson. New York: Free Press, 1951.

Eisenstadt, S. "Delinquency Group Formation among Immigrant Youth." *British Journal of Delinquency* 2:34–43, July 1951.

Ellis, Desmond P., and P. Austin. "Menstruation and Aggressive Behavior in a Correctional Center for Women." *Journal of Criminal Law, Criminology, and Police Science* 62:388–96, September 1971.

Empey, Lamar T. "Delinquency Theory and Recent Research." *Journal of Research in Crime and Delinquency* 4:28–32, January 1967.

———. "Delinquent Subcultures: Theory and Recent Research." *Journal of Research in Crime and Delinquency* 4:32–42, January 1967.

———, and Jerome Rabow. "The Provo Experiment in Delinquency Rehabilitation." *American Sociological Review* 26:679–95, October 1961.

Erickson, Maynard L., and Lamar T. Empey. "Court Records, Undetected Delinquency and Decision-Making." *Journal of Criminal Law, Criminology, and Police Science* 54:456–69, December 1963.

Erikson, Kai. *Wayward Puritans.* New York: John Wiley and Sons, 1966.

Exner, Franz. *Biología Criminal.* Barcelona, Spain: Bosch, Casa Editorial, 1946.

Ferentz, Edward A. "Mental Deficiency and Crime." *Journal of Criminal Law, Criminology, and Police Science* 45:299–307, September-October 1954.

Ferracuti, Franco, and Marvin E. Wolfgang. *The Prediction of Violent Behavior. Studies in Sociology,* Vol. IX, pp. 92–100. Buenos Aires: Edit. Omeba, 1965.

Fink, Arthur E. *Causes of Crime: Biological Theories in the United States, 1800–1915.* Philadelphia: University of Pennsylvania Press, 1938.

Fox, Sanford J. "Delinquency and Biology." *University of Miami Law Review* 16:65–91, Fall 1961.

Friedlander, Kate. *The Psychoanalytic Approach to Juvenile Delinquency.* New York: International Universities Press, 1947.

García Ramírez, Sergio. *La Reforma Penal de 1971.* Mexico: Botas, 1971.

Geis, Gilbert. "Statistics Concerning Race and Crime." *Crime and Delinquency,* April 1965, pp. 142–50.

Gibbons, Don C. *Society, Crime and Criminal Careers.* Englewood Cliffs, N.J.: Prentice-Hall, 1968.

Glaser, Daniel, and Kent Rice. "Crime, Age and Employment." *American Sociological Review* 24:679–86, October 1959.

———. *Social Deviance.* Chicago: Markham Publishing Company, 1972.

Glueck, Sheldon, and Eleanor T. Glueck. *Physique and Delinquency.* New York: Harper and Row, 1956.

Gómez Grillo, E. *Introducción a la Criminología.* Caracas: Universidad de Venezuela, 1966.

Gordon, Milton. "The Concept of the Subculture and Its Application." *Social Forces* 26:40–42, October 1947.

Gough, Harrison G. "Theory and Measurement of Socialization." *Journal of Consulting Psychology* 24:23–30, 1960.

Grant, Douglas J. *Current Trends of Individual and Interpersonal Approaches to the Rehabilitation of the Offender. Studies in Sociology,* Vol. IX, pp. 101–17. Buenos Aires: Edit. Omeba, 1965.

Greer, Scott. *The Logic of Social Inquiry.* Chicago: Aldine, 1969.

Hall, Jerome. *Theft, Law, and Society.* 2d ed. Indianapolis: Bobbs-Merrill, 1952.

———. *Foundations of Jurisprudence.* Indianapolis: Bobbs-Merrill, 1973.

Hartung, Frank E. *Crime, Law and Society.* Detroit: Wayne State University Press, 1965.

————. "A Critique of the Sociological Approach to Crime and Correction." *Law and Contemporary Problems* 23:703–34, Autumn 1958.

————. "Methodological Assumption in a Social Psychological Theory of Criminality." *Journal of Criminal Law, Criminology, and Police Science* 45:652–61, March-April 1955.

————. "White Collar Crime: Its Significance for Theory and Practice." *Federal Probation* 17:31–36, June 1953.

Henry, Andrew F., and James R. Short, Jr. *Suicide and Homicide.* New York : Free Press, 1954.

Herrera Figueroa, Miguel. *Sociología del Derecho.* Buenos Aires: Depalma, 1970.

Hewitt, John P. *Social Stratification and Deviant Behavior.* New York: Random House, 1970.

Hirschi, Travis, and Hanan C. Selvin. *Delinquency Research: An Appraisal of Analytic Methods.* New York: Free Press, 1967.

Hollingshead, August D., and Fredrick C. Redlich. *Social Class and Mental Illness.* New York: John Wiley and Sons, 1958.

Howells, W. W. "A Factorial Study of Constitutional Type." *American Journal of Physical Anthropology* 10:91–118, March 1952.

Husserl, E. *Investigaciones Lógicas.* Buenos Aires: Revista de Occidente, 1949.

Inciardi, James. "The Adult Firesetter." *Criminology, an Interdisciplinary Journal,* August 1970, p. 145.

————. "Visibility, Societal Reaction and Criminal Behavior." *Criminology, an Interdisciplinary Journal* 10:217–35, August 1972.

Irey, E. L., and W. J. Slocum. *The Tax Dodgers.* New York: Greenberg, 1948.

Jacobs, J. *The Death and Life of Great American Cities.* New York: Random House, 1961.

Jeffery, C. R. *Crime and Prevention through Environmental Design.* Beverly Hills and London: Sage Publications, 1971.

Johnson, Guy B. "The Negro and Crime." *Annals of the American Academy of Political and Social Science* 217:93–104, September 1941.

Joplin, Glenn H. "Self-concept and the Highfields Program: Recidivists and Non-recidivists." *Criminology, an Interdisciplinary Journal* 19:491–97, February 1972.

Kelly, Harold H., and Edmund H. Volkart. "The Resistance to Change of Group-Anchored Attitudes." *American Sociological Review* 17:453–65, August 1952.

Kephart, William H. "The Negro Offender." *American Journal of Sociology* 60:46–50, July 1954.

Klapper, Joseph T. *The Effects of Mass Communication.* New York: Free Press, 1961.

Klein, Malcolm W., ed. *Juvenile Gangs in Context.* Englewood Cliffs, N.J.: Prentice-Hall, 1967.

Kobrin, Solomon. "The Conflict of Values in Delinquency Areas." *American Sociological Review* 16:653–61, October 1951.

Kozol, H. L., M.D., R. J. Boucher, and R. F. Garofalo. "The Diagnosis and Treatment of Dangerousness." *Crime and Delinquency* 18:371–92, October 1972.

Laing, R. D. *The Politics of Experience.* New York: Ballantine Books, 1967.

Larsen, Otto N., ed. *Violence and the Mass Media.* New York: Harper and Row, 1968.

Lemert, Edwin M. *Human Deviance, Social Problems and Social Control.* Englewood Cliffs, N.J.: Prentice-Hall, 1972.

Lindesmith, Alfred R. *The Addict and the Law.* Bloomington, Ind.: Indiana University Press, 1965.

Lyra, Roberto Filho. *Criminología Dialéctica.* Rio de Janeiro: Borsoi, 1971.

————. *Addiction and Opiates.* Chicago: Aldine, 1968.

————. *Opiate Addiction.* Bloomington, Ind.: Principia Press, 1947.

————. "Organized Crime." *Annals of the American Academy of Political and Social Science* 217:119–27, September 1941.

Mannheim, Hermann. *Comparative Criminology.* Boston: Houghton Mifflin, 1965.

————. *Group Problems in Crime and Punishment.* London: Routledge and Kegan Paul, 1955.

Matza, David, and Gresham M. Sykes. "Juvenile Delinquency and Subterranean Values." *American Sociological Review* 26:712–19, October 1961.

Mayorca, Juan Manuel (H.). *Criminología*. Caracas, Venezuela: Ministerio de Educación, 1970.

McClellan, John L. *Crime without Punishment*. New York: Duell, Sloan and Pearce, 1962.

Mendoza, José Rafael T. *La Protección y el Tratamiento de los Menores*. Buenos Aires: Bibliográfica, 1960.

Menninger, Karl. *The Crime of Punishment*. New York: Viking Press, 1966.

Meyer, John C., Jr. "Marijuana Use by White College Students." *Crime and Delinquency* 19:79–90, January 1973.

Moran, Richard. "Criminal Homicide: External Restraint and Subculture of Violence." *Criminology, an Interdisciplinary Journal*, February 1971, p. 357.

Musgrove, F. *Youth and the Social Order*. Bloomington, Ind.: Indiana University Press, 1965.

National Commission on the Causes and Prevention of Violence, *Staff Report: Firearms and Violence in American Life* (Washington, D.C., U.S. Government Printing Office, 1970).

————, *Staff Report: Shut It Down! A College in Crisis* (Washington, D.C., U.S. Government Printing Office, June 1969).

National Council on Crime and Delinquency, *Fifty Projects: Citizen Action to Control Crime and Delinquency* (New York, April 1969).

Nieves, Hector. *Investigación Sobre un Sistema de Prioridades*. Valencia, Venezuela, 1972.

Nye, F. Ivan. *Family Relationships and Delinquent Behavior*. New York: John Wiley, 1958.

Palmer, Stuart. *Deviance and Conformity*. New Haven, Conn.: College and University Press, 1970.

Pollack, Otto. *The Criminality of Women*. Philadelphia: University of Pennsylvania Press, 1950.

Piaget, Jean, and L. Goldmann. *Las Nociones de Estructura y Genesis*. Buenos Aires: Proteo, 1969,

Pinatel, Jean. *La Societé Criminogene*. Paris: Calman-Levy, 1971.

President's Commission on Campus Unrest, *Report* (Washington, D.C., U.S. Government Printing Office, 1970).

President's Commission on Law Enforcement and Administration of Justice, *The Challenge of Crime in a Free Society* (1967).

————, Task Force on Assessment, *Task Force Report: Crime and Its Impact—An Assessment* (1967).

————, Task Force on Drunkenness, *Task Force Report: Drunkenness* (Annotations, Consultants' Papers, and Related Materials) (1967).

————, Task Force on Juvenile Delinquency, *Task Force Report: Juvenile Delinquency and Youth Crime* (Report on Juvenile Justice and Consultants' Papers) (1967).

Quinney, Earl R. "The Study of White Collar Crime: Toward a Reorientation in Theory and Research." *Journal of Criminal Law, Criminology, and Police Science* 55:208–14, June 1964.

Quinney, Richard. *The Social Reality of Crime*. Boston: Little, Brown, 1940.

Radzinowicz, Leon. *In Search of Criminology*. London: Heinemann, 1961.

————, and Marvin E. Wolfgang. *Crime and Justice*. Vols. I, II, and III. New York: Basic Books, 1971.

Rawlings, L. M. "Self-Control and Interpersonal Violence: A Study of Scottish Male Severe Offenders." *Criminology, an Interdisciplinary Journal* 19:23–49, May 1973.

Reasons, Charles E., and Jack L. Kuykendall. *Race, Crime and Justice*. Pacific Palisades, Calif.: Goodyear, 1972.

Reckless, Walter C. *The Etiology of Delinquent and Criminal Behavior*. New York: Social Science Research Council, 1943.

Research Analysis Corporation. *A Comprehensive Research Program in Crime Prevention*. McLean, Va., August 1969.

Reuterman, N. A., M. J. Love, and F. Fiedler, "A Partial Evaluation of Block and Niederhoffer's Theory of Gang Delinquency." *Criminology, an Interdisciplinary Journal* 10:415–27, February 1973.

Rosen, George. *Madness in Society*. New York: Harper Torchbooks, 1969.

Rosenberg, Chaim M., and J. J. Paine. "Female Juvenile Delinquency: A Nineteenth Century Followup." *Crime and Delinquency* 19:72–78, January 1973.

Rubington, Earl, and Martin S. Weinberg. *Deviance*. New York: Macmillan, 1973.

Rudoff, Alvin. "The Incarcerated Mexican-American Delinquent." *Journal of Criminal Law, Criminology, and Police Science* 62:224–39, June 1971.

Salerno, Ralph F. "Organized Crime and Criminal Justice." *Federal Probation* 33:11–17, June 1969.

Szasz, Thomas S. *The Manufacture of Madness*. New York: Dell, 1970.

Scheff, Thomas J., ed. *Mental Illness and Social Processes*. New York: Harper and Row, 1967.

Schur, Edwin M. *Labeling Deviant Behavior*. New York: Harper and Row, 1971.

Sellin, Thorsten. *Culture Conflict and Crime*. New York: Social Science Research Council, 1938.

―――. *Research Memorandum on Crime in the Depression*. New York: Social Science Research Council, 1937.

―――, and Marvin E. Wolfgang. *The Measurement of Delinquency*. New York: John Wiley, 1964.

Schoenfeld, C. G. "A Psychoanalytic Theory of Juvenile Delinquency." *Crime and Delinquency* 17:469–80, October 1971.

Shore, Milton F. "Psychological Theories of the Causes of Anti-Social Behavior." *Crime and Delinquency* 17:456–68, October 1971.

Short, James F., Jr., and Fred L Strodtbeck. *Group Process and Gang Delinquency*. Chicago: University of Chicago Press, 1965.

―――. *Gang Delinquency and Delinquent Subcultures*. New York: Harper and Row, 1968.

Shulman, Harry M. *Juvenile Delinquency in American Society*. New York: Harper and Row, 1961.

Spergel, Irving. *Street Gang Work: Theory and Practice*. Reading, Mass.: Addison-Wesley, 1966.

Spitzer, Stephan P., and Norman K. Denzin. *The Mental Patient*. New York: McGraw-Hill, 1968.

Stofflet, E. H. "The European Immigrant and His Children." *Annals of the American Academy of Political and Social Science* 217:84–92, September 1941.

Stratton, John R., and Robert M. Terry, eds. *Prevention of Delinquency: Problems and Programs*. New York: Macmillan, 1968.

Sussman, Frederick B. *Laws of Juvenile Delinquency*. New York: Oceana Publications, 1950.

Sutherland, Edwin H. *The Professional Thief*. Chicago: University of Chicago Press, 1937.

―――, and Donald R. Cressey. *Criminology*, Philadelphia: J. B. Lippincott, 1970.

Tobias, J. J. *Urban Crime in Victorian England*. New York: Schocken Books, 1967.

Toby, Jackson. "Social Disorganization and Stake in Conformity: Complementary Factors in the Predatory Behavior of Hoodlums." *Journal of Criminal Law, Criminology, and Police Science* 48:12–17, May-June 1957.

Toro Calder, J. *Survey of Personnel Working in Criminology in Puerto Rico*. Rio Piedras: University of Puerto Rico, 1966.

Trice, Harrison. *Alcoholism in America*. New York: McGraw-Hill, 1966.

Vaz, Edmund W., ed. *Middle-class Juvenile Delinquency*. New York: Harper and Row, 1961.

Vincent, Clark E. "Mental Health and the Family." *Journal of Marriage and the Family* 29:18–39, February 1967.

Volkman, Rita, and Donald R. Cressey. "Differential Association and the Rehabilitation of Drug Addicts." *American Journal of Sociology* 69:129–42, September 1963.

Von Hentig, Hans. "The First Generation and a Half: Notes on the Delinquency of Native Whites of Mixed Parentage." *American Sociological Review* 10:792–98, December 1945.

Voss, Harwin L. *Society, Delinquency and Delinquent Behavior*. Boston: Little, Brown, 1970.

Weinberg, Kirson S. "Urbanization and Male Delinquency in Ghana." *Journal of Research in Crime and Delinquency* 2:85–94, July 1965.

―――. *Urbanization and Delinquency in West Africa*. Studies in Sociology, Vol. IX, pp. 139–54. Buenos Aires: Edit. Omeba, 1965.

Wheeler, Stanton, and Leonard S. Cottrell, Jr., with the assistance of Anne Romasco. *Juvenile Delinquency: Its Prevention and Control.* New York: Russell Sage Foundation, 1966.

Whyte, William F. *Street Corner Society.* Chicago: University of Chicago Press, 1943.

Wilkins, Leslie T. *Social Deviance: Social Policy, Action and Research.* Englewood Cliffs, N.J.: Prentice-Hall, 1965.

Wirth, Louis. "Culture Conflicts and Delinquency." *Social Forces* 9:484–92, June 1931.

Witmer, Helen L., and Edith Tufts, *The Effectiveness of Delinquency Prevention Programs,* U.S. Children's Bureau Publication 350 (Washington, D.C., U.S. Government Printing Office, 1954).

Witmer, Helen L., ed. *Parents and Delinquency* (Washington, D.C., Department of Health, Education and Welfare, 1954).

Wolfgang, Marvin E. *Crime and Race: Conceptions and Misconceptions.* New York: Institute of Human Relations Press, American Jewish Congress, 1964.

———. "Criminology and the Criminologist." *Journal of Criminal Law, Criminology, and Police Science* 54:155–62, June 1963.

———, and Franco Ferracuti. *The Subculture of Violence.* London: Social Science Paperbacks, 1967.

Wood, Arthur Lewis. "Minority-Group Criminality and Cultural Integration." *Journal of Criminal Law and Criminology* 37:498–510, March-April 1947.

———. "Political Radicalism in Changing Singalese Villages." *Human Organization* 23:99–107, Summer 1964.

Wooton, Barbara. *Social Science and Social Pathology.* London: Macmillan, 1959.

Yablonsky, Lewis. *Synanon: The Tunnel Back.* Baltimore: Penguin Books, 1967.

Yinger, J. Milton, "Contraculture and Subculture." *American Sociological Review* 25:625–26, October 1960.

II. Law Enforcement

Alex, Nicholas, *Black in Blue: A Study of the Negro Policeman.* New York: Appleton-Century-Crofts, 1970.

Banton, Michael. *The Policeman in the Community.* London: Tavistock, 1964.

Bennett, James V. *I Chose Prison.* New York: Alfred A. Knopf, 1970.

Bittner, Egon. *The Functions of the Police in a Modern Society,* National Institute of Mental Health, Center for Studies of Crime and Delinquency (Washington, D.C., U.S. Government Printing Office, 1970).

———. "The Police on Skid-Row: A Study of Peace Keeping." *American Sociological Review* 32:699–715, October 1967.

Bordua, David. *Police: Six Sociological Essays.* New York: John Wiley, 1967.

Chevigny, Paul. *Police Power.* New York: Pantheon, 1968.

Cicourel, Aaron V. *The Social Organization of Juvenile Justice.* New York: John Wiley, 1968.

Cipes, Robert M. *The Crime War.* New York: New American Library, 1968.

Clark, Kenneth. *Dark Ghetto.* New York: Harper and Row, 1965.

Cole, Donald, et al. "The Negro Law Enforcement Officer in Texas." Criminal Justice Monograph (Huntsville, Tex.) 1(4):1–73, 1969.

Conot, Robert. *Rivers of Blood: Years of Darkness.* New York: Bantam Books, 1967.

Cray, Edward. *The Big Blue Line.* New York: Coward-McCann, 1967.

Donnelly, Richard C. "Police Authority and Practices." *Annals of the American Academy of Political and Social Science* 339:90–110, January 1962.

Ehrlich, H. J., J. W. Rinehart, and J. C. Howell. "The Study of Role Conflict: Explorations in Methodology." *Sociometry* 25:85–97, March 1962.

Fanon, Franz. *The Wretched of the Earth.* New York: Grove Press, 1965.

Fort, Joel. *The Pleasure Seekers.* New York: Bobbs-Merrill, 1968.

Germann, A. C., et al. *Introduction to Law Enforcement.* Springfield, Ill.: Charles C Thomas, Publisher, 1970.

Goldman, Nathan. *The Differential Selection of Juvenile Offenders for Court Appearance.* New York: National Council on Crime and Delinquency, 1963.

Hacker, Andrew. *The End of an American Era.* New York: Atheneum Publishers, 1970.

Hall, Jerome. "Police and Law in a Democratic Society." *Indiana Law Journal* 18:133–77, Winter 1953.

Institute of Contemporary Corrections and the Behavioral Sciences. *Police-Community Relationships.* Huntsville, Tex., 1969.

International Association of Chiefs of Police. *Police and Their Opinions.* Washington, D.C., 1969.

————. *Police and the Changing Community.* Washington, D.C., 1965.

————. *Police-Community Relations.* Washington, D.C., 1966.

Jacobs, Paul. *Prelude to Riot.* New York: Random House, 1966.

Kadish, S. H. "Legal Norms and Discretion in the Police and Sentencing Processes." *Harvard Law Review* 75:904–31, March 1962.

Koehne, Frederic W., with W. R. Partridge. *Region V Criminal Justice Information and Communications System Plan.* Berkeley, Calif.: Association of Bay Area Governments, 1969.

LaFave, Wayne R. *Arrest: The Decision to Take a Suspect into Custody.* Boston: Little, Brown, 1965.

Lester, Julius. *Look Out Whitey, Black Power's Gonna Get Your Mama!* New York: Grove Press, 1969.

Lunden, Walter A. "The Police Image." Prepared for the Des Moines Police Department, Des Moines, Iowa. Ames, Iowa: Iowa State University, 1971.

Mayer, Milton. *On Liberty: Man vs. the State.* Center for the Study of Democratic Institutions, 1969.

National Council on Crime and Delinquency, Washington Council. *The Use of Juveniles as Paid Informants in Drug Abuse Matters (Position Statement).* Seattle, Wash.: 1971.

Nelson, Jack, and Jack Bass. *The Orangeburg Massacre.* New York: Ballantine, 1972.

Newman, David. *Conviction.* Boston: Little, Brown, 1966.

Niederhoffer, Arthur. *Behind the Shield: The Police in Urban Society.* New York: Doubleday, 1967.

————, and Abraham Blumberg. *The Ambivalent Force: Perspectives on Police.* Boston: Ginn, 1970.

Packer, Herbert L. *The Limits of the Criminal Sanction.* Stanford, Calif.: Stanford University Press, 1968.

Partridge, William R., with F. W. Koehne and H. C. Flinner. *Evaluation Plan—Police Information Management Systems.* North American Rockwell, 1968.

"Police and Community Relations." *Police Chief* 38:6–64, 1971.

Randano, Gene. *Walking the Beat.* New York: World, 1968.

Rolph, C. H., ed. *The Police and the Public.* London: Heinemann, 1962.

Schutz, Alfred. *On Phenomenology and Social Relations.* Chicago: The University of Chicago Press, 1970.

Short, James F., Jr., and Ivan Nye. "Reported Behavior as a Criterion of Deviant Behavior." *Social Problems* 5:207–13, Winter 1957–58.

Skolnick, Jerome H. *Justice without Trial.* New York: John Wiley, 1966.

————. *The Politics of Protest.* New York: Simon and Schuster, 1968.

Sowle, Claude R., ed. *Police Power and Individual Freedom: The Quest for Balance.* Chicago: Aldine, 1962.

Thorwald, Jurgen. *Crime and Science.* New York: Harcourt, Brace & World, 1966.

Turner, William W. *Invisible Witness.* New York: Bobbs-Merrill, 1968.

————. *The Police Establishment.* New York: G. P. Putnam's Sons, 1968.

U.S., Chamber of Commerce, *Marshaling Citizen Power against Crime* (Washington, D.C., 1970).

U.S., Justice Department, *Police-Community Relations Training* (Washington, D.C., U.S. Government Printing Office, 1970).

Vollmer, August. "Police Progress in the Past Twenty-Five Years." *Journal of Criminal Law and Criminology* 24:161–75, May-June 1933.

Walker, Daniel. *Rights in Conflict.* New York: Bantam Books, 1968.

Wheeler, Stanton. "Criminal Statistics: A Reformation of the Problem." *Journal of Criminal Law, Criminology, and Police Science* 58:317–24, September 1967.

Whittemore, L. H. *Cop! A Closeup in Violence and Tragedy.* New York: Holt, Rinehart and Winston, 1969.

Willett, T. C. *Criminal on the Road.* London: Tavistock, 1964.

Wilson, James Q. "Generation and Ethnic Differences among Career Police Officers." *American Journal of Sociology* 69:522–28, March 1964.

———. *The Varieties of Police Behavior.* Cambridge, Mass.: Harvard University Press, 1968.

Wilson, O. W. *Police Administration.* New York: McGraw-Hill, 1950.

Winick, Charles. *Juvenile Delinquency as a Function of the Mass Society. Studies in Sociology,* Vol. IX, pp. 155–66. Buenos Aires: Edit. Omeba, 1965.

Wolfgang, Marvin E. "Uniform Crime Reports: A Critical Appraisal." *University of Pennsylvania Law Review* 111:708–39, April 1963.

III.   The Judicial Process

American Bar Association Project on Minimum Standards for Criminal Justice. *Standards Relating to Appellate Review of Sentences.* New York, March 1968.

———. *Standards Relating to Electronic Surveillance.* New York, March 1971.

———. *Standards Relating to Joinder and Severance.* New York, September 1968.

———. *Standards Relating to Pleas of Guilty.* New York, March 1968.

———. *Standards Relating to Pretrial Release.* New York, September 1968.

———. *Standards Relating to Post-Conviction Remedies.* New York, January 1967.

———. *Standards Relating to Providing Defense Services.* New York, June 1967.

———. *Standards Relating to Sentencing Alternatives and Procedures.* New York, September 1968.

———. *Standards Relating to Speedy Trial.* New York, May 1967.

———. *Standards Relating to Trial by Jury.* New York, September 1968.

American Bar Association Project on Standards for Criminal Justice. *Standards Relating to Criminal Appeals.* New York, October 1970.

———. *Standards Relating to Discovery and Procedure before Trial.* New York, October 1970.

———. *Standards Relating to Probation.* New York, February 1970.

———. *Standards Relating to the Prosecution Function and the Defense Function.* New York, March 1970.

Block, Richard L. "Police Action as Reported by Victims of Crime." *Police* 15:43–49, 1970.

Bok, Curtis. "The Jury System in America." *Annals of the American Academy of Political and Social Science* 287:92–96, May 1953.

Cerrada, José. "Estudio sobre el Erotismo como Fenómeno de Desvio Social." *Relación Criminológica,* año 4, no. 6. Valencia, Venezuela: 1971.

Chappell, D., and P. R. Wilson. *The Police and the Public in Australia and New Zealand.* St. Lucia, Queensland: University of Queensland Press, 1969.

Cohen, William M. "Due Process, Equal Protection and State Parole Revocation Proceedings." *University of Colorado Law Review* 42:197–299, 1970.

Correctional Association of New York. *The Rights of Prisoners.* New York, November 1970.

Criminal Justice Coordinating Council and Vera Institute of Justice. *The Manhattan Court Employment Project.* New York, 1970.

David, Pedro. *Sociología Criminal Juvenil*. Buenos Aires: Edit. Depalma, 1968.

———. *Conducta, Integrativismo y Sociología del Derecho*. Buenos Aires: Ediciones de Zavalia, 1970.

Dobson, Mary Virginia. "The Juvenile Court and Parental Rights." *Family Law Quarterly* 4:393–408, 1970.

Downie, Leonard, Jr. *Justice Denied*. Baltimore: Penguin Books, 1971.

Fahey, Richard P. "The Enforcement of the Illinois Felony Marijuana Law in Chicago." *Washington University Law Quarterly*, Vol. 2, Spring 1971.

Fox, Sanford J. "Juvenile Justice Reform: An Historical Perspective." *Stanford Law Review* 22:1187–1239, 1970.

Graham, Fred P. *The Self-Inflicted Wound*. Macmillan, 1970.

Hall, Jerome. "Justice in the Twentieth Century." *California Law Review*, Vol. 59, No. 3, May 1971.

Harris, Richard. *Justice*. New York: E. P. Dutton, 1970.

Hobaica, Chibly A. *El Menor en el Mundo de Su Ley*. Caracas: Gaceta Legal, 1970.

Ichica, Wesley W. "Prisoners' Rights: Access to Courts." *University of Colorado Law Review* 42:275–303, 1970.

James, Rita M. "Status and Competence of Jurors." *American Journal of Sociology* 64:563–70, May 1959.

Kraft, Larry. "Prison Disciplinary Practices and Procedures: Is Due Process Provided?" *North Dakota Law Review* 47:9–75, 1970.

Ladinsky, Jack. "Career of Lawyers, Law Practice, and Legal Institutions." *American Sociological Review* 28:47–54, February 1963.

Lemert, Edwin. "The Grand Jury as an Agency of Social Control." *American Sociological Review* 10:751–58, December 1945.

Mayer, Martin. *The Lawyers*. New York: Harper and Row, 1967.

Mayers, Lewis. *The American Legal System*. Rev. ed. New York: Harper and Row, 1964.

McIntyre, Donald M., and David Lippman. "Prosecutors and Early Disposition of Felony Cases." *American Bar Association Journal* 56:1154–59, 1970.

Miller, Dawson, Dix, and Parnas. *The Police Function*. Mineola, N.Y.: Foundation Press, 1971.

New York State, Systems Development Bureau, *Name Search Techniques* (Albany, New York, 1970).

Newman, Donald J. *Conviction: The Determination of Guilt or Innocence without Trial*. Boston: Little, Brown, 1966.

Nieves, Hector. *Los Valores Criminológicos del Hecho Punible*. Valencia, Venezuela: University of Carabobo, 1972.

Pfiffner, John M. *The Function of the Police in a Democratic Society*. Occasional Papers, University of Southern California, School of Public Administration Civic Center Campus, Center for Training and Career Development, Series 7. Los Angeles, April 1967.

Reale, Miguel. *Pluralismo e Libertade*. São Paulo: Saraiva, 1963.

Rubin, Sol. *The Law of Criminal Correction*. St. Paul, Minn.: West Publishing Co., 1963.

Saari, David J. "Management and Courts: A Perplexing Nexus." *American University Law Review* 20:601–19, 1970–71 Supplement.

Schulman, Sidney. *Toward Judicial Reform in Pennsylvania*. Philadelphia: University of Pennsylvania Law School, 1962.

Serna, Patricio. "The Court Executive in Modern Court Management." A paper prepared for the course Issues in Law Enforcement and the Administration of Justice, Harvard Law School, 1971.

———. "A Legal Services Program for the Barrio." A paper prepared for the course Legal Services for the Poor, Harvard Law School, 1971.

———. "The Preliminary Hearing—What's It All About?" Unpublished third-year paper in fulfillment of requirements for Juris Doctor's Degree, Denver University College of Law, 1970.

Subin, Harry I. "New York's Jail Riots." *Legal Aid Review* 67:23–31, 1970.

Sudnow, David. "Normal Crimes: Sociological Features of the Penal Code in a Public Defender Office." *Social Problems* 12:255–76, Winter 1965.

U.S., Justice Dept., Law Enforcement Assistance Administration, Indian Justice Planning Project, *The People Will Judge!* (1971).

U.S., National Commission on Reform of Federal Criminal Laws, *Final Report: A Proposed New Federal Criminal Code (Title 18, United States Code)* (Washington, D.C., U. S. Government Printing Office, 1971).

Vera Institute of Justice. *Toward Justice for the Poor: The Manhattan Bail Project.* New York.

Wood, Arthur Lewis. "Informal Relations in the Practices of Criminal Law." *American Journal of Sociology* 62:48–55, July 1956.

IV. Corrections and Rehabilitation: The Criminal Law

Adamson, LaMay, and H. Warren Dunham. "Clinical Treatment of Male Delinquents: A Case Study in Effort and Result." *American Sociological Review* 21:312–20, June 1956.

Alexander, Myrle E. *Jail Administration.* Springfield, Ill.: Charles C Thomas, 1957.

Allen, Francis A. "Criminal Justice, Legal Values and the Rehabilitative Ideal." *Journal of Criminal Law, Criminology, and Police Science* 50:226–32, September-October 1959.

American Correctional Association. *Manual of Correctional Standards.* 5th printing, 1969.

———. *Proceedings: Current Trends in Prison Design and Construction, 1956.*

———. *Proceedings: 96th Annual Congress of Correction, 1966.* Washington, D.C., 1966.

American Foundation. *Description of Program and Architectural Requirements for a New State Correctional Institution in Philadelphia Area.* Philadelphia, 1964.

American Institute of Architects. *Conference on Correctional Architecture.* Washington, D.C., 1961. Papers.

Anson, Grove, Haack and Associates. *Community Based Correctional Center,* Vol. 2. Fort Lauderdale, Fla., 1970.

Argentina, Comisión Nacional de Construcciones Penitenciarias, Ministerio de Educación y Justicia de la Nación, Sub-secretaría de Justicia, *Informe Anual* (Buenos Aires, 1965).

Aristeguieta Gramcko, A. *Algunas Consideraciones sobre la Medida de Observación del Menor.* Caracas: 1972.

Bailey, Walter C. "Correctional Outcome: An Evaluation of 100 Reports." *Journal of Criminal Law, Criminology, and Police Science* 57:153–60, June 1966.

Barnes, H. E. *The Evolution of Penology in Pennsylvania.* Indianapolis: Bobbs-Merrill, 1927.

Bates, Sanford. "How Many Years?" *Crime and Delinquency* 19:15–18, January 1973.

Bedau, Hugo A. *The Death Penalty in America.* New York: Anchor Books, 1967.

Bennett, James V. *Of Prisons and Justice: A Selection of the Writings of James V. Bennett.* Prepared for the Subcommittee on National Penitentiaries of the Committee on the Judiciary, U.S. Senate (Washington, D.C., U.S. Government Printing Office, 1964).

Board of Directors, NCCD. "Parole Decisions—A Policy Statement." *Crime and Delinquency* 19:137, April 1973.

Bolivar León, Delia. *Derecho de Menores.* Caracas: 1972.

Bonnie, Richard J., and Charles H. Whitebread. "The Forbidden Fruit and the Tree of Knowledge: An Inquiry into the Legal History of American Marijuana Prohibition." *Virginia Law Review* 56:971–1203, 1970.

Brooker, Frank. "The Deterrent Effect of Punishment." *Criminology, an Interdisciplinary Journal* 9:469–91, February 1972.

Burns, Henry, Jr. "The American Jail in Perspective." *Crime and Delinquency* 17:446–55, October 1971.

California, Youth Authority, *Compensatory Education in the California Youth Authority,* 1969–1970 (Sacramento, 1970).

————, *The Los Angeles Community Delinquency Control Project: An Experiment in the Rehabilitation of Delinquents in an Urban Community* (Los Angeles, 1970).

————, *Youth Service Bureaus in California: A Progress Report,* by Elaine B. Duxbury (Sacramento, 1971).

Chambliss, William J. *Crime and the Legal Process.* New York: McGraw-Hill, 1969.

Christie, Nils. "Scandinavian Criminology Facing the 1970's." In *Council of Europe: Current Trends in Criminological Research.* Strasbourg, 1970.

Cossio, Carlos. *El Derecho en el Derecho Judicial.* Buenos Aires: Kraft, 1945.

Cloward, Richard A., Donald R. Cressey, George H. Grosser, Richard McCleery, Lloyd E. Ohlin, Gresham M. Sykes, and Sheldon L. Messenger. *Theoretical Studies in Social Organization of the Prison.* New York: Social Science Research Council, 1960.

Conrad, John. *Crime and Its Correction: An International Survey of Attitudes and Practices.* Berkeley and Los Angeles: University of California Press, 1965.

Cooper, H. A. "Toward a Rational Doctrine of Rehabilitation." *Crime and Delinquency* 19:228–40, April 1973.

"Correctional Buildings of Today." *Empire State Architect* 26:6–9, 1966.

"Correctional Institutions: Security and Rehabilitation." *Empire State Architect* 26:12–15, 1966.

Council of Judges, NCCD. "Model Sentencing Act." *Crime and Delinquency* 18:335–70, October 1972.

Cressey, Donald R. "The Nature and Effectiveness of Correctional Techniques." *Law and Contemporary Problems* 23:754–71, Autumn 1958.

————. "Prison Organizations." In *Handbook of Organizations,* James G. March, ed. New York: Rand McNally, 1965.

Curran, J. W. *Trends in Prison Labor: Proceedings of the American Prison Association.* 1946.

Curtis, Nathaniel C., Jr. "Medium Security Institution: Programming and Design." *Architectural Record* 1959 (Sept.):221–25.

De Castro, Lola Aniyar. *Delitos de Bigamia.* Maracaibo, Venezuela: Universidad del Zulia, Facultad de Derecho, 1970.

————. *Victimología.* Maracaibo, Venezuela: Universidad del Zulia, Facultad de Derecho, 1969.

Dembo, Richard. "Recidivism: The Criminal's Reaction to Treatment." *Criminology, an Interdisciplinary Journal,* February 1971, p. 345.

District of Columbia, Department of Corrections, *A Study of Post-Release Performance of Women's Detention Center Releases,* by Colleen Barros, Virginia McArthur, and Stuart Adams, Research Report no. 31, Washington, D.C., 1970.

Duncan, D. F. "Psychedelic Drugs in Correctional Treatment." *Crime and Delinquency* 18:291–97, July 1972.

England, Ralph W., Jr. "New Departures in Prison Labor." *Prison Journal* 41:21–26, Spring 1961.

————. *Prison Labour.* New York: United Nations Department of Economic and Social Affairs, 1955.

Erikson, Erik H. *Young Man Luther.* New York: W. W. Norton, 1962.

Galaway, B., and J. Hudson. "Restitution and Rehabilitation—Some Central Issues." *Crime and Delinquency* 18:402–10, October 1972.

Galtung, Johan. "The Social Functions of a Prison." *Social Problems* 6:127–40, Fall 1958.

Garabedian, Peter G. "The Natural History of an Inmate Community in a Maximum Security Prison." *Journal of Criminal Law, Criminology, and Police Science* 61:78–85, 1970.

Gibson, Evelyn. *Time Spent Awaiting Trial.* Home Office Research Unit Report no. 2. London: Her Majesty's Stationery Office, 1960.

Glaser, Daniel. *The Effectiveness of a Prison and Parole System.* Indianapolis: Bobbs-Merrill, 1964.

————. "A Reconsideration of Some Parole Prediction Factors." *American Sociological Review* 19:335–41, June 1954.

Godoy Troconis, Diego. *El Organo Jurisdiccional de Menores.* Caracas: 1972.

Goffman, Erving. *Stigma*. Englewood Cliffs, N.J.: Prentice-Hall, 1965.

———. *Asylum*. New York: Doubleday, 1961.

Goodsell, James N. "The Penal Press: Voice of the Prisoner." *Federal Probation* 23:53–57, June 1959.

Grinnell, Frank W. "The Common Law History of Probation." *Journal of Criminal Law and Criminology* 32:15–34, May-June 1941.

Hakeem, Michael. "The Validity of the Burgess Method of Parole Prediction." *American Journal of Sociology* 53:376–86, March 1948.

Hall, Jay, Martha Williams, and Louis Tomaino. "The Challenge of Correctional Change: The Interface of Conformity and Commitment." *Journal of Criminal Law, Criminology, and Police Science* 57:493–503, December 1966.

Hall, Jerome. *General Principles of Criminal Law*. 2d ed. Indianapolis: Bobbs-Merrill, 1960.

———. *Studies in Jurisprudence and Criminal Theory*. Indianapolis: Bobbs-Merrill, 1958.

———. *Comparative Law and Social Theory*. Baton Rouge: Louisiana State University Press, 1963.

Hammer, Max. "Hypersexuality in Reformatory Women." *Corrective Psychiatry and Journal of Social Therapy* 15:20–26, 1969.

Haskell, Martin R., and H. Ashley Weeks. "Role Training as Preparation for Release from a Correctional Institution." *Journal of Criminal Law, Criminology, and Police Science* 50:441–47, January-February 1960.

Heckel, Robert V., and Elizabeth Mandell. *Crime and Delinquency: A Study of Incarcerated Offenders in South Carolina*. Columbia, S.C.: University of South Carolina Social Problems Research Institute, 1970.

Hendrick, Edward J. "The House of Correction." *American Journal of Correction* 20:36ff., May-June 1958.

Herrera Figueroa, M. *Psicología y Criminología*. Buenos Aires: Edit. Omeba, 1966.

Hippchen, Leonard J. *Experience in Application of the Team Treatment Approach, to the Rehabilitation of AIR Offenders*. Studies in Sociology, Vol. IX, pp. 118–28. Buenos Aires: Edit. Omeba, 1965.

Holt, Norman. "Temporary Prison Release—California's Prerelease Furlough Program." *Crime and Delinquency* 17:441–30, October 1971.

Howell, Lewis, Shay and Associates. *Juvenile Delinquent . . . Training and Treatment: A Study of Youth Development Centers for the General State Authority*. Philadelphia: Commonwealth of Pennsylvania, 1966.

Hughes, William H. "New Construction—Who's Building What, and Why." National Association of Training Schools and Juvenile Agencies *Proceedings* 56:187–93, 1960.

Hulin, Charles L., and Brendan A. Maher. "Changes in Attitudes toward Law Concomitant with Imprisonment." *Journal of Criminal Law, Criminology, and Police Science* 50:245–48, September-October 1959.

Humbert, W. H. *The Pardoning Power of the President*. Washington: American Council on Public Affairs, 1941.

Illinois, Detention Facilities and Jail Standards Bureau, *Jail Planning and Construction Standards* (Springfield, Ill., 1971).

Ives, George. *A History of Penal Methods*. London: Stanley Paul, 1914.

Johnston, Norman. "Recent Trends in Correctional Architecture." *British Journal of Criminology* 1:317–38, 1961.

"Juvenile Rehabilitation: California Branch Facility." *Architectural Record* 1959 (Sept.):219–21, 1959.

Kirkpatrick, Ronald E., et al. *Functional and Space Requirements for a Juvenile Justice Center in Fairfax County, Virginia*. Research Analysis Corporation, McLean, Va., 1969.

Langley, Michael H., H. R. Graves, and B. Norris. "The Juvenile Court and Individualized Treatment." *Crime and Delinquency* 18:79–92, January 1972.

LaPierre, Litchfield, and Partners. *Catalog of Designs and Plans of Correctional Institutions, Hospitals, Schools and Other Public Buildings.* New York, 1957.

Lindsey, E. "A Historical Sketch of the Indeterminate Sentence and Parole System." *Journal of Criminal Law and Criminology* 16:9–16, May-June 1925.

Litchfield, Clarence B. "Principles of Good Correctional Institution Design." *Canadian Journal of Corrections* 10:232–38, 1968.

————. "Some Modern Trends in Architecture for Correctional Institutions." *International Review of Criminal Policy* 1961 (17–18):37–61, 1961.

López Rey, M. *Qué es el Delito?* Buenos Aires: Edit. Atlantida, 1946.

————. *Crime, An Analytical Appraisal.* London, New York: 1970.

Madge, John. "Prison Design and Penal Reform." *International Review of Criminal Policy* 1961 (17–18):1–21, 1961.

Mannheim, Hermann. "Comparative Sentencing Practice." *Law and Contemporary Problems* 23:447–582, Summer 1958.

————, and Leslie T. Wilkins. *Prediction Methods in Relation to Borstal Training.* London: Her Majesty's Stationery Office, 1955.

Manwell, Francis H. "Building for a Better Treatment Program." National Association of Training Schools and Juvenile Agencies *Proceedings* 56:182–86, 1960.

Mathiesen, Thomas. "The Sociology of Prisons: Problems for Future Research." *British Journal of Sociology* 17:359–80, December 1966.

Mathis, F. O., and M. B. Rayman. "The Ins and Outs of Crime and Corrections." *Criminology, an Interdisciplinary Journal* 10:366–74, November 1972.

"Maximum Security Prison that Emphasizes Rehabilitation." *Architectural Record* 1965 (4):187–92.

McCorkle, Lloyd W., and Richard Korn. "Resocialization within Walls." *Annals of the American Academy of Political and Social Science* 293:88–98, May 1954.

Mayer, Charles H. Z. "A Half Century of Probation and Parole." *Journal of Criminal Law, Criminology, and Police Science* 43:707–28, March-April 1952.

Mayer, Joel. "Reflections on Some Theories of Punishment." *Journal of Criminal Law, Criminology, and Police Science* 59:595–99, December 1968.

Mayorca, Juan Manuel. *Delincuencia y Folklore.* Caracas: 1972.

Michael, J., and M. J. Adler, *Crime, Law, and Social Science.* New York: Harcourt, Brace, 1933.

Moos, Rudolf R. "The Assessment of the Social Climates of Correctional Institutions." *Journal of Research in Crime and Delinquency* 5:174–88, July 1968.

Morris, Norval. *The Habitual Criminal.* Cambridge, Mass.: Harvard University Press, 1951.

————. "Lessons from the Adult Correctional System of Sweden." *Federal Probation* 30:3–13, December 1966.

Mueller, Gerhard O. W. *Essays in Criminal Science.* New York: New York University Press, 1961.

Murphy, G. F. "The Courts Look at Prisoners' Rights." *Criminology, an Interdisciplinary Journal* 10:441–61, February 1973.

Murphy, J. E. "The Planning of Jail Facilities." *Police Chief* 37:42–48, 1970.

New York City, Chamber of Commerce, *Drug Abuse as a Business Problem* (New York, July 1970).

————, Probation Office, *An Inquiry into the Juvenile Centers Operated by the Office of Probation,* by Joseph Stone, Robert K. Ruskin, and Donald H. Goff (New York, 1970).

Nieburg, H. L. "Agnostics—Rituals of Conflict." *Annals of the American Academy of Political and Social Science* 391:56–73, 1970.

Nieves, Hector. *El Comportamiento Doloso del Ofendido.* Valencia, Venezuela: Universidad de Carabobo, 1972.

Ohlin, Lloyd E., and Otis Dudley Duncan. "The Efficiency of Prediction in Criminology." *American Journal of Sociology* 54:441–52, March 1949.

Oppenheimer, H. *The Rationale of Punishment.* London: University of London Press, 1913.

Orfield, Lester B. *Criminal Procedure from Arrest to Trial.* New York: New York University Press, 1947.

Penrose, L. W. "Mental Disease and Crime: Outline of a Comparative Study of European Statistics." *British Journal of Medical Psychology* 18:1–15, March 1939.

Piaget, Jean. *Psicología y Pedagogía.* Barcelona: Ariel, 1969.

———. *Biología y Conocimiento.* Mexico: Siglo XXI, 1969.

Polk, Kenneth. "Delinquency Prevention and the Youth Service Bureau." In Jorden, Daniel C., and Larry L. Dye. *Delinquency: An Assessment of the Juvenile Delinquency Prevention and Control Act of 1968.* Amherst, Mass.: University of Massachusetts, 1970.

Pound, Roscoe. *Criminal Justice in America.* New York: Holt, 1930.

President's Commission on Law Enforcement and Administration of Justice, Task Force on Corrections, *Task Force Report: Corrections* (1967).

Price, John. "Private Enterprise in a Prison." *Crime and Delinquency* 19:218–27, April 1973.

Public Systems, Inc. *A Study of the Characteristics and Recidivism Experiences of California Prisoners.* 2 vols. San Jose, Calif., 1970.

Purcell, F. P., and John C. Scanlon. *The Social Work Profession and Delinquency Prevention Programs. Studies in Sociology,* Vol. IX, pp. 128–38. Buenos Aires: Edit. Omeba, 1965.

Quiroz Cuaron, A. *La Nueva Penitenciaria de México.* Revista Penal y Penitenciaria, XXIII, 1958.

Quinney, Richard. *Crime and Justice in Society.* Boston: Little, Brown, 1969.

Reale, Miguel. *O Direito Como Experiencia.* São Paulo: Saraiva, 1968.

Reiss, Albert J., Jr. "The Accuracy, Efficiency, and Validity of a Prediction Instrument." *American Journal of Sociology* 56:552–61, May 1951.

Roberts, John W., and James S. Palermo. "A Study of the Administration of Bail in New York." *University of Pennsylvania Law Review* 106:685–730, March 1958.

Rose, Gordon. *The Struggle for Penal Reform.* London: Stevens and Sons, 1961.

Ross, Alf. *On Law and Justice.* London: Stevens and Sons, 1958.

Rubin, Sol. "The Indeterminate Sentence—Success or Failure?" *Focus* 28:47–52, March 1949.

Rusche, George, and Otto Kirchheimer. *Punishment and Social Structure.* New York: Columbia University Press, 1939.

Sajon, Rafael. *Teoria del Derecho de Menores.* Caracas: 1972.

Schafer, Stephen. *Restitution to Victims of Crime.* London: Stevens and Sons, 1960.

———. *Theories in Criminology.* New York: Random House, 1969.

Schrag, Clarence. "A Preliminary Criminal Typology." *Pacific Sociological Review* 4:11–16, Spring 1961.

Schur, Edwin M. *Law and Society.* New York: Random House, 1969.

Schubert, G., and David J. Danelsky. *Comparative Judicial Behavior.* New York: Oxford University Press, 1969.

Sellin, Thorsten. *Culture Conflict and Crime.* New York: Social Science Research Council, 1938.

———. "Philadelphia Prisons of the Eighteenth Century." *Transactions of the American Philosophical Society* 43:326–30, 1953.

———, ed. *Capital Punishment.* New York: Harper and Row, 1967.

Shoham, Shlomo. *The Mark of Cain: The Stigma Theory of Crime and Social Deviation.* Dobbs Ferry, N.Y.: Oceana Press, 1970.

Sindwani, K. L., and W. C. Reckless. "Prisoners' Perceptions of the Impact of Institutional Stay." *Criminology, an Interdisciplinary Journal* 10:461–73, February 1973.

Skolnick, Jerome H. "The Sociology of Law in America: Overview and Trends." In *Law and Society, a Supplement to Social Problems,* Summer 1965.

———. "Toward a Developmental Theory of Parole." *American Sociological Review* 25:542–49, August 1960.

Solis Quiroga, Hector. *La Atención a la Familia del Preso Como Medida de Prevención.* Mexico: Rev. Mexicana de Prevención y Readaptación Social, 1973, pp. 57–67.

Stout, Ellis. "Should Female Officers Supervise Male Offenders?" *Crime and Delinquency* 19:61–71, January 1973.

Studt, Elliott, Sheldon L. Messinger, and Thomas P. Wilson. *C-Unit: Search for Community in Prison.* New York: Russell Sage Foundation, 1968.

Sturz, Herbert. "An Alternative to the Bail System." *Federal Probation* 23:12–17, December 1962.

Sutherland, Edwin H. *White Collar Crime.* New York: Dryden Press, 1949.

Sykes, Gresham M. *The Society of Captives: A Study of a Maximum Security Prison.* Princeton, N.J.: Princeton University Press, 1958.

Szabo, Denis, and Pierre Landreville. "Research at the Department of Criminology of the University of Montreal." In *Council of Europe: Current Trends in Criminological Research.* Strasbourg: 1970.

Tapp, June L., and Felice J. Levine. "Persuasion to Virtue." *Research Contributions of American Bar Foundation* 4:565–82, 1970.

Tappan, Paul W. "Objectives and Methods in Correction." In *Contemporary Corrections,* Paul W. Tappan, ed. New York: McGraw-Hill, 1951.

Teeters, Negley K. *The Cradle of the Penitentiary: The Walnut Street Jail at Philadelphia, 1773–1835.* Philadelphia: Pennsylvania Prison Society, 1955.

Timasheff, N. A. *An Introduction to the Sociology of Law.* Cambridge, Mass.: Harvard University Committee on Research in the Social Sciences, 1939.

———. *One Hundred Years of Probation.* New York: Fordham University Press, 1941.

Trojanowicz, Robert C. "Factors that Affect the Functioning of Delinquency Prevention Programs." *Police Chief* 38:42–47, 1971.

Turk, Austin. *Criminality and Legal Order.* Chicago: Rand McNally, 1969.

University of Hawaii, Juvenile Delinquency and Youth Development Center, *Application of Behavior Modification Techniques in Hawaii* (Honolulu, 1968).

U.S., Bureau of Narcotics and Dangerous Drugs, *Handbook of Federal Narcotic and Dangerous Drug Laws* (Washington, D.C., U.S. Government Printing Office, January 1969).

U.S., Bureau of Prisons, *Handbook of Correctional Institution Design and Construction* (Washington, D.C., 1949).

U.S., Congress, House, Select Committee on Crime, *Marijuana, First Report,* H. Rept. 91–978 (Washington, D.C., U.S. Government Printing Office, 1970).

U.S., Department of Health, Education and Welfare, *A Community Mental Health Approach to Drug Addiction* (Washington, D.C., U.S. Government Printing Office, 1968).

———, *Rehabilitation in Drug Addiction* (Washington, D.C., U.S. Government Printing Office, 1964).

U.S., Justice Department, *Prisoner Management and Control* (Washington, D.C., 1969).

———, Law Enforcement Assistance Administration, *National Jail Census 1970: A Report on the Nation's Jails and Types of Inmates,* Statistic Center Report SC-1 (Washington, D.C., U.S. Government Printing Office, 1971).

U.S., National Commission on the Causes and Prevention of Violence, Task Force on Individual Acts of Violence. "Biological Bases of Social Behavior with Specific Reference to Violent Behavior," by Gerald E. McClearn, in *Crimes of Violence,* vol. 13 (Washington, D.C., U.S. Government Printing Office, 1969, pp. 1037–1115).

———. "Compensation for Victims of Violent Crimes," by Gilbert Geis, in *Crimes of Violence,* vol. 13 (Washington, D.C., U.S. Government Printing Office, 1969, pp. 1559–97).

———. "Crimes of Violence by Women," by David A. Ward, Maurice Jackson, and Renee E. Ward, in *Crimes of Violence,* vol. 13 (Washington, D.C., U.S. Government Printing Office, 1969, pp. 843–909).

———. "Critical Analysis of Sociological Theories," by Clarence C. Schrag, in *Crimes of Violence,* vol. 13 (Washington, D.C., U.S. Government Printing Office, 1969, pp. 1241–89).

———. "Cross-Cultural Comparison of Aggression and Violence," by Paul Bohannan, in *Crimes of Violence,* vol. 13 (Washington, D.C., U.S. Government Printing Office, 1969, pp. 1189–1239).

―――. "Drugs and Violence," by Richard Blum, in *Crimes of Violence*, vol. 13 (Washington, D.C., U.S. Government Printing Office, 1969, pp. 1461–1523).

―――. "Invocation and Constraint of Religious Zealotry," by Samuel Z. Klausner, in *Crimes of Violence*, vol. 13 (Washington, D.C., U.S. Government Printing Office, 1969, pp. 1291–1325).

U.S., National Council on Crime and Delinquency, *Adult Correctional Program, Commonwealth of Kentucky: A Study and Recommendations for the Kentucky Committee for Correctional Research* (1963).

―――, *Indiana Citizens Council: Report on the Indiana Girls School*, by Sherwood Norman (Indianapolis, November 1964).

―――, New Mexico Council, *Juvenile Forestry Camps: A Survey of National Experience with Application to New Mexico* (Albuquerque, N.M., 1963).

―――, Standard Act for State Correctional Services (New York, 1966).

―――, *Standards and Guides for the Detention of Children and Youth*, 2d ed. (New York, 1961).

―――, *Suggested Floor Plan for Overnight to 48-hour Hold-over Facility* (New York, 1970).

U.S., National Institute of Mental Health, Center for Studies of Crime and Delinquency. *Perspectives on Deterrence*, by Franklin E. Zimring (Washington, D.C.: U.S. Government Printing Office, 1971).

Vetter and Adams. "Effectiveness of Probation Caseload Sizes." *Criminology, an Interdisciplinary Journal*, February 1971, p. 33.

"Violence." *Police Chief* 38:16–63, 1971.

Ward, David A., and Gene G. Kassebaum. *Women's Prison: Sex and Social Structure.* Chicago: Aldine, 1965.

Wilkins, Leslie T. *Evaluation of Penal Measures.* New York: Random House, 1969.

―――, and P. Macnaughton-Smith. "New Prediction and Classification Methods in Criminology." *Journal of Research in Crime and Delinquency* 1:10–32, January 1964.

Williams, Vergil L., and M. Fish. "Rehabilitation and Economic Self-Interest." *Crime and Delinquency* 17:406–13, October 1971.

Wolfgang, Marvin E. *Patterns of Criminal Homicide.* Philadelphia: University of Pennsylvania Press, 1958.

―――, ed. *Crime and Culture.* New York: John Wiley, 1968.

Young, Pauline V. *Social Treatment in Probation and Delinquency.* 2d ed. New York: McGraw-Hill, 1952.

"Youth Care, Inc.: A Dream Come True." *Juvenile Court Journal* 20:144–49, 1969.

Zeisel, Hans, Harry Kalven, Jr., and Bernard Buchholz. *Delay in Court.* Boston: Little, Brown, 1959.

Zerpa, Dora Aguado-Hernández. *Legislación, Prevención y Tratamiento do los Menores en Situación Irregular*, Valencia, Venezuela, 1971.